Don't Ask, Don't Tell

Don't Ask, Don't Tell

Debating the Gay Ban
in the Military

edited by
Aaron Belkin and Geoffrey Bateman

LYNNE
RIENNER
PUBLISHERS

BOULDER
LONDON

Published in the United States of America in 2003 by
Lynne Rienner Publishers, Inc.
1800 30th Street, Boulder, Colorado 80301
www.rienner.com

and in the United Kingdom by
Lynne Rienner Publishers, Inc.
3 Henrietta Street, Covent Garden, London WC2E 8LU

Library of Congress Cataloging-in-Publication Data
Don't ask, don't tell : debating the gay ban in the military /
    edited by Aaron Belkin and Geoffrey Bateman.
    Includes bibliographical references and index.
    ISBN 1-58826-121-2 (alk. paper)
    ISBN 1-58826-146-8 (pbk. : alk. paper)
    1. United States—Armed Forces—Gays—Government policy.
I. Belkin, Aaron, 1966–   II. Bateman, Geoffrey, 1974–
UB418.G38 D65   2003
355'0086'640973—dc21   2002031836

British Cataloguing in Publication Data
A Cataloguing in Publication record for this book
is available from the British Library.

Printed and bound in the United States of America

        The paper used in this publication meets the requirements
  ∞   of the American National Standard for Permanence of
        Paper for Printed Library Materials Z39.48-1984.

        5 4 3 2 1

Contents

Preface

THE DISCUSSION OF GAYS AND LESBIANS IN THE MILITARY HAS ALL TOO OFTEN generated more heat than light. Thus, it is with great pleasure that we have been involved in the project that culminated in this volume, which brings together thoughtful, often opposing, interacting views on the issue.

A conference titled "Don't Ask, Don't Tell: Is the Gay Ban Based on Military Necessity or Prejudice?" was held in December 2000, cosponsored by the Center for the Study of Sexual Minorities in the Military (CSSMM) at the University of California, Santa Barbara, and the Commonwealth Club of California. The Commonwealth Club is the oldest and largest public affairs forum in the United States, and the CSSMM is a research institute whose mission is to promote the study of sexual minorities in the armed forces. We are very proud that the conference participants included many of the leading scholarly and official voices on this issue.

As conference organizers, we sought to involve a critical mass of experts of all political persuasions to discuss the topic. That being said, we should acknowledge candidly that opponents of allowing open gays in the military were underrepresented—and thus, are underrepresented in this volume—and we feel it important to explain why. The reasons are threefold.

First, eight of the country's leading opponents of gays in the military, representing the American Enterprise Institute, the Family Research Council, the Center for Military Readiness, the Army Research Institute, and other organizations, declined invitations to participate. All invitees were offered reimbursement for travel expenses. One individual asked us to change our discussion format as a condition of his participation; we agreed to modify the format, but he declined anyway. Another invitee said that she feared being outgunned unless accompanied by a group of her colleagues; we offered to invite any colleagues whom she nominated, but she declined to provide additional names or to participate.

Second, one expert who was invited to participate as an opponent of gays in the military actually switched his position prior to attending the conference. Finally, a last-minute scheduling conflict prevented a leading opponent of allowing open gays in the military—a scholar who helped craft the "Don't Ask, Don't Tell" policy—from attending.

To compensate for the lack of perfect balance, the moderator of our deliberations probed repeatedly and explicitly for opposing views. Although the discussions would have been even richer had we been able to assemble a perfectly balanced group, the dialogue reported in this book reflects a wide variety of perspectives, attesting to the success of this project.

* * *

This project was sponsored generously by Jim Follis and Ray Hurst and the R. Gwin Follis Foundation, the Institute on Global Cooperation and Conflict at the University of California, the Michael Palm Foundation in New York, the Office of the President of the University of California, and three private donors in San Francisco: Steven Gorosh, Jon Kouba, and Arthur Collingsworth. We offer thanks to all of these individuals and institutions. In addition, Gloria Duffy, the chief executive officer of the Commonwealth Club of California, and all of the staff at the Commonwealth Club, were incredibly helpful, generous, and supportive colleagues. Alix Sabin provided extensive and irreplaceable help in organizing the project. Lynn Eden of Stanford University volunteered to serve as moderator of our discussions. Michele Sieglitz made an excellent documentary film based on our deliberations. And Lynne Rienner provided extensive feedback and comments that strengthened the volume considerably. We are grateful to all of these individuals, without whom the project would not have come to fruition. Finally, we thank Rhonda Evans, Jason McNichol, and the entire board and staff of CSSMM for their years of unending and tireless support.

—*Aaron Belkin,*
Geoffrey Bateman

I

Introduction

On July 3, 1999, Private Calvin Glover challenged Private First Class
Barry Winchell to a fistfight in front of their barracks at Fort Campbell,
Kentucky. Glover lost, and two days later, on July 5, he took his re-
venge after ceaseless taunting about having had "his ass kicked by a
faggot." Glover borrowed a baseball bat from his friend Justin Fisher
and then beat Winchell to death while he slept in the barracks. There is
widespread agreement across the political spectrum as to the tragic nature of Winchell's murder. How could anyone, after all, endorse the
senseless, brutal beating of a service member whose life was cut short
at age twenty-one? Despite consensus about the tragic dimensions of
Winchell's death, however, there is almost no agreement about its lessons or wider meaning.

On one side of the issue, proponents of gays in the military point to a
lack of leadership at Fort Campbell, where Winchell was stationed. They
gathered evidence of widespread antigay harassment at the base, including
senior leaders' failure to discipline numerous reported instances of homophobic abuse. According to this point of view, Winchell's murder was the
predictable result of a pattern of blatant antigay harassment that leaders
chose to ignore. For example, Fort Campbell's inspector general took no
disciplinary action after learning that Winchell's sergeant called him a
"faggot" on a repeated basis. Even after Winchell was murdered, soldiers
at Fort Campbell sang the following cadence during group runs: "Faggot,
faggot down the street. Shot him, shot him, till he retreats." Proponents of
gays in the military argue that the commander of Fort Campbell, Major
General Robert T. Clark, could have prevented Winchell's death by refusing to tolerate antigay abuse. They suggest that known gays can serve
effectively in the armed forces as long as leaders insist on tolerance and
set an example by punishing service members who refuse to obey.

On the other side, however, opponents of gays in the military cite the very same evidence from the Winchell case to confirm their point that known homosexuals cannot serve in uniform. According to this perspective, the military is not a gay-friendly environment, and it never will be a safe space for gay and lesbian personnel. As much as leaders might try, there is nothing they can do to prevent other soldiers from being harassed or even beaten to death if their peers perceive them to be gay. In addition, opponents focus on the possibility that Justin Fisher, the soldier who taunted Calvin Glover for having "his ass kicked by a faggot" and who provided Glover with the baseball bat he used to kill Winchell, was romantically or sexually attracted to his victim. To the extent that Fisher may have been sexually attracted to men, opponents of gays in the military interpret the murder as a case of gay-on-gay violence that illustrates how allowing known gays into the military would introduce a destructive potential for jealousy and subsequent violence in every unit.

As the reactions to the Winchell murder suggest, the issue of gays in the military is one of the most contentious, hot-button topics in the U.S. culture war. The authors of a recent study, titled "Women, Men, and Media," identified 1,021 news stories about military personnel that were aired by the three major networks during the 1990s, and found that "gays in the military was the single most-heavily covered peacetime Pentagon story of the decade." In addition to extensive media coverage of the issue, powerful networks of activists, scholars, and grassroots organizations have lined up on both sides of the debate. Descriptions of the behind-the-scenes mobilizing that occurred when President Bill Clinton attempted to lift the gay ban at the beginning of his first administration, for example, show that gay rights as well as family-values organizations used the issue to orchestrate massive fund-raising and membership drives.

People who believe that open gays and lesbians should not serve in the armed forces advance a variety of arguments to justify their positions. Some justifications concern military necessity while others seem to be grounded in personal values. Positions grounded in military necessity argue that gays and lesbians undermine unit cohesion and that combat performance would decline if open homosexuals were allowed to serve in the U.S. armed forces. A position grounded more in prejudice claims that gay soldiers are "perverts in uniform" who should not be allowed to serve *even if* they do not undermine military performance. According to this perspective, homosexuality is so inconsistent with the norms of loyalty, honor, and patriotism that gays and lesbians have no place in the armed forces.

On the other side of the issue, of course, many people believe that gays and lesbians should be allowed to serve in uniform. Similar to the opponents of gays in the military, some supporters also justify their positions in terms of military effectiveness by claiming that military performance would improve if gays and lesbians were allowed to serve openly. At the same time, other supporters of gays in the military seem to prioritize gay rights over a concern for military capability, and they claim that known gays should be allowed to serve in uniform *even if* they undermine the military.

The positions presented above are brief summations of very rich arguments, many of which appear in this volume. While these arguments do represent the authentic views of many participants in the conversation about gays and lesbians in the military, we suggest that the intensity of the political debate has had very little to do with whether or not lifting the gay ban would undermine combat effectiveness. Rather, we attribute the passion of the debate to other factors that are addressed only rarely in public. What factors actually motivate participants in the debate over gays in the military, and why can participants not express these factors in polite company?

On one side of the issue, gay-rights advocates see access to the military as a metaphor for full citizenship rights. In addition to the right to marry, own property, and enter into contracts, military service has been a fundamental marker of citizenship throughout history. According to gay-rights advocates, gays and lesbians will not be able to lock in their hard-won citizenship rights in other realms until they obtain the right to serve in the military. It is certainly true that gay-rights advocates are concerned about antigay harassment in the military as well as the principles of workplace nondiscrimination and fairness. At the same time, however, we suggest that they are equally, if not more, motivated by the symbolic stakes of the debate. The military is the largest employer in the country and roughly a quarter of all men in the United States today are veterans. Gay-rights advocates believe that when the largest employer in the country goes out of its way to fire people who say that they are gay, this sends a terrible message to the civilian sector. While gay-rights advocates believe passionately in the symbolic effects of the military ban, however, they often hesitate to raise this issue in public, because they do not want to appear to press for a narrow, parochial, self-interested agenda that could undermine the effectiveness of the military.

On the other side of the issue, opponents of gays in the military sometimes are likewise motivated by unstated factors. For example, they may recall how President Harry Truman's 1948 decision to integrate African Americans into the armed forces on an equal basis set an important racial precedent that helped shatter the separate-but-equal standard in civilian settings. We suggest that President Clinton's attempt to lift the gay ban served as a powerful fund-raising vehicle for the religious right, not because of concerns about unit cohesion and combat performance, but because family-values groups believed that the open acceptance of gays and lesbians in the military would lead to the progress of gay rights in other realms. Leaders of family-values groups, however, often refrain from articulating this perspective because they do not want to appear homophobic, and because they can cloak the real reason for their opposition to allowing gays in the military under the mantle of attempting to preserve combat effectiveness.

The issue of gays in the military is complicated in part by the mixture of facts and values that people on both sides invoke to support their positions. It occupies a sort of middle zone between more purely social-scientific debates (such as the question of whether poverty causes crime) and more purely moral debates (such as the question of whether an unborn fetus should be considered a person entitled to full human rights). Both social-scientific as well as moral debates, of course, include facts and values. But the standards for adjudicating such arguments are perhaps more clear than is the case with claims concerning gays in the military. For example, there are very few facts that could convince the average U.S. citizen to switch his or her position on abortion because most positions in the abortion debate are driven by personal values. Conversely, social-scientific arguments (such as the claim that poverty is a cause of crime) are at least in theory subject to falsification depending on the quality of evidence for and against any particular position.

Like arguments in other social-scientific realms, claims about gays in the military may sometimes be subject to falsification. For example, the argument that gays undermine the military can be at least partially empirically tested by studying military units that have included gay and lesbian soldiers, or by polling service members to probe their attitudes toward gays and lesbians. Or, to take another example, the claim that gays and lesbians undermine privacy in the shower may be subject to confirmation or falsification by studying the experiences of heterosexual service members who have served in units with known homosexual peers. On the other hand, some arguments in the gays-in-the-military debate may not be subject to testing. To take an extreme example, how could one confirm or falsify the argument that gay soldiers are "perverts in uniform" who do not belong in the military?

Further complicating the issue is the tortured political history of the "Don't Ask, Don't Tell" policy. When President Clinton attempted to force the military to allow known gays and lesbians to serve at the beginning of his administration, Congress and the Pentagon reacted by adopting a compromise policy known as "Don't Ask, Don't Tell." According to the policy, the military is not allowed to ask new recruits if they are gay, but service members who reveal a homosexual identity must be fired from the armed forces. Many people on both the left and the right would agree that the "Don't Ask, Don't Tell" policy was perhaps the greatest blunder of the Clinton administration. According to proponents of gays in the military, the policy is even worse than the previous, outright ban because it has been implemented unfairly and because even more soldiers currently are discharged for homosexuality than was the case prior to its adoption. According to some opponents of gays in the military, however, even closeted homosexuals who do not reveal their sexual orientation should not be allowed into the military. Hence, some people believe that the "Don't Ask, Don't Tell" policy goes too far while others believe that it does not go far enough. A third group believes that the policy is a fair compromise that has given the military time to adjust to society's increasing tolerance of gay and lesbian people.

Our view is that advocates on both sides of the debate may bear special burdens as they advance their arguments. On the one hand, experts who favor allowing known gays and lesbians to serve in the armed forces should always keep in mind the importance of safety in combat. Given that service members can be asked to risk their lives, Pentagon leaders understandably shy away from changes that are imposed on them by civilians who may not understand military operations, and that may undermine soldiers' safety during combat. On the other hand, given the abhorrence of discrimination, experts who oppose allowing known gays and lesbians to serve in the armed forces should, in our opinion, take special care to show why lifting the gay ban would undermine military effectiveness. Rather than relying on anecdotes or attitudinal surveys, opponents would be well served by basing their arguments on studies of what actually happens when militaries lift their gay bans.

Our discussions in this book are structured in terms of a cost-benefit framework. In order to provide an answer to the guiding question behind the project—Is the gay ban based on military necessity or prejudice?—it is important to determine whether the ban's benefits outweigh its costs. If they do not, this may suggest that the policy is based more on prejudice than on military necessity.

Chapter 2 of the book provides a historical context to the issue of gays and lesbians in the armed forces by explaining how and why the military has changed the way it defines homosexuality and manages and regulates gay people. Written by Timothy Haggerty of Carnegie Mellon University, the chapter shows that the issue is not new, and that military regulations concerning same-sex sex date back to World War I. In addition, Haggerty provides a historical overview of the military's own internal studies concerning homosexuality.

Chapter 3 asks whether the gay ban preserves soldiers' privacy. Like the subsequent chapters, it is presented as an edited transcript of one of the sessions at the "Don't Ask, Don't Tell" conference. According to some supporters of "Don't Ask, Don't Tell," the gay ban preserves heterosexual soldiers' privacy by preventing open homosexuals from serving in the U.S. armed forces. As a result, the policy benefits heterosexual soldiers by preserving their privacy in the showers. Critics argue, however, that there are large numbers of open gays and lesbians currently serving in the military and that lifting the ban would have no implication for privacy. In this chapter, scholars use the most recent scholarly evidence to discuss whether the ban preserves heterosexual privacy in the showers and the barracks, and whether lifting the ban would have implications for privacy.

In Chapter 4, the participants consider whether the gay ban preserves unit cohesion. Supporters of "Don't Ask, Don't Tell" have argued that heterosexual soldiers do not like gays and lesbians, and that as a result the presence of open homosexuals in the armed forces would undermine unit performance and cohesion. In other words, the ban preserves unit cohesion and lifting it would undermine combat performance. Some critics have responded that whether or not group members like each other has no impact on organizational performance. Even if heterosexuals dislike gays and lesbians, in other words, lifting the ban would not undermine military performance. This chapter is devoted to a discussion of the latest scholarly evidence on the relationship between dislike, cohesion, and performance.

Chapter 5 discusses whether the experiences of foreign militaries that have lifted their gay bans are relevant to the U.S. case. Opponents of "Don't Ask, Don't Tell" claim that when foreign militaries lift their gay bans, unit cohesion and performance do not suffer. Some advocates of "Don't Ask, Don't Tell" have responded that the experiences of foreign militaries are not relevant to the United States because of cultural differences, because few if any foreign militaries extend full rights to homosexuals in practice, and because few gays and lesbians come out of the closet even after foreign militaries lift their bans. The participants consider scholarly data on the topic.

Shifting away from the issue of benefits, Chapter 6 concentrates on the possible costs of the gay ban. According to some gay and lesbian advocates, "Don't Ask, Don't Tell" is a financially expensive policy that leads to loss of talent and to violence against women. Others respond that the gay ban does not lead to violence and if the ban were lifted, gay bashing would increase. This chapter is devoted to the academic evidence on the costs of "Don't Ask, Don't Tell."

Chapter 7 consists of testimony from two gay service members who have served openly in the U.S. Army and in the Royal Navy: former Arizona state representative and U.S. Army reservist Steve May, and British submariner Rob Nunn. The volume concludes with a summary and discussion of various areas of agreement and disagreement among opponents and proponents of gays in the military and suggestions for future areas of research and investigation.

2

History Repeating Itself: A Historical Overview of Gay Men and Lesbians in the Military Before "Don't Ask, Don't Tell"

Timothy Haggerty

IN EARLY 1993, STEVEN SCHLOSSMAN, THEN HEAD OF THE HISTORY DEPART-
ment at Carnegie Mellon, asked me to participate as a researcher in the
RAND study that ultimately resulted in the publication *Sexual Orientation and U.S. Military Personnel Policy: Options and Assessment*. Our
study team, which included Tanjam Jacobsen, Ancilla Livers, and
Sherie Mershon, consisted of a dozen sets of researchers who were
being organized to study the social, political, and cultural consequences
of addressing the issue of sexual orientation and U.S. military personnel
policy. Including the reviewers, directors, and RAND staff, I was one of
approximately seventy individuals who worked on the report from
inception to publication.[1]

I had the unusual opportunity—particularly for a historian—to have
my research become immediately relevant in a national debate. My
prior work had examined the social impact of war and, by implication,
military service; my dissertation examined how men used war service—
in this case, service in the Union armies of the U.S. Civil War—to
remake their identities. I was also a gay man who had a fairly firm grasp
of the historiography of the gay and lesbian literature and was frankly
lucky enough to be in the right place at the right time. When President
Bill Clinton issued a memorandum that directed Secretary Les Aspin to
submit the draft of an executive order "ending discrimination on the
basis of sexual orientation in the armed forces," the secretary of defense
asked RAND to provide information and analysis that would be useful
in helping formulate the executive order. RAND asked Steve Schlossman. Steve asked me.

A decade later, the historical record may not seem acutely pertinent to those examining how "Don't Ask, Don't Tell, Don't Pursue" played out. If you had been involved in gay and lesbian politics in the early 1990s, the whole issue of gays and lesbians in the military seemed to come out of right field, or at least out of the conservative wing of the gay movement. But over time, I think, the issue of military participation has become a symbol for open citizenship and full participation in U.S. culture, and I find myself agreeing, surprisingly, with people whose politics were far more conservative than my own in 1992.

This particular volume's subject—"Is the gay ban based on military necessity?"—is a question that, as a historian, I can answer rather simply: "no." Unlike heterosexuality, which has (at least in the modern era) been presupposed as a normative and therefore preferred course of development, homosexual behaviors have been subject to a wider variety of interpretations and theories that have directly affected the social and legal circumstances of those that practice them. To risk a gross generalization, psychological models of causation have posited either that homosexuality is innate and immutable or, conversely, that homosexual behaviors are a learned or adaptive response that strays from an ideal developmental pattern. Like the early sexologists Havelock Ellis and Richard von Krafft-Ebing, current psychological and biological theorists favor a model that stresses the inborn propensity of some individuals to seek erotic outlet with members of their same sex. Others, including Sigmund Freud, Alfred Kinsey, and Irving Bieber, have argued that the adoption of a homosexual persona is a result of an individual's life circumstance.

These two conflicting paradigms—homosexuality as an immutable component of a person's psyche on the one hand, and as a deliberate behavioral choice with social and criminal consequences on the other—confounded military personnel (and doctors, jurists, and theologians, for that matter) for the greater part of the twentieth century. As accepted paradigms shifted, the military found itself in the unenviable position of having to develop policies that could balance the manpower demands of a fighting force with the political formulations of representation in a democratic society.

In this chapter, I would like to place the existing "Don't Ask, Don't Tell, Don't Pursue" policy, which this volume's other authors will discuss with greater familiarity, in historical context. Despite the pyrotechnic display that accompanied "Don't Ask, Don't Tell," the policy was really a continuation and elaboration of those military policies that have been selectively enacted, enforced, rationalized, ignored, and repealed since the Articles of War went into effect in 1917.

Since 1900, there have been several marked shifts in an accepted psychological understanding of homosexual activity. Early criminal constructions were already on the wane by the turn of the nineteenth century; by the 1920s, attempts at defining homosexuality as being biologically determined, a brain disease model, had given way to theories that suggested that homosexuality was part of an abnormal developmental pattern. According to these theories, those engaging in homosexual activity were not directly responsible for their decisions; rather, they were subconsciously acting out fundamental personality characteristics over which they had little or no control. Following World War II, developmental rationales for homosexuality were undermined by the publications of the Kinsey reports, which contended that homosexuality was far more widespread than previously believed. This gave rise to the impression that while some homosexuals were compelled to adopt the inverted persona of the Sapphist or Fairy, most could keep their vice secret.

Reacting to a postwar world characterized by the development of small gay communities within larger environments of persecution, deception, and isolation, a homosexual or gay-rights movement coalesced in the United States during the second half of the twentieth century. As economic and demographic trends quickened the pace of urbanization and as the rhetorics of civil rights and feminism gave rise to the concept of "identity politics," gay-rights advocates increasingly reacted to the systematically exclusionary policies and strategies of local, state, and federal agencies as well as overarching social opprobrium. The emergence of a small homophile political movement in the 1950s gave way to a larger, more politicized gay-liberation movement in the early 1970s, which in turn engendered both a mainstream gay political movement and a radical "queer" faction during the AIDS crisis of the 1980s and 1990s. During the past quarter century, direct political action increasingly confronted those institutions that discriminated on the basis of sexual preference, including the military.

The shifting frameworks of medical discourse and political practice altered the realities of gay life from a deviant characteristic to a lifestyle with its own institutions, rituals, and normative behaviors. As homosexuality underwent several stylistic transformations in the twentieth century, its once-marginalizing stigma became an organizing principle for a substantial minority of lives. In reaction, the social mechanisms regulating homosexual behavior, including those of the military, have increasingly attempted to discover and regulate both homosexual "behavior," or same-sex acts, and the homosexual "personality," or those that have adopted gay, lesbian, or other nonnormative sexual identities.

The questions persistently raised by the presence of homosexuality within the U.S. military are neither new nor unique to that particular institution. As policy evolved, however, and the homosexual "personality type" was increasingly recognized as inherently disruptive to the morale and cohesion of troop discipline and order, the armed forces systematically began initiating separation procedures against individuals who may not have committed any disorderly acts. The constitutional protection accorded military justice made successful appeals virtually impossible for most of the twentieth century; regardless, these separation proceedings were the basis of the first legal challenges by homosexuals against existing policies. In turn, these lawsuits engendered new regulation.

Rather than being a new topic of investigation, the place of gay men and lesbians within the military has been an ongoing area of policy inquiry for seventy years. Despite the best efforts of the armed forces to deny their existence or, in extreme instances, to disavow their findings or destroy documentation, journalists, litigants, and scholars have uncovered an opus of sponsored research that documents the Department of Defense's concern with the incidence of homosexuality within its ranks. The transition from prosecuting "sodomists" to separating homosexuals that occurred during World War II, for example, was preceded by psychological and legal research that tried to rationalize the varied practices within the services before the war.

Particularly in the postwar period, the armed forces were a virtual laboratory of social policy experimentation. After World War II, when manpower needs lent such research greater utility and when academia provided more sophisticated social-science methodologies, analysts concluded that many of the long-standing rationales for excluding gay and lesbian service members were unjustified. In 1957, the navy's Crittenden Report exposed the perception that homosexuals were greater security risks than their heterosexual counterparts as a red herring; additionally, it argued that the widely held belief that gay men and lesbians acted as "sexual predators" had no basis in empirical data, long before this argument gained wider currency.

The earliest attempts to regulate homosexual behaviors within the armed forces were sporadic and inchoate. An investigation into immoral behaviors in the naval facilities in 1919 in Newport, Rhode Island, uncovered a flourishing subculture of homosexual activity within and outside the navy. While the rationale behind the investigation, originally initiated by a sailor and expanded under the orders of then assistant secretary of the navy Franklin D. Roosevelt, remains unclear, the investigation may have helped initiate policy toward the punishment of those caught in homosexual activity. The resulting court-martial sentenced sailors to prison or immediate dishonorable discharge; however, insufficient evidence allowed some men to escape conviction and remain in service. The notoriety of the events in Newport eventually led to a Senate investigation.[2] The bad publicity of this case, as well as a desire to expedite cases of homosexuality as quickly as possible, may have established military policy toward homosexuals.

According to prison data from between the wars, the navy incarcerated extremely few sailors for sodomy. All men convicted of moral perversion were imprisoned at Portsmouth, New Hampshire. According to censuses for 1929–1932, approximately 10 percent of the prison system's population (which also included jails on Mare Island, Parris Island, and Cavite in the Philippines) were imprisoned for either sodomy or scandalous conduct tending to the destruction of good morals, a lesser charge that could have included homosexual activity. At Portsmouth, less than 1 percent of the inmates were serving time for sodomy.[3]

The military discharged homosexuals more frequently than they court-martialed them, despite the official stance that sodomists were to be convicted under the Articles of War. Individuals suspected of homosexual acts were released under a "Section VIII" discharge for unsuitability. While in theory these could be honorable discharges, in cases of psychopathic behavior, it was normally less-than-honorable, or "blue."[4] In 1931, the commanding general of the Seventh Corps Area recommended that "sex perverts" be summarily discharged without bringing them to trial. He supported his recommendation with medical testimony from the staff psychiatrist at Alcatraz, who divided sodomists into two different classes of offender. The "accidental" or "acquired" sodomist had temporarily strayed from the normative path of heterosexual development. The "true" sodomist, on the other hand, had been imprisoned because of his detrimental effects upon the functioning of the service. When confined and cut off from his sexual outlets, the true pervert became a danger to those around him. The medical officer concluded that it was in the best interest of the military service that all sexual perverts be released.[5]

In an attempt to rationalize policy concerning homosexuals, the army's judge advocate general (JAG) tried to separate criminal behaviors from behavioral problems. In 1941, members of the advocate general's staff attempted to reform the existing sodomy code. In a tour of court-martial jurisdictions in the United States, Lieutenant Colonel Earnest H. Burt came to the conclusion that most presiding officers did not consider sodomists as penal problems, and therefore did not send such cases to trial. In the absence of aggravating factors, the army removed most sodomists from service through administrative proceedings. In Burt's opinion, this widespread practice was congruent with leading medical and psychiatric opinions of the day, and he sought to modify official procedure to reflect reality.[6] In a draft memo, he proposed that soldiers "ascertained to have engaged willfully and knowingly, in an act of sodomy will be separated from the service through administrative processes as distinct from a court-martial to that end." Court-martial was indicated, however, in those cases where force was employed, when minors were involved, or when the sexual partner was incapable of consent due to intoxication or other impairing conditions.[7]

A review of sodomy cases tried under the JAG between 1938 and 1941 supported Burt's contention that there was a wide disparity in the adjudication of sodomy cases. In the thirty-four cases, sentences ranged from immediate dismissal with no confinement to the maximum allowable sentence of ten years. In those cases where there were no mitigating factors involving youths or force, the range of sentences was between eight months and five years, with the average sentence slightly more than two and one half years' confinement. The sheer paucity of cases further suggested that most homosexuals were separated administratively.[8]

Despite attempts to standardize policies and procedures concerning homosexuality in the service, the U.S. military did not have any uniform procedure for the handling of men accused of sodomy before World War II. While in theory all sodomists were to be court-martialed, in practice men were administratively discharged, allowed to resign their commissions, or, in cases where there was insufficient evidence to convict them, allowed to return to service.

During World War II, a debate occurred among military authorities concerning the policies and practices surrounding homosexual activity in the armed forces. Within the army alone, for example, there were twenty-four separate revisions of existing regulations concerning homosexuality between 1941 and 1945, compared with eleven revisions before the war and seventeen between the end of the war and the passage of the Uniform Code of Military Justice in May 1950.[9] This debate had several causes. First, there was a widespread variance in the treatment of individual cases within the service.[10] Second, military authorities seemed more willing to confer with and accept the recommendations of medical and psychiatric personnel in the development of policy concerning homosexual tendencies or behaviors. Finally, the utility of incarcerating or segregating the homosexual was called into question, as were efforts to treat the condition while in the service.

While the initial instructions for the screening of young men did not include any reference to homosexuality, the Army Surgeon General's Office included "homosexual proclivities" as a disqualifying condition in its May 1941 revision of the circular.[11] Under these regulations, suspected homosexuals were to be referred to regional medical advisory boards for further psychiatric examination. Like the army, the navy declared the "neuropsychiatrically unfit" to be a danger or disturbance to the functioning of the military unit. By the beginning of the war, both branches of service along with the Selective Service System itself had determined that overt homosexual (or effeminate) behavior could be used to deny entry into the military.[12]

During the war, the services turned to the expertise of psychiatry to understand and refine their understanding and treatment of the confirmed homosexual. In 1942, the members of the Committee on Neuropsychiatry of the National Research Council (NRC), composed of leading psychiatrists from academia and clinical practice and chaired by Winfred Overholser, the superintendent of Saint Elizabeth's Hospital, met to establish a policy concerning the disposition of homosexuals in the military.

This committee came to several conclusions, including the development of a typology that divided homosexuals into three personality types. The first was the homosexual who committed additional offenses in connection with sexual gratification; the second was the confirmed homosexual whose activities were confined to seeking out other contacts; and the third, and most problematic, was the casual homosexual who yielded to seduction due to immaturity, curiosity, or inebriation. According to the committee, this third type might have been reclaimable. In response to the changing makeup of the armed forces, the committee of the NRC also expanded the definition of sodomy to include the sexual relations between women.

On January 10, 1943, the adjutant general's office issued Memorandum No. W615-4-43, which rescinded the 1941 policy statement. The new policy was notable for several changes in both policy and the discretion allowed each individual case:

• First, the act of sodomy was denounced as an offense of the Articles of War, and it was reiterated that the sexual pervert, or "the true sodomist," should be tried by court-martial, unless the circumstances surrounding the particular case made a conviction unlikely. In these cases, the individual should be separated under the provisions of Section VIII and issued a blue discharge. However, all acts involving force or against a minor would be brought to trial.

• Second, when the accused was the pathic, rather than the aggressor, and where evidence suggests that he was not a confirmed pervert, the policy was to reclaim the individual through treatment. This condition could be met, for example, if the individual engaged in homosexual activity due to intoxication or curiosity.

• Finally, the disposition of any one case was left to the discretion of the officer exercising general court-martial jurisdiction.[13]

In December, G. C. Marshall, the chief of staff, issued another revision of code, rescinding the memorandum of January. In this revision, the accused could demand a trial by court-martial but was to be offered the opportunity to resign his commission or accept a Section VIII discharge if enlisted. The exceptions concerning the use of force and the onetime offender remained in place.

On January 3, 1944, the secretary of war issued Circular No. 3, entitled "Homosexuals," that rescinded Memorandum No. W615-4-43 on sodomists. This circular made the following revisions of existing regulatory practices: First, homosexuality was part of the criminal denunciation of Article of War 93. Second, the "true" or confirmed homosexual was not deemed reclaimable, and was thus separated from service through the resignation of commission, discharge under the provisions of Section VIII, or court-martial through his own demands or the circumstances of his case. Third, some homosexuals could be deemed "reclaimable," particularly if their actions were motivated by immaturity, intoxication, or the influence of superior age or grade.[14]

While there is less archival evidence available to document the formation of naval policy during the war, it appears that the navy command was concerned with many of the same issues as their army counterparts. Like the army, the navy consulted with leading civilian and federal psychiatric experts, including the NRC committee, to help reformulate their own internal policy.[15] In reconsidering navy policy, the chief of the Bureau of Medicine and Surgery (BuMed) believed that in reconceptualizing homosexuality as a medical rather than a legal problem, the navy's policy would ultimately result in a more humane, uniform, and intelligent handling of the homosexual problem.[16]

In the opinion of BuMed, the legal punishment of the homosexual, like the punishment of other congenitally deformed individuals, was meaningless. While those homosexuals whose activities included criminal behavior should be prosecuted, those who were simply benign homosexuals should be separated from their navy service after confirmation of their irreclaimable status by a medical board. Like army policy, this humane approach to the problem of homosexuality detained, discharged, or decommissioned personnel without benefit of due process.[17]

Early studies of the characteristics of homosexual offenders confirmed many of the conclusions that the armed forces were making independently through their legal and administrative systems. Clement Fry and Edna Rostrow tracked 183 individuals who had evidenced "homosexual problems" at induction. Of these 183, 51 were rejected at the induction station; approximately a third of the rejections were for neuropsychiatric reasons. Of the 132 who were permitted to enter the service, 118 served honorably for a period of one to five years; only 14 people were discharged. Over half of the inductees attained officer rank.[18]

Lewis H. Loeser, a lieutenant colonel in the Medical Corps, undertook a study of 270 men admitted as sexual offenders to the 36th Station Hospital during the war years. Among his conclusions were that homosexuals, overall, were less likely to have criminal records, were more likely to be of above-average intelligence, and, excepting a higher-than-average incidence of alcohol use, were generally physically fit for service. In his observations of his subjects, he came to the conclusion that there was still little uniformity in the administrative handling of these cases, and in general the military was performing a disservice in the exclusion and prosecution of these men as a group. His final conclusion reads:

> The author does not believe that sodomy per se should be a punishable offense, that discharge from the military is necessary for most cases, or that deferment in the draft is advisable in all known cases. A large percentage of homosexuals possess sufficient restraint and insight, and have sufficient talents to justify careful examination of the individual case.[19]

By the end of the war, military policy concerning homosexuality had undergone several important changes. First and most importantly, the "homosexual" had replaced the "sodomist" although the criminal aspects of same-sex behaviors had been neither eliminated nor elucidated in any clear manner. People who engaged in same-sex behaviors could be separated from the service through their resignation or by administrative discharge. Even if no sexual activity had occurred, a growing body of policy supported the conceptualization of a homosexual personality who was to be barred from military service at induction or separated from the service upon his discovery. The military definition of homosexuality was extended to women engaged in same-sex behavior for the first time during this conflict.

Starting in World War II, official policy allowed for commanding officers to exercise discretion in their handling of homosexual personnel. Sodomy remained in violation of the Articles of War, and could lead to trial, dishonorable discharge, and confinement. Those caught in homosexual acts could be tried, allowed to resign, or discharged administratively with a less-than-honorable discharge. Those who exhibited homosexual tendencies, or who confided those tendencies to chaplains, doctors, or other military personnel, could resign or be separated with an honorable, general, or less-than-honorable discharge.

The results of these policies were that hundreds of men, and an uncalculated but presumably smaller number of women, were denied entry into the service, treated for pathological sexuality, or discharged during their service. One estimate, admittedly not complete, is that approximately four to five thousand men were denied entry into the services under Selective Service because of their homosexuality. There were approximately five thousand admissions to army medical installations for pathological sexuality during the war;[20] due to their conflation with other discharges, there does not appear to be any reliable estimate of the number of men discharged primarily because of homosexuality during the war, though the best guess is probably one to two thousand discharges a year.[21]

While policies were designed to exclude or separate gay men and lesbians from service, the majority of homosexuals in the military during the war served their hitch without any disciplinary action. As Allan Bérubé has documented, men and women who entered the screening process encountered the first hurdle they would have to clear in order to serve honorably. Men who presented effeminate qualities were placed under suspicion; men who knew themselves to be homosexual began to learn how to cover their tracks. Paradoxically, then, the revision of policies toward homosexuals in the military gave rise to an environment that encouraged the wider application of these policies in intelligence operations. Since servicemen and women could now be discharged for homosexual tendencies as well as behaviors, an incentive developed to identify and prosecute behaviors that had previously gone undetected.

Homosexuality emerged as a mainstream social issue in the decade following World War II. This public debate had profound effects on the everyday lives of homosexuals, as well as upon the formulation and enforcement of public and legal policies concerning their behaviors. In the military as well as the larger society, policies concerning homosexuals and their behavior came under heightened attention; as the Cold War escalated, homosexuals found themselves under increasing scrutiny as possible risks to the security and welfare of the United States. Locally as well as nationally, gay men and women found themselves victims of systematized prosecution. In reaction to both new scientific evidence and political pressures, some gay men and women began to organize into social and political groups that would form the nucleus of the latter-day gay-rights movement.

If the war engendered a new rhetoric among gay men and lesbians, the 1948 publication of Alfred Kinsey's *Sexual Behavior in the Human Male* sparked a very public discussion about homosexuality in U.S. society at large. Unlike the earlier writings of Ellis or Freud, which were disseminated relatively slowly through the medical and psychiatric professions, the Kinsey reports' startling data, which presented homosexual activity as far more prevalent than conventionally believed, exploded into popular consciousness. Kinsey's estimates (which are still used as ballpark figures) were that 37 percent of the male population had physical contact to the point of orgasm with other men between adolescence and old age; one in eight men was or had been primarily homosexual for at least a three-year period in his adult life. Approximately one in eight women was engaged in homosexual behaviors during adulthood.[22]

By the postwar period, the rationales for excluding homosexuals from positions of security or authority had developed a long if dubious history. To baldly state the tenets of what might be thought of as the "commie-pinko-queer" syndrome, homosexuals were secretive and pervasive and had infiltrated key positions in the government and civilian life. Since they did not reproduce themselves, homosexuals needed to recruit the previously innocent into their ranks. Once introduced to the codes, passwords, and secret meeting places of homosexuals, the newly initiated gay man or lesbian was free to convert others (particularly impressionable youths) into their devious ways and means. Once an individual had tasted the forbidden fruit of homosexuality, he or she had entered a world from which few ever returned.[23]

Within the military, the growing conceptualization of the homosexual as a threat to society and to the discipline of the service was introduced into the training procedures for new recruits. In a lecture prepared for navy recruits dated January 14, 1948, the homosexual was portrayed as a psychologically unsound person who expended a great deal of energy in the seduction of the innocent in order to fulfill his own sexual needs. While some homosexuals were easily identified, others were indistinguishable from the normal men and women that the sailor could encounter on or off the base. Since it was presumed that recruits were uniformly heterosexual, the navy's advice was to avoid all contacts with suspicious characters, as well as to report any homoerotic tendencies among service personnel.[24] Like their male counterparts, WAVES received instructions concerning homosexuality. In remarkable contrast to the respect accorded homosocial relationships between women during the wartime years, WAVES were lectured as to the inherent risk involved in emotional or sexual relationships with their comrades. WAVES, at all costs, were impelled to remove themselves from contact with the alleged homosexual, and any suspicious acts or characters were to be reported to military authorities.[25]

Military policy reflected these changing social attitudes concerning homosexuality. Even though the military had liberalized policies toward homosexual personnel immediately after the war, by 1948 this liberalization had begun to erode. The provision for honorable discharge was deleted; however, those men and women with good service records were to be separated from the service with a general, rather than a dishonorable, discharge.[26]

On October 11, 1949, the Department of Defense issued a memorandum that unified military policy toward homosexual behavior. While still allowing each branch of the service to develop its own regulations concerning the separation of homosexual personnel, the memorandum reiterated the belief that lesbians and gay men posed security risks and proved unsuitable for military service.

As well as reflecting social attitudes, the military's revision of policy was part of a postwar political environment notable for an increasingly systematized prosecution of homosexuals by police forces and state agencies.[27] Like communists, homosexuals were singled out as security risks who had infiltrated governmental positions of authority.[28] In 1950, the Senate Committee on Expenditures in the Executive Department's subcommittee on Investigations, chaired by Senator Clyde R. Hoey of North Carolina, issued "Employment of Homosexuals and Other Sex Perverts in Government."[29] This report outlined the unsuitability and incidence of sexual perversion among government employees, including members of the Department of Defense.

Like previous documents that adhered to a social-contagion theory, the Senate's report did not outline the difference between the risk posed by the homosexual and that of heterosexual drug addicts or adulterers. It did, however, document the extent to which federal employees had been separated for homosexual practices. From 1947 to 1950, there were 4,954 cases involving homosexuality in the federal government, of which 88 percent involved military personnel.[30] Of these 4,380 cases, 470, or slightly more than 10 percent, were removed through court-martial, while the rest were separated by administrative actions.[31] Of the three services, the navy was more likely to discharge an individual on the basis of homosexuality; if accused of homosexual practices, however, an individual was more likely to undergo court-martial proceedings in the army than in the navy. The air force was the least likely of the services to either separate an individual for homosexuality or try the accused in a military court.[32]

Despite the Senate's attention, the incidence of administrative discharge for homosexuality within the armed services remained a relatively small problem. In the navy, for example, there were 5 administrative discharges per 10,000 officers and 10 discharges per 10,000 enlisted men. In the Marine Corps, there were 7 discharges per 10,000 servicemen for the period from 1947 to 1949.[33]

The 1950 revision of army regulations divided homosexuals into three classes that corresponded to the typology developed by the NRC during the war years. As Jeffrey Davis writes:

> Class I homosexuals were those whose homosexual offenses involved assault or coercion. . . . A general court-martial was mandatory for this category. Class II homosexuals were those who engaged in or attempted to engage in homosexual acts. Preferral of court-martial charges was mandatory, but a resignation in lieu of court-martial could be accepted from officers, or a statement accepting a dishonorable discharge could be accepted from enlisted soldiers. Class III homosexuals were personnel who exhibited, professed, or admitted homosexual tendencies, but who had not committed any provable acts or offenses. . . . Class III homosexuals could receive either an honorable or dishonorable discharge.[34]

Like army policy, air force regulations further distinguished between the onetime offender and the confirmed homosexual, while the navy declined to make this distinction.[35] In practice, there seem to be no documented cases of accused Class III homosexuals receiving an honorable discharge. However, the admission of homosexual behaviors, in and of itself, was now evidence enough to be separated from service. The Uniform Code of Military Justice, revised in 1950, broadened the legal definition of sodomy from the intent or act of anal intercourse to include any "unnatural carnal copulation with another person of the same or opposite sex. . . . Penetration, however slight, is sufficient to complete the offense."[36]

By adopting Executive Order 10450 in 1953, the Eisenhower administration codified "sexual perversion" as grounds for dismissal from federal jobs. By some estimates, dismissals from federal employment increased tenfold; within the military, where the charge of perversion could be circumvented by the use of an administrative discharge, the annual rate of separations doubled between the end of the war and the early 1950s.[37]

In the armed services, the decade following the war was marked by a retreat from the more lenient practices that had developed during wartime. Even though many homosexuals previously appear to have served their country either openly or without overt recrimination, official Cold War policies attempted to close the loopholes through which many homosexuals escaped detection or punishment. While wartime policies viewed homosexuals as individuals who, through no fault of their own, were undesirable members of the armed forces, postwar practices emphasized the subversive nature of homosexuality and its inherently disruptive effect on the operations of the military. The abandonment of the honorable discharge as a means of separation, the increased use of intelligence operations to separate individuals suspected of homosexual activity, and the heightened suspicion placed upon those who did not conform to traditional sex roles forced a minority of homosexuals into administrative discharges and the majority deeper into hiding.

In 1956, the secretary of the navy convened a board of naval and Marine Corps personnel to study the current situation and offer recommendations on the place of homosexuals within the U.S. Navy. The board, headed by Captain S. H. Crittenden, issued its "Report of the Board Appointed to Prepare and Submit Recommendations to the Secretary of the Navy for the Revision of Policies, Procedures, and Directives Dealing with Homosexuals" in the following spring. The Crittenden Report, as it has become known, is the most thorough review of homosexual policies that any of the services have released to this date. Besides detailing the internal workings of the navy in regard to homosexual policy and personnel, its recommendations presage current policy debates by more than a quarter century.[38]

The original charge to Crittenden and the board has been destroyed, along with much of its supporting documentation. Among gay and lesbian scholars, some speculation exists as to why the report was originally commissioned, including the need to reexamine policies in the light of the discovery that prominent navy personnel were homosexual. Even without this impetus, however, the review of policies would not have been surprising. Both the army and the air force had recently revised their separation policies for homosexual personnel; since navy policy differed from the other branches' policies in a few particulars, a cross-service comparison might have been warranted. As the report itself remarked, the social climate of the immediate postwar period had changed to some extent: the shock waves from the Kinsey reports had subsided, as had the most virulent anticommunist rhetoric of the early

Cold War. The Crittenden Board, finally, was used as a means of evaluating the effectiveness of the implementation strategies surrounding the 1949 Department of Defense directive that substantially rationalized military policies concerning homosexuals.[39]

The Crittenden Report opens a window into the practices of the military of the 1950s as well as offering further evidence that there have long been competing viewpoints concerning the role of homosexuals within the military itself. The recommendations made by the board generally argue for the relaxation of separation criteria of homosexual personnel. These recommendations do not appear to have been enacted into any substantive policy; therefore, it might be reasonable to assume that within the service there were competing forces that argued against those conclusions reached by the Crittenden Board.

Among the report's findings:

- "Many exclusively homosexual persons have served honorably in all branches of the military service without detection."
- "The concept that homosexuals necessarily pose a security risk is unsupported by adequate factual data."
- "The concept of homosexuality as a clinical entity has been discarded."[40]

The committee also came to the following conclusions:

- "Based on testimony of record, the practice of the other services and its own experience, the Board has little difficulty in reaching the conclusion that mandatory discharge for all one-time, non-habitual offenders is not in the best interest of the Naval service."
- On this basis, the board recommended that the Class III homosexual classification, including those individuals that displayed homosexual tendencies or associated with homosexuals, be abolished, and that new means of evaluation be developed that weighed each Class III offense on its own merit.
- "The exclusion from service of all persons who, on the basis of their personality structure, could conceivably engage in homosexual acts is totally unfeasible in view of the large proportion of the young adult male population which falls in this category."
- No attempt should be made to differentiate between men and women in the instruction with respect to procedures or disposition for homosexual activity.

The report summarized the differences between the different branches of service in their disposition toward homosexuals. While these administrative differences were relatively minor, variations existed, particularly in the directives determining the inclusion of an individual in the Class III category. The army favored the retention of those men or women who were determined to have engaged in an isolated homosexual act. The air force was less lenient in its desire to retain Class III homosexuals, and the navy refused to make these distinctions in its statement of policy and further "provides that pychiatric opinion that a homosexual offender is not a 'true homosexual' is immaterial."[41]

The Crittenden Report made several recommendations to change procedure concerning homosexual personnel. These included the elimination of the Class III homosexual as an administrative distinction. In existing administrative code, a "Class III" homosexual was defined as "those rare cases wherein personnel only exhibit, profess, or admit homosexual *tendencies* and wherein there are no specific provable acts or offenses, or court-martial jurisdiction does not exist."[42]

The tendency clause was seen as the most problematic aspect of existing policy for two reasons. First, even psychiatrists hesitated to label individuals solely on the basis of their statements. Second, even exclusively homosexual persons could not be identified solely through mannerisms or behaviors. Finally, "the exclusion from service of all persons who, on the basis of their personality structure, could conceivably engage in homosexual acts is totally unfeasible in view of the large proportion of the young male adult population which falls into this category."[43]

The report also recommended that the policies surrounding the one-time offender be reevaluated. In the board's opinion, the present policies were too inflexible, and the board "has little difficulty in reaching the conclusion that mandatory discharge for all one-time, non-habitual offenders is not in the best interest of the naval service." The board also stated that other-than-honorable discharge should not be mandatory for any class of offender.[44]

Some of the problems uncovered by the board in connection with homosexual personnel were definitional. While the board recommended the separation of the confirmed homosexual, it believed that both the one-time offender as well as the individual who had homosexual tendencies should be retained in service. As Colonel Albert Glass, chief psychiatry and neurology consultant to the Office of the Surgeon General, argued, one of the foremost problems was in defining the "confirmed" homosexual. In the absence of subjective criteria, many confirmed homosexuals served honorably while many members of the service who had tendencies were separated and stigmatized for life.[45]

Glass remarked in his testimony that earlier studies of the problem had come to the conclusion that there was no way to separate the confirmed homosexual from personnel who might exhibit stereotypical manner-isms or occasional tendencies. After discussing the 1945 studies of Fry and Rostrow, Glass remarked upon an army study that

> followed 75 overt homosexuals [who] were retained in the service. All were followed at least a year and some a little more than a year. Of these 75 individuals, 44% were retained in the service at the end of this year, 23% had received an honorable discharge and 7% an un-desirable discharge. One individual had died as a result of combat wounds. Of the 44% retained in service, 11 of these were promoted; 17 had served overseas in some combat theater; one had been pro-moted and demoted, and two were AWOL. In summary, 48% made a fair service adjustment, 7% were of doubtful value, and 45% proved to be a definite liability.

In comparing this group with the average inductees, it was found that 90 percent of the inductees were expected to give creditable service.[46]

The incidence of cases involving sexually aberrant conduct during the period from July 16 to November 26, 1956, was approximately 1 per 440 enlisted persons per year in the whole navy, ranging from a mini-mum of about 1 per 1,200 or 1,300 in rating groups III (electronics), VIII (construction), IX (aviation), and XII (stewards) to an extreme rate of more than 1 per 200 per year among hospital men and hospital corpsmen, seamen, WAVES, yeomen, and certain other personnel clas-sifications. This analysis, completed for the purposes of the Crittenden Board, further characterized the service person accused of homosexu-ality. The great majority were under twenty-five years of age and had served for less than seven years. They did not fall into any particular pattern of educational attainment, preservice environment, or family background. Their previous criminal records were so negligible that the authors of the report concluded that "individuals involved in reported sexual aberrations are, on the whole, an otherwise well behaved lot."

It is perhaps safe to conclude that those individuals who fell under the working definition of the "confirmed" homosexual were rarely caught in their behaviors while within the service. Of those individuals who were caught, the majority were younger naval personnel who were likely to fall into either the category of Class III homosexual or of the onetime offender. In addition, there is some evidence to suggest that those individuals accused of homosexuality had manifested other psy-chological or neurological disorders.

The most startling aspects of the navy's procedures toward homo-sexual behavior were the procedures of investigation and interrogation carried out by the Office of Naval Intelligence. Since, according to the chief of naval personnel, two-thirds of the aberrant sexual behavior of those accused of homosexuality occurred off-base, it was unlikely that these individuals had been caught *in flagrante delicto*. Instead, the naval personnel report documented that "only 15.3% of cases derived from unsolicited voluntary admissions of homosexual activity or tendencies. Nearly 50% of all individual cases were developed through follow-up. . . [and] some 20% or less involved voluntary admission."[47] In theory, the Office of Naval Investigation (ONI) was only supposed to initiate an investigation by the request of a commanding officer. However, it became apparent that by 1956 the ONI was using evidence collected in one investigation to initiate proceedings against other naval personnel.

In his testimony, Mr. S. Frank Scinta of the Office of Naval Intelligence described the interrogation procedures of those accused of homosexual acts or tendencies. According to Scinta, the accused was not interrogated until enough information was gathered to initiate court-martial proceedings. When confronted, the accused was offered neither the promise of immunity nor the advice of counsel (though the latter would be provided on demand). Instead, the individual was confronted with a prima facie case and offered the opportunity to either resign his or her commission or accept a separation from service under less-than-honorable discharge.[48]

As the only extant report released by the military in the postwar period, the recommendations issued by the Crittenden Report stand at odds with the official policies of the navy and the armed services. In historical context, however, the report's recommendations logically extended some of the trends that had emerged in the fifteen years since the war. In the aggregate, the Crittenden Board concluded that homosexuality was not a major problem to the everyday functioning of the navy. It did not believe that revision of existing code would significantly alter the incidence of homosexuality and while it did not recommend that confirmed homosexuals be kept within the service, it concluded that many had served their country with honor, and did not pose any extraordinary security risk to their nation.

By recommending the elimination of the Class III homosexual, the Crittenden Report further suggested that people accused of quasi-criminal behavior had the right to some form of due process. The Class III homosexual either exhibited "homosexual tendencies" or was disruptive in his or her behaviors. The board did *not* favor the retention of the confirmed homosexual but realized that the elimination of all those who might possibly have homosexual tendencies was an unworkable solution to the dilemma posed by homosexuals within the service.

The recommendations offered by the Crittenden Report articulated a double standard of behavior and policy within the military. Gay men and women who successfully hid their orientation, proclivities, or tendencies were to be rewarded by honorable completion of their tour of duty. When behavior became disruptive to the smooth functioning of the military unit in the eyes of their superior officers, however, a gay man or lesbian could be labeled as a "confirmed homosexual" and be discharged under a Class II administrative proceeding. While the Crittenden Board attempted to circumvent any abuse of this proviso by specifying the psychiatric and administrative steps that should be undertaken in the determination of a Class II status, even the liberal policies and findings of the board stopped short of recommending the inclusion of openly gay men and women into the navy's ranks.

In the decade following the Crittenden Report, U.S. society saw the emergence of a new discourse surrounding homosexuality within the behavioral sciences as well as the beginnings of a political movement that championed the civil rights of gay men and women. Within the U.S. government, congressional officials and legal scholars began to question the administrative proceedings that had been developed to separate homosexuals from the armed services, laying the groundwork for the legal challenges that would occur in the 1970s and 1980s.

The use of police power in maintaining behavioral norms was not new to individual lesbians or gay men. What *was* new, however, was the use of homosexuality as a scare tactic in the political arena as well as the systematic nature of political oppression. Regardless of the nuances of medical causality, the homosexual was becoming an individual who equated his affectionate preferences with a legal system that left him vulnerable to arrest, extortion, or blackmail. As they became increasingly visible and identifiable within an urban milieu, and as they were increasingly unprotected by law enforcement agencies themselves, violent attacks against gay men and women became part of postwar urban life.[49]

Like the induction screening processes of World War II, the heightened rhetoric of antigay crusaders in the 1950s engendered an unexpected consequence: increasingly, gay men and women were given clues and indications that networks, institutions, and comrades existed where before there were no known contacts. For many isolated homosexuals, bad news about moral decline was good news. If the Kinsey reports had informed U.S. heterosexuals about a specter in their midst that it responded to both viscerally and violently, the same report had also helped inform gay men and lesbians that they were not alone.

Early homosexual advocacy, or "homophile," organizations were founded in U.S. cities during the 1950s. Henry Hay founded the Mattachine Society in April 1951; the Daughters of Bilitis, the first political organization for lesbians, was founded on September 21, 1955.[50] By the end of the decade, both groups would have several branches, or in the Mattachine Society's case, cells, in several U.S. cities. The year 1953 saw the publication of *ONE*, the first homophile periodical, as an off-shoot of the Los Angeles chapter of the Mattachine Society.

Several characteristics separate the Mattachine and the Daughters of Bilitis from previous social groups that had existed in the gay or lesbian community. The two groups argued for the civil rights of homosexuals within a larger society, without advocating their treatment or cure. When under the influence of Hay, whose previous political activity had been with the Communist Party, the Mattachine Society originally argued that homosexuals were a discrete class of individuals who were subject to distinctive social conditions given the structural nature of their oppression; as such, they had developed their own subculture that could act as a basis for future political and cultural expression.[51] The Daughters of Bilitis, meanwhile, developed a feminist rhetoric that connected the interests of lesbians to other homophile organizations and the political rights of women.

The impact of early homophile organizations should not be overemphasized, however. The combined memberships of these groups probably never exceeded a thousand at any one time during the 1950s; *ONE* never published more than two thousand issues. For the vast majority of gay men and lesbians in U.S. society, isolation remained the overriding characteristic of their affectionate preferences; even within the relatively more tolerant environments of those U.S. cities that had rudimentary gay subcultures, fear of prosecution and harassment remained part of everyday lives.

In San Francisco, overt protest took an unusual form. José Sarria, a well-known drag entertainer at the Black Cat, one of the more venerable gay bars in the city, decided to run for city supervisor in the fall elections. Previously, Sarria had performed a weekly operatic satire, whose invariable subtext was that gay men and lesbians had legal rights, could plead not guilty to morals charges, and could demand a trial by jury. In the election, Sarria polled over seven thousand votes, enough to beat several established politicos, if not enough to put him on the board. This was the nation's first run for office by an avowed homosexual.

Activists on the East Coast rethought their political positions, as well. The Mattachine Society, whose early radicalism had been tempered by the late 1950s, was transformed again as new members took control of the existing organizations. Frank Kameny, taking his organizational cues from black civil rights leaders, argued for direct, confrontational action as well as chiding those who sought an etiologic explanation for homosexuality:

> I do not see the NAACP and CORE worrying about which chromo-some and gene produces [a] black skin or about the possibility of bleaching the Negro. I do not see any great interest on the part of the B'nai B'rith Anti-Defamation League in the possibility of solving problems of anti-semitism by converting Jews to Christianity.
>
> In all of these minority groups, we are interested in obtaining rights for our respective minorities as Negroes, as Jews, and as homo-sexuals. Why we are Negroes, Jews, or homosexuals is totally irrele-vant, and whether we can be changed to whites, Christians, or hetero-sexuals is equally irrelevant.[52]

The Mattachine Society of New York picketed the United Nations, Independence Hall, and the White House in the summer of 1965. "Sip-Ins," or protests at bars that enforced liquor control laws that prohibited the serving of homosexuals, were used to defuse the state liquor author-ity's harassment of gay men and women; early attempts were made at coalition building between existing homophile organizations to turn sporadic protests and actions into a mass movement.[53]

Concurrently within psychology and sociology, the late 1950s and early 1960s saw the origin of a debate over the proper classification of homosexuals in U.S. culture. A small number of psychiatrists, Evelyn Hooker chief among them, saw homosexuality as a condition that was neither pathological nor congenital; instead, it was an immutable part of a person's makeup.[54] Rather than belonging to a diagnostic category, some homosexuals began to consider themselves as part of a class of individuals, with a separate and distinctive relationship to the larger society. Like feminists who questioned the medical and psychological formulations of hysteria or depression, gay men and women became increasingly suspicious of psychiatric explanations of their conditions.[55] By 1960, homosexuality had been listed as a sociopathic personality disorder in the American Psychiatric Association's *Diagnostic and Sta-tistical Manual, Mental Disorders* (*DSM-I*) for eight years.[56] In the 1960s, psychiatrists and psychoanalysts continued to redefine the prac-tice of homosexual behaviors in both clinical behaviors and social con-texts. In what might be thought of as the last gasp of the homosexual as a clinical entity, sociologists redefined homosexuality as a heterodoxy of personality types, rather than a category of deviance.[57]

Within the military, the separation of homosexuals proceeded unchal-lenged throughout the late 1950s and early 1960s. In *Homosexuals and*

the Military: A Study of Less Than Honorable Discharge, Colin S.
Williams and Martin J. Weinberg concluded that if current estimations as
to the extent of homosexual activity in the general population were at all
congruent with the incidence of homosexuality in the military, then the
vast majority of homosexual personnel received honorable discharges.[58]
As the authors conclude, "the stereotyped view of the homosexual as having uncontrollable sex drives that demand constant satisfaction" is a perception that was not based in the facts of the period.[59] However, separations of homosexuals within the service were a substantial (between
one-quarter and one-third) proportion of less-than-honorable discharges.[60]

Williams and Weinberg then undertook a study of members from
homophile groups who had served in the military to analyze the variables
that might predict the type of discharge that a homosexual would receive
at the end of his military service. In terms of personal characteristics, neither age nor educational attainment seemed to influence the type of discharge that the service member received. After discharge, there was no
difference in the income or occupational level between those who
received an honorable and those who received less-than-honorable discharge, nor was there a difference between the type of discharge received
and the sexual-orientation level of the sample group (the authors
employed the scale developed originally by Alfred Kinsey, which places
sexual orientation on a scale where zero is an exclusively heterosexual
individual, and six indicates an exclusively homosexual orientation).

Thus, less-than-honorable discharge resulting from discovery was
not necessarily an arbitrary decision by military authorities. Williams
and Weinberg further examined the effects of the less-than-honorable
discharge, and concluded that those who were labeled as deviant did not
suffer any greater effects than those homosexuals who had completed
their service with an honorable discharge. The application of the deviant
label by military authorities did not seem to affect the life course of
those individuals to whom it was applied.[61]

For those members of the service who were accused of homosexual
activity, the procedure from accusation to discharge took approximately
two to three months, including interrogation, a psychiatric evaluation, a
board hearing, and a court-martial. It was here that the application of the
deviant label was at its most successful. There were virtually no cases
of gay men or women who chose to fight their discharges.[62] Instead,
most people accused of homosexuality cooperated to protect others, to
avoid being threatened, to avoid more severe punishment, or to finally
come clean. Most of the accused waived the right to an administrative
hearing, which virtually guaranteed them an undesirable discharge. After
interrogation, the accused service member was segregated from his

or her unit; in rare instances, he or she was tried and sentenced to hard time.

By the early 1960s, however, the rationales developed to explain the separation of homosexuals from the services had been altered to reflect a new understanding of homosexual behavior. The new justifications for exclusion were not based on the inherent unsuitability of the homosexual or upon their perceived risk to national security. Instead, new theories centered upon the homosexual's inability to maintain proper discipline or command his or her fellow comrades. As John A. Everhard wrote in the *Air Force Judge Advocate General's Bulletin:* "In addition to strong moral and social taboos, sexual perverts are a corrosive influence because they must have partners and often prey upon the youthful, naive, and greedy. Hence they are conducive to a general lowering of the moral fiber of the military community. They are, in short, military liabilities and must be discharged."[63]

Within other governmental circles, however, there seemed to be some discomfort with the means by which homosexual servicemen and women were being separated. As documented in the Crittenden Report, procedure generally involved presenting the accused with the options of voluntarily accepting either a resignation for the good of the service, if an officer, or an administrative discharge, if an enlisted person. If the accused refused one of these two options, he or she was liable to court-martial and the possibility of being discharged dishonorably. This confrontation occurred without the benefit of counsel.

In August 1963, Senator Sam Ervin proposed a series of legislation that would alter the civil liberties enjoyed by members of the armed forces.[64] In an atmosphere that questioned the military's right to determine and enforce the legal code necessary for its required discipline, several legal scholars challenged the administrative proceeding as a means of separation from the service. Among the legal challenges were the right to legal counsel, the right to confront and cross-examine witnesses, and the right to request a court-martial for alleged misconduct.[65]

By the end of the decade, military legal authorities, like behavioral scientists, were moving away from attempts to define the homosexual. "In 1970," one analyst writes, "the homosexuality regulation was superseded and was integrated into regulations that covered all types of unfitness and unsuitability discharges. Unsuitability could be demonstrated by evidence of homosexual 'tendencies, desires, or interests.'"[66] The army's posture, then, was that there was discretion to retain homosexuals in this period.[67] Contrary to what would later be argued in court, however, the navy regulation of July 31, 1972, reiterated the policy of separating homosexuals without exception.[68]

On June 27, 1969, police attempted to make a routine raid on the Stonewall Inn, a gay bar in New York's Greenwich Village. Instead of complying, the bar's patrons, joined by onlookers and passersby, erupted into violence, forcing the arresting officers back into the bar. By the next night, the rioting spread; sporadic confrontations between police and gay protesters occurred over the next several days.[69]

The American Psychiatric Association (APA) became one of the first targets of the new gay radicalism. During their annual meetings from 1970 to 1973, the APA was confronted with gay men and lesbians who were disruptive, confrontational, and adamant in their goal of removing homosexuality as a psychiatric diagnosis per se. At the 1972 convention, panelists presenting gay-liberationist views included Barbara Gittings, a founding member of the Daughters of Bilitis. Over the course of the year, various subcommittees and affiliated organizations either were confronted by activists or initiated their own dialogues concerning the place of homosexuality in their profession. Finally, the nomenclature of diagnosis was altered; "sexual orientation disturbance" was substituted for "homosexuality" in the *DSM-II*. For the first time, gay activists had achieved a victory over a group with whom they had, at times, an adversarial relationship.[70]

The archetypes of gay life began to change as well. Historically, lesbian personae were dichotomized into the categories of "butch" and "femme," while gay male characterizations were uniformly derogatory and powerless. As more men and women publicly declared their sexual orientation and the diversity of the homosexual community became apparent, these old characterizations were quickly replaced by newer stereotypes. Lillian Faderman has argued that the "femme" disappeared from the lesbian scene as women cast off roles imposed by a sexist society. In the gay male community, an ideal developed that was based on the imagery of working-class men and was overtly virile, masculine, and sexually aggressive. Both politically and personally, gay men and women developed characteristics that rejected the imposition of powerlessness.[71]

Within the military, the procedures of accusation, interrogation, and separation of homosexuals from service continued. What began to occur after Vietnam, however, were a series of court cases that challenged the procedures of the military. During the late 1970s and early 1980s, openly homosexual service members brought to court each branch of the service. The three cases generally thought to be legal benchmarks concerning U.S. military policy toward homosexuals are, for the navy, *Berg v. Claytor;* for the army, *Ben-Shalom v. Secretary of the Army;* and for the air force, *Matlovich v. Secretary of the Air Force.*[72] In each of these instances, the plaintiff argued that his or her conduct negated the assumption made by the military that homosexuality was incompatible with military service.

These proceedings differed from earlier cases because of the nature of the complaint against the service. Earlier plaintiffs had denied homosexuality and protested the nature and the effects of their separations from the service. In general, these earlier plaintiffs questioned the due process of administrative discharge proceedings and the irreparable harm caused by the mislabeling of themselves as homosexuals.[73] Matlovich, Berg, and Ben-Shalom, on the other hand, freely admitted to their homosexual proclivities, and protested existing policy that separated them on this basis. All argued that their sexuality had little or no effect upon their ability to complete their duties satisfactorily and presented their service records as their evidence.

Leonard Matlovich, the best known of the three plaintiffs, had the effect of bringing the military's policies into public discourse. In a remarkable speech from the bench, Judge Gerhard Gesell remarked:

> This is a distressing case. It is a bad case. It may be that bad cases make bad law. Having spent many months dealing with aspects of this litigation, it is impossible to escape the feeling that the time has arrived or may be imminent when branches of the Armed Forces need to reappraise the problem which homosexuality unquestionably presents in the military context. . . .
>
> We all recognize that by a gradual process there has come to be a much greater understanding of many aspects of homosexuality. Public attitudes are clearly changing. Some state legislatures have already acted to reflect these changing attitudes, moving more in the direction of tolerance. Physicians, church leaders, educators, and psychologists are able now to demonstrate that there is no standard, no stereotype of a homosexual which, unfortunately, some of the Air Force knee-jerk reaction to these cases would suggest still prevails in the Department.[74]

Upon appeal in federal court, Matlovich was reinstated. Rather than reenlisting, however, he eventually made a cash settlement with the air force. In Vernon "Copy" Berg's case, the separation board had been instructed that it could recommend retention, which in fact was contrary to military policy. Eventually, Berg's discharge was upgraded to honorable, and since his case was legally joined to Matlovich's, he was technically reinstatable. The case of Miriam Ben-Shalom, an army reservist, had the most profound policy effects of the three cases. As Randy Shilts writes, "in 1980 a Federal district court ruled that she should be reinstated on the grounds that her first amendment rights had been violated when she was discharged because of her comments to . . . a reporter."[75] The army ignored the ruling.

The challenges to policy in these cases helped to redefine the military's rationale for excluding gay men and lesbians from the services. Rather than upholding moral standards, separating the criminal from the innocent, or removing security risks, the basis for military policy now rested upon the proposition that homosexuals were incapable of efficiently carrying out procedures and policy due to the lack of deference and respect they would receive from their compatriots. Given the traditional deference accorded to the military in regard to personnel matters by the civil courts, legal challenges invoking due process or equal protection arguments on behalf of their plaintiffs found little success.

In 1981, the Department of Defense issued a directive that made this policy uniform in all service branches. Perhaps the most startling aspect of the new policy was the working definition of a homosexual: Department of Defense directive 1332.14 stated that "homosexual means a person, regardless of sex, who engages in, desires to engage in, or intends to engage in homosexual acts."[76] By this definition, the Department of Defense contradicted the findings of the Crittenden Report issued twenty-five years earlier; rather than understanding homosexuality as a physical expression that close to half of all men would experience during their adult lives, the new regulation defined homosexuals as a discrete, identifiable group.

By the early 1980s, the U.S. political climate had been substantially altered by the emergence of a gay and lesbian subculture. Rather than accepting the judgments of some psychiatric or religious spokespeople that their condition was deviant or morally wrong, lesbians and gay men began to challenge the institutional frameworks that discriminated against them. As a political movement, homosexuals began to perceive themselves as a minority group with special interests and needs in U.S. culture. In the U.S. military, the "confirmed" homosexual, rather than accepting his or her ouster quietly, began to question the rationales that had facilitated his or her separation from the armed services.

The 1970s and 1980s also saw the emergence of a homosexual subculture in the United States that increasingly articulated its political desires through the rhetoric of diversity and inclusion. For a minority of gay men and lesbians, homosexual orientation became an organizing characteristic of personal and community life; this orientation, fueled by the increased demands of AIDS and the increasingly radical stance of AIDS activists, became part of a unifying political identity. As a political plank, gay rights moved from a radical fringe to an accepted subject of national party politics.

The period after the Vietnam conflict also saw the development of a gay and lesbian subculture within the military itself. The informal networks that had existed previously grew and expanded as more homo-sexual men and women integrated their sexual orientation into their everyday lives; while previously lesbians and gay men had been cir-cumspect in their behaviors, more joined "The Family" as specific duties, bases, and off-base institutions developed reputations for toler-ance or acceptance. While certain stations remained the stereotyped province of gay men and lesbians (hospital corpsmen in the navy, for example, or female drill sergeants in the marines), gay men and women began to develop a presence throughout the armed services.[77]

The procedures that had developed among the military intelligence services for investigating and separating gay men and lesbians grew alongside the emergent subculture. According to a report compiled by the General Accounting Office (GAO), there were 16,919 discharges for homosexuality within the armed services between 1980 and 1991. These discharges comprised 1.7 percent of all involuntary discharges in the Department of Defense for this period.[78] Like all involuntary sepa-rations for this period, the numbers of homosexual-related discharges peaked in 1982 and declined for the remainder of the decade. On aver-age, however, over 1,400 service personnel were separated per year.

Both between and within the services, there were significant varia-tions in the rates of discharge for homosexuality. While the navy accounted for 27 percent of the active force, it discharged 8,638 mem-bers, accounting for 51 percent of all homosexual discharges. The army, accounting for 37 percent of the active force, had 25 percent of all homosexual discharges, whereas the Marine Corps and air force, at 27 and 9 percent of the active force, accounted for 18 and 6 percent of all homosexual separations, respectively.

While the Department of Defense does not maintain cost figures pursuant to the processing and separation of personnel, the GAO esti-mated that the cost of replacing each member separated from the service would be approximately $28,226 per enlisted member and $120,772 for each officer. Using the more conservative figure for enlisted personnel, and an average discharge rate of 1,400 members per year, the cost of replacing those discharged for homosexuality in the period between 1980 and 1990 would have approximated $39.5 million annually.

Within the military, the policies surrounding AIDS or the incidence of the human immunodeficiency virus (HIV) again brought the issues of separation of homosexuals into public discussion. While many HIV-positive service members stated that they had been infected through het-erosexual contact, the enormous preponderance of AIDS cases in the 1980s were contracted through homosexual contact or intravenous drug use. When the military began testing for the presence of HIV antibodies in late 1985, it predicted that it would find approximately one thousand infected soldiers and dependents. By later 1987, when the testing program had been under way for two years, the number of HIV-positive personnel (excluding dependents) was 3,336, or roughly two-and-a-half times the number of men who had been discharged for homosexuality in each calendar year.[79]

The armed services' policies concerning the exclusion and separation of homosexual personnel continued to come under increasing internal and external criticism. Legal challenges continued after the new Department of Defense polices went into effect in 1981; among the most publicized were *Secora v. Fox*, *Pruitt v. Cheney*, *Steffan v. Cheney*, and *Watkins v. United States Army*. In each case, different aspects of the new regulations were contested in federal court.

Like the earlier ruling in *Matlovich v. Secretary of the Air Force*, the Secora case questioned the relationship between an individual's homosexuality and the right of the armed services to discharge them solely on that basis. Like Matlovich, Secora's record was unblemished; the district court questioned the air force's discharge and agreed with the magistrate that Secora was entitled to a reasoned explanation as to why he was being discharged.[80]

Dusty Pruitt, an ordained Methodist minister, was separated from the army reserves in 1986. Pruitt, who had no previous allegations of homosexual conduct while within the service, was separated because of her public admission of homosexuality in 1982. Under appeal, the federal bench held that Pruitt should have been allowed to present the evidence to support an equal-protection argument, and that the army needed to provide a rational nexus between the behavior of homosexual soldiers and their separation from service.[81]

Joseph Steffan, a midshipman at the United States Naval Academy at Annapolis, was separated from service six weeks before his graduation. An outstanding midshipman, Steffan filed suit in the United States District Court challenging the Department of Defense policy on the grounds that his separation violated his rights of free speech, due process, and equal protection. After refusing to answer questions concerning his sexual behavior while at the academy, Steffan's case was dismissed. On appeal, however, the bench reversed the earlier court's decision, claiming that because Steffan's dismissal was predicated on his own admissions rather than any substantive evidence, his sexual activity was irrelevant to the ruling. The district court, however, held that the military ban on homosexuals was justifiable both on military grounds and as a protection against the spread of AIDS in the armed forces.[82]

Perhaps the most intriguing challenge to the military's policies concerning homosexuality came from Perry Watkins, an army staff sergeant whose fourteen-year career included tours in Vietnam and Korea. Watkins, who admitted to his homosexuality upon enlistment in 1968, had been permitted to reenlist in 1971, 1974, and 1979. By all accounts an exemplary soldier (he had, on at least one occasion, received eighty-five out of a possible eighty-five points on a service evaluation), Watkins's security clearance was revoked in 1982, prompting him to file suit to have his clearance reinstated as well as to prevent his discharge under the new Department of Defense regulations.

The Western District Court of Washington enjoined the army from separating Watkins; however, the service subsequently denied his reenlistment. On appeal, the federal bench ruled that the reenlistment regulations violated the equal-protection clause and held the army to be stopped from barring Watkins's reenlistment. In 1990, the United States Supreme Court denied the army's petition to review. Watkins was promoted, collected his back pay, and voluntarily retired from the service.[83]

Like the Crittenden Report thirty years earlier, the PERSEREC report investigated the policies surrounding homosexuals and issued recommendations that stood in opposition to many established procedures and rationales. Unlike the Crittenden Report, which was essentially an in-house review of navy procedures, the PERSEREC report was developed largely independent of service review, and its conclusions were suppressed immediately by the Department of Defense.

In June 1986, the undersecretary for defense (policy) approved ten top research areas, including the validation of personnel security clearances. In this research area, one question addressed the possibility of rationalizing the disposition of the cases involving homosexuality and adultery, as well as the adjudication of those who abused alcohol or other drugs. Part of this research agenda was directed to the recently established Personnel Security Research and Education Center, known by the acronym PERSEREC.

In the fall of 1987, the assistant deputy to the undersecretary of defense wrote PERSEREC, amplifying the research that the office of the undersecretary felt was necessary. Rather than comparing the job performance of heterosexuals and homosexuals, the memo stated:

> The governing factors . . . are whether a particular individual has engaged in acts which are criminal, notoriously disgraceful, reckless or irresponsible, constitute sexual perversion, or indicate lack of judgment or stability. It is also relevant whether the particular conduct is criminal in the jurisdiction in which the subject resides (which sodomy is in many States), the extent to which it involves

minors, and whether it is indicative of instability or lack of good judgment.[84]

The working draft of the report, entitled "Nonconforming Sexual Orientations and Military Suitability," by Theodore Sarbin, Ph.D., and Kenneth E. Karols, M.D., Ph.D., was submitted to the undersecretary of defense on December 15, 1988.

The Department of Defense's first response to the report was that the work was fundamentally misdirected in its research objectives. In a memorandum dated February 10, 1989, the Department of Defense was concerned with the possibility that a connection existed between homosexual orientation and security risks for both its civilian and military personnel, not with whether homosexuals could serve in the military. Craig Alderman Jr., the author of the memo, further stated that while the report might prove to have some utility in the future, it would be used by critics of PERSEREC to undermine the usefulness of that institution. As well, "It most probably will cause us in Washington to expend even more time and effort satisfying concerns in this whole issue area both in Congress and the media, and within the Department itself." Alderman concluded the memo by stating, "If it were not for all of the above, the situation could be humorous. It is as if *Consumer Reports* commissioned research on the handling characteristics of the Suzuki Sammurai [*sic*], and received instead a report arguing that informal import quotas for Japanese automobiles were not justified."[85]

Prior research concerning the suitability of homosexuals for security clearances had concluded that gay men and lesbians posed no extraordinary risks.[86] Jerel McCrary and Lewis Gutierrez, writing in 1979, remarked that while there was no explicit exclusion of homosexuals from receiving security clearances, gay men and lesbians fell under the exclusion criteria for sexual perversion under Department of Defense Directive 5220.6. By 1980, legal challenges to the denial or withdrawal of security clearances on the basis of homosexuality had achieved a limited number of narrow successes. Having established the defendant's homosexuality, the government was required to offer evidence or proof that this constituted a basis for blackmail or reckless behavior.[87]

Rather than reexamine the rationales for the exclusion of homosexuals from positions requiring security clearances, Theodore Sarbin and Kenneth Karols authored a report that widely interpreted their charge to investigate the military suitability of homosexuals through an analysis of cultural, legal, and scientific explanations for the incidence of homosexuality within U.S. culture.

They came to the conclusion that U.S. culture had undergone a shifting series of attitudinal changes in its folkways, legal codes, and social constructions of sexual deviance that could be best characterized by an attitude of intolerance being replaced by one of indifference, if not acceptance.[88] After outlining current biological and psychological theories of sexual orientation, Sarbin and Karols present a typology of social constructions that had characterized the social perceptions of sexual deviance. After noting the incidence of separation, and the discrepancy between that number and the expected number of homosexuals within the military given the estimated percentage who claimed a same-sex preference, the authors concluded that the sodomy statutes under Article 125 of the Uniform Code of Military Justice were unenforceable and should thus be deleted from the legal code under the principle of desuetude.[89]

Sarbin and Karols also argued that since previous studies have concluded that military performance was not compromised by homosexuality per se, then the effects of openly homosexual men and women upon discipline, group morale, and cohesiveness should be the object of further study.[90] Working through analogy, the authors suggest that some paramilitary organizations, such as selected police and fire departments, had integrated homosexual personnel without incident, and that the time had come for the U.S. military to act as a model for the integration of homosexual men and women within its ranks. Finally, Sarbin and Karols reiterated the conclusions of the Crittenden Report that, overall, homosexuals prove no greater a security risk than heterosexuals.

While Sarbin and Karols's analysis of homosexuals within the military is a relatively straightforward exposition of liberal scientific and sociological thought, the report had several problems that limited its utility to the Department of Defense. As remarked previously, it did not specifically address the dilemma of homosexual orientation within the framework of security clearances, nor had the Department of Defense asked PERSEREC for a position paper outlining the feasibility of integrating homosexuals within the services. There had, in fact, been several recent challenges to Department of Defense policies surrounding security clearances among homosexual contractors or military personnel that remained unaddressed in this report.[91] The exposition of social constructions, while valid, was decidedly positivistic in its outlook, ignoring the possibility that differing paradigms could exist at the same time in a pluralistic society. Finally, Sarbin and Karols's discussion of military policy was ahistoric in nature, ignoring variations in service practices that may have effected change regardless of their argument that U.S. society was becoming more tolerant of homosexuality overall.

Similar to the navy's efforts to suppress the Crittenden Report, the Department of Defense refused to release the PERSEREC report to interested parties, citing "deliberative process privilege," or simply that the report was a draft discussion of internal policy and therefore not subject to public review. When finally released to congressional staff members as part of the deposition in Joseph Steffan's case, the Sarbin and Karols report was accompanied by another document, "Preservice Adjustment of Homosexual and Heterosexual Military Accessions: Implications for Security Clearance Suitability," that was released by PERSEREC to the Department of Defense in January 1989.[92]

Authored by Michael A. McDaniel, this second report was a quantitative analysis that compared the preservice adjustment of two different groups of service people: men and women who had been discharged for homosexuality and those men and women who either had been separated for other reasons, did not enter the services, or remained in the military. McDaniel linked self-reported data from the 1983 Educational and Biographical Information Survey (a survey administered to military applicants) and discharge data obtained from the Defense Manpower Data Center. Like the Sarbin report or the earlier Crittenden study, McDaniel's conclusions reiterated the lack of a relationship between homosexuality and service suitability: "Although [the] . . . limitations [of the study] should be carefully considered, the preponderance of the evidence presented in this study indicates that homosexuals show preservice suitability-related adjustment that is as good or better than the average heterosexual."[93] McDaniels further concluded that with the exception of preservice adjustment in the area of drug and alcohol use, "homosexuals resemble those who successfully adjust to military life more so than those who are discharged for unsuitability."[94]

CONCLUSION

In the aggregate, these documents suggest that the military has grappled with the issue of a gay and lesbian presence in the armed forces for far longer and with far more sophistication and complexity than it has been willing to acknowledge. In most reports that have become public, the military has admitted openly that most lesbians and gay men have served honorably and without incident, regardless of their admission or denial of their affectionate preferences.

Homosexuality, however, has not been a constant in U.S. military history. The meanings attached to the same-sex behaviors of men and women have been subject to a series of changing social constructions and ideologies for nearly the past eighty-two years. Like all sexual behaviors, homosexuality has undergone a transformation from an intimate and private activity to a behavior that is increasingly part of a public and political discourse.

The desire to fully understand homosexuality—or to put it less kindly, to solve its puzzle—has essentially stripped gay men and lesbians in the service of their civil liberties under either federal or military code. This is as true under the Articles of War in 1917 as it is under "Don't Ask, Don't Tell." The standard of behavior that has existed for putatively heterosexual service members has, unfortunately, never existed for those suspected of being gay or lesbian, regardless of their behavior, demeanor, or performance.

In the twentieth century, the social history of gay men and lesbians in the United States suggests that public policies and medical discourses have had a substantial impact upon the lives of those who identify themselves as homosexual. During the 1950s, a medical model posited that homosexual behavior was part of a faulty developmental pattern, was used as a justification to remove homosexuals from government or military service, and was used as a rationale to justify their entrapment, arrest, and persecution. On the other hand, in periods in which homosexuality was considered an innate or biologically determined characteristic, the rationale for policies that exclude or punish homosexual behavior became less clear; in the late nineteenth century or in the prewar period, criminal behavior and homosexuality were not popularly conflated.

In part, social perceptions and political consequence have been the result of the application of behavioral models to public policy. In the postwar period, gay men and lesbians underwent a period of heightened visibility and political persecution. The synergistic nature of this political environment helped give rise to a small but growing political movement that adopted the rhetoric and tactics of the civil-rights movements to argue for the inclusion of homosexual men and women in the body politic. While only a few men and women embraced homophile politics, many more began to think of themselves as part of a discrete minority who shared personality characteristics, affectionate preferences, and oppressions.

The growth of a gay subculture became one of the notable social developments in the United States after World War II. The rise of an identifiable gay and lesbian milieu was an indication not only that the incidence of openly homosexual behaviors had increased in U.S. society, but that gay men and lesbians had achieved the means and places in which to construct social institutions and identities that incorporated their sexual behaviors.

Increasingly, lesbians and gay men have come to see themselves as part of a minority or protected class. While there have always existed tensions between those men and women who seek inclusion in the mainstream of life and those who reject this goal, the once dominant themes of maladjustment and treatment have given way to a political discourse centered upon the rights and responsibilities of homosexual citizens.

NOTES

1. National Defense Research Institute, *Sexual Orientation and U.S. Military Personnel Policy: Options and Assessment* (Santa Monica, Calif.: RAND, 1993).

2. Lawrence R. Murphy, *Perverts by Official Order: The Campaign Against Homosexuals by the United States Navy* (New York, N.Y.: The Haworth Press, 1988), pp. 62–64. See also "Report of the Committee on Naval Affairs, United States Senate, Sixty-Seventh Congress, First Session, Relative to Alleged Immoral Conditions and Practices at the Naval Training Station, Newport, R.I." (Washington, D.C.: Government Printing Office, 1921).

3. These figures are tabulated from information found in a memo from the judge advocate general to the chief of the Bureau of Navigation, "Statistics Relative to Prison Population and Classification of Offenses," February 8, 1933, in Office of the Secretary, General Correspondence 1926–1940 (Washington, D.C.: National Archives), box 1224, folder P13-10/A to A9-9.

4. See the discussion of discharges in Jeffrey Davis, "Military Policy Toward Homosexuals: Scientific, Historical, and Legal Perspectives," *Military Law Review* 131 (1991): 75.

5. These opinions are quoted in a letter from Major General Blanton Winship, Judge Advocate General to the Adjutant General Record, October 16, 1931, in the U.S. Army Office of the Judge Advocate General Record Group 407, JAG (Washington, D.C.: National Archives), box 992, 250.1, folder 12-31-41 to 4-1-41. These documents are a collection of the intra- and interservice correspondence concerning the policy around homosexuality cases in the period July 1938 to May 1941, and will be referred to henceforth as the JAG Sodomists File.

6. See letter from Lietutenant Colonel Ernest H. Burt, JAGD, Chief, Military Justice Section, JAG Sodomists File.

7. Ibid., attached draft of proposed policy.

8. "Sodomy Cases Review, July 1938–May 1941," JAG Sodomists File.

9. This enumeration of revisions is from the figures found in memorandum "Miscellaneous Regulations and Source Material Pertinent to Army Homosexual Policies," June 23, 1950, Army Judge Advocate General (JAG) Precedent and History Section, Department of the Army (Washington, D.C.: National Archives), box 101.

10. "Sodomy Cases Review, July 1938–May 1941," JAG Sodomists File.

11. Allan Bérubé, *Coming out Under Fire: The History of Gay Men and Women in World War Two* (New York, N.Y.: The Free Press, 1990), p. 10.

12. Ibid., pp. 10–18.

13. Memorandum No. W615-4-43 from H. B. Lewis, Brigadier General, "Sodomists," January 10, 1943, JAG Sodomists File.

14. In certain circles, this is still referred to as the "queen for a day" loophole.

15. For example, see the correspondence from Winfred Overholser, M.D., National Research Council, Committee on Neuropsychiatry to Captain Forrest M. Harrison, Bureau of Medicine and Surgery, November 3, 1941, JAG Sodomists File.

16. Memorandum from the Chief of the Bureau of Medicine and Surgery to the Chief of Navy Personnel, "Proposed Procedure for the Disposition of Cases of Homosexuality Among Personnel of the U.S. Naval Service," September 21, 1942, in Record Group 52, Bureau of Medicine (Washington, D.C.: National Archives), folder P13-7/P19-1.

17. Wartime navy policy is codified in Bureau of Naval Personnel (BuPer) Regulation C44-12, "Procedure for the Disposition of Homosexuals Among Personnel of the United States Armed Service Pers-651-cdr, P13-7," January 28, 1944, Record Group 52, Bureau of Medicine (Washington, D.C.: National Archives).

18. Clement Fry and Edna Rostrow, "Some Observations on Homosexuality in Military Service," Interim Report No. 337, April 1, 1945, Committee on Medical Research of the Office of Scientific Research and Development (Washington, D.C.: Archives of the National Academy of Sciences). See also the testimony brief of Colonel Albert Glass, in S. H. Crittenden Jr. et al., "Report of the Board Appointed to Prepare and Submit Recommendations to the Secretary of the Navy for the Revision of Policies, Procedures, and Directives Dealing with Homosexuals, 21 December 1956–15 March 1957" (henceforth referred to as the Crittenden Report), part II, enclosure 1e. The Crittenden Report is difficult to obtain but copies may be requested for a nominal photocopying fee from the editors: belkin@polsci.ucsb.edu.

19. Lewis H. Loeser, "The Sexual Psychopath in the Military Service," *American Journal of Psychiatry* 102 (July 1945): 101.

20. Selective Service and psychiatric admission estimates are from memorandum from Charles O. Perrin, June 22, 1950, Army JAG Precedent and History Section, box 101.

21. For a discussion of the incidence of military administrative action taken against homosexuals, however, see William C. Menninger, *Psychiatry in a Troubled World: Yesterday's War and Today's Challenge* (New York, N.Y.: Macmillan, 1948), p. 255.

22. Alfred Kinsey et al., *Sexual Behavior in the Human Male* (Philadelphia, Pa.: W. B. Saunders, 1948). Kinsey's companion volume, *Sexual Behavior in the Human Female,* appeared in 1953. Quoted in John D'Emilio and Estelle Freedman, *Intimate Matters: A History of Sexuality in America* (New York, N.Y.: Harper & Row, 1988), p. 292.

23. The synonymous nature of communist and homosexual witch-hunts in the McCarthy period awaits an extensive analysis. For an introductory article on the sexual politics of the McCarthy era, see Allan Bérubé and John D'Emilio, "The Military and Lesbians During the McCarthy Years," *Signs: Journal of Women in Culture and Society* 9 (1984): 759–775. For the sexual proclivities of a few of the leading anticommunist agitators, however, see

Nicholas Von Hoffman, *Citizen Cohn* (New York, N.Y.: Doubleday, 1988) and Curt Gentry, *J. Edgar Hoover: The Man and the Secrets* (New York, N.Y.: Norton, 1991).

24. "Lecture to Be Utilized in the Indoctrination of Recruits," Bureau of Naval Personnel for Training Activity, January 14, 1948, Record Group 52, General Correspondence Bureau of Medicine (BuMed) (Washington, D.C.: National Archives), box 190, folder P11-4/A21.

25. "Indoctrination of WAVE Recruits on Subject of Homosexuality" [1952], reprinted in Bérubé and D'Emilio, "The Military and Lesbians During the McCarthy Years," *Signs: Journal of Women in Culture and Society* 9 (1984): 764–770.

26. Davis, "Military Policy Toward Homosexuals," p. 75.

27. This is not to suggest that gay men and lesbians were not persecuted for their affectionate preferences before the 1950s. As Jonathan Katz remarks in an introduction to his documentary history *Gay American History: Lesbians and Gay Men in the USA* (New York, N.Y.: Thomas Y. Crowell Co., 1976):

> During the four hundred years documented here, American homosexuals were condemned to death by choking, burning and drowning; they were executed, jailed, pilloried, fined, court-martialed, prostituted, fired, framed, blackmailed, disinherited, declared insane, driven to insanity, to suicide, murder, and self-hate, witch-hunted, entrapped, stereotyped, mocked, insulted, isolated, pitied, castigated, and despised . . . They were also castrated, lobotomized, shock-treated, and psychoanalyzed. (p. 11)

The documents collected by Katz detail some of the conditions of legal prosecution experienced by homosexual men and women before the war.

28. See Katz, *Gay American History,* pp. 91–108.

29. U.S. Senate, Committee on Expenditures in the Executive Departments, Subcommittee on Investigations, "Employment of Homosexuals and Other Sex Perverts in Government" (Washington, D.C.: Government Printing Office, 1950).

30. Calculated from figures in U.S. Senate Subcommittee on Investigations, "Employment of Homosexuals and Other Sex Perverts in Government," p. 7.

31. Thus, the incidence of homosexual separations from the armed services in the immediate postwar period would seem to follow a pattern roughly consistent with what we know about the World War II era.

32. Air force figures are included in army figures until the separation of these services in January 1948.

33. Figures are from "Administrative Discharges for Homosexuality" attached to letter from Captain C. G. McCormack to Dr. Richard L. Meiling, August 15, 1950, Record Group 52, General Correspondence Bureau of Medicine (Washington, D.C.: National Archives), box 190, folder P11-4/A21.

34. Davis, "Military Policy Towards Homosexuals," p. 76.

35. On speculation, this regulatory difference may account for the navy's higher incidence of separations during this period.

36. Quoted in Davis, "Military Policy Towards Homosexuals," p. 73.

37. John D'Emilio, *Sexual Politics, Sexual Communities: The Making of a Homosexual Minority in the United States 1940–1970* (Chicago, Ill.: University of Chicago Press, 1983), pp. 44–45. Unfortunately, there are no consistently

reliable statistics of separations for homosexual behavior across the different branches of the armed services, nor are there any internally consistent statistics for any one service over the entire time period. While many analysts make the logical assumption that most separations for moral charges were indeed for homosexual behavior, unfortunately medical, legal, and administrative statistics within the armed forces were not tabulated in any consistent manner.

38. Despite rumors as to its existence, the Crittenden Report was kept confidential for twenty years. According to Randy Shilts, it first came to light when navy lawyers found it during a search of Pentagon files in 1976; a copy of the report was released to Vernon Berg's attorneys under a Freedom of Information Act request. Previous requests by members of Congress, among others, were met by the reply that no work had been conducted. See Randy Shilts, *Conduct Unbecoming: Gays and Lesbians in the U.S. Military* (New York: St. Martin's Press, 1993), pp. 281–282. Other scholars have had difficulty obtaining the entire document, as well. Allan Bérubé received the completed text of the report, but an incomplete copy of its supporting documentation, while researching *Coming out Under Fire*. See his "A Note on Sources," pp. 283–285. While Berg's lawyers and Shilts's estate now possess the completed text and most of the second part of the report, the verbatim testimony included in the second part of the report and the entire third part or "confidential supplement" has never been released by the navy. When requesting a copy of the report for the writing of this document, the investigators were told that "a portion is no longer in the files . . . it is believed to have been destroyed." See personal correspondence from Major Cherie Zadlo, Office of the Assistant Secretary of Defense for Force Management and Personnel to Steve Schlosser [*sic*], RAND Corporation, May 10, 1993. This may be the first statement issued by the navy that indicates that it has destroyed its own reports concerning the incidence and effects of homosexuality in the service.

The army, like the navy, maintains that there is "no evidence of special studies pertaining to homosexuals" for the period before 1982 (see Bérubé, *Coming out Under Fire,* pp. 278–279). However, the Crittenden Report contains substantial evidence that the armed services had made several detailed studies of its homosexual servicemen and women. This evidence includes the following references:

1. Wartime Documentation. Fry and Rostrow's works are cited by the Crittenden Report, but the completed report has never been made available. Bérubé cites their reports, "Some Observations on Homosexuality in Military Service" and "Reflections on Some Aspects of Homosexuality as It Relates to Military Administration," May 10, 1948, Record Group 330 (Washington, D.C.: National Archives), box 65, entry 356. In the Crittenden Report, Fry and Rostrow's project is summarized on fiche 2, image 96.

2. 1947. On fiche 4, image 357, there is a summary of a report by the Department of Defense in preparation of the 1949 revision of policy (Colonel John M. Caldwell Jr., Chairman, "A Study to Revise Regulations for the Handling of Homosexuals in the Armed Forces [Project M-46]," August 24, 1947).

3. 1948. On fiche 4, image 368, of the Crittenden Report, in a memo from Acting Secretary of the Navy John Nicholas Brown to the

Chief of Naval Personal, Bureau of Medicine, Com, USMC, JAG, October 18, 1948, he states, "I am attaching herein the 'Report of the Committee for the Review of the Procedures for the Disposition of Naval Personnel Involved in Homosexual Offenses,' which includes a proposed draft of a letter to all ships and stations, which will replace all current directives."

Image 370 contains the title page of the report, "Committee Report of 24 August 1948," known extant copy held by G. N. Raines, Medical Corps.

4. 1949. In the Chronological Development of Naval Personnel, fiche 4, image 313, there is a reference to the "Report of Military Personnel Policy Committee (Project N146[?])" of August 24, 1949. This report was done in the preparation of the Secretary of Defense's memorandum of October 11, 1949. The question, here, of course, is whether these three citations (II, III, and IV) are actually the same report with different titles. While the year changes, they were all issued on August 24, and "N146" and "M-46" could very well be a typographical error.

5. 1952. In the same chronology (fiche 4, image 313), there is reference to a Department of Defense study that was ordered in the summer of 1952, in a memo from the Assistant Secretary of Defense (MP&R), "Directing Study of Processing Class III [Homosexuals]," July 28, 1952. The result of this order was Colonel John A. Schindler's "Report of Committee to Review Policy on Discharge of Homosexuals," October 24, 1952.

6. Postwar Documentation. In their brief before the Crittenden Board, on fiche 1, image 89 [Enclosure 1d], Captain J. E. Nardini, MC, Chief, Neuropsychiatric Service; Captain M. Cooperman, MC, USN Acting Chief of Psychiatry; and Captain S. V. Thompson, MC, USN, Med. Officer in Charge, Neuropsychiatric Service, USNH, Bethesda, commented upon a study that was completed, in which "a total of 267 men were examined in connection with investigations for homosexuality during a 33 month period at USNH, Yokosuka."

39. Shilts, *Conduct Unbecoming,* p. 288.

40. These findings are included in the summary found on pages 11–12 of the Crittenden Report.

41. Crittenden Report, p. 59.

42. Ibid., p. 25. Emphasis in the original.

43. Ibid., p. 38.

44. Ibid., p. 24.

45. Ibid., enclosure 1e.

46. Ibid.

47. Ibid., enclosure 3a.

48. Ibid., enclosure 1h.

49. Ibid., p. 51.

50. These dates are from Toby Marotta, *The Politics of Homosexuality* (Boston, Mass.: Houghton Mifflin, 1981) and from D'Emilio, *Sexual Politics, Sexual Communities,* p. 102.

51. D'Emilio, *Sexual Politics, Sexual Communities,* pp. 58–91.

52. Quoted in Marotta, *The Politics of Homosexuality,* p. 24.

53. Ibid., pp. 48–68.

54. For example, see Evelyn Hooker, "A Preliminary Analysis of Group Behavior of Homosexuals," *Journal of Psychology* 42 (1956): 217–225; and "Homosexuality: Summary of Studies," in *Sex Ways in Fact and Faith: Basis for Christian Family Policy,* Evelyn M. and Sylvanus M. Duvall, eds. (New York, N.Y.: Association Press, 1961).

55. For a patient's recounting of his psychological treatment, see Martin Duberman, *Cures: A Gay Man's Odyssey* (New York, N.Y.: Dutton, 1991).

56. A sociopathic personality disorder is one in which the patient does not exhibit anxiety or distress, despite the presence of pathological behavior. See Ronald Bayer, *Homosexuality and American Society: The Politics of Diagnosis* (New York, N.Y.: Basic Books, 1981), pp. 39–40.

57. For example, see William Simon and John H. Gagnon, "Homosexuality: The Formulation of a Sociological Perspective," *Journal of Health and Social Behavior* 8 (1968): 177–185.

58. Besides extrapolating from the published sources of the government, primarily the U.S. Senate Subcommittee on Constitutional Rights, "Constitutional Rights of Military Personnel," 87th Congress, 2d Session, 1962, and "Military Justice," 89th Congress, 2d Session, 1966, Williams and Weinberg draw upon other studies, including Fry and Rostrow, "Some Observations on Homosexuality in Military Service," and Loeser, "The Sexual Psychopath in the Military Service." See Colin J. Williams and Martin S. Weinberg, *Homosexuals and the Military: A Study of Less Than Honorable Discharge* (New York, N.Y.: Harper & Row, 1971), p. 50, note 17.

59. Ibid., p. 61.

60. Ibid., pp. 38–53.

61. Ibid., pp. 177–185. In *Conduct Unbecoming,* Shilts uses these statistics from this study to argue that, in the period of the Korean conflict when military manpower demands grew, the military's separation of homosexual personnel dropped dramatically. There is relatively little statistical information to support this claim. During the Korean conflict, all administrative separations dropped dramatically, including honorable, general, and undesirable discharges. With the exception of 1951, bad conduct and dishonorable discharges remain consistently below 1 percent of all military separations between 1951 and 1965. The proportion of all administrative separations that are "undesirable," or those that would be on account of homosexual activity, do not vary significantly during this time. See Williams and Weinberg, *Homosexuals and the Military,* pp. 39–40.

62. Williams and Weinberg, *Homosexuals and the Military,* p. 102. The procedures of interrogation are outlined on pages 100–114.

63. John A. Everhard, "Problems Involving the Disposition of Homosexuals in the Service," *Air Force Judge Advocate General's Bulletin* 11 (1960): 20.

64. S. 2001 to S. 2019, 88th Congress, 1st Session, 109th Congressional Record (Washington, D.C.: Government Printing Office, 1963), p. 120.

65. Among the analysts examining the procedural issues surrounding the military's use of the administrative discharge are William A. Creech, "Congress Looks to Serviceman's Rights," *American Bar Association Journal* 49 (1963):

1070–1074; Clifford A. Dougherty and Norman B. Lynch, "The Administrative Discharge: Military Justice?" *George Washington Law Review* 33 (1964): 498–528; Jerome A. Susskind, "Military Administrative Discharge Boards: The Right to Confrontation and Cross-Examination," *Michigan State Bar Journal* 46 (1965): 25–32; and Richard J. Bednar, "Discharge and Dismissal as Punishments in the Armed Services," *Military Law Review,* DA Pam. 27-100-16 (April 1962): 1–42.

66. Army Reg. 635-212, Personnel Separations, Discharge, Unfitness and Unsuitability, para. 6 (July 15, 1966) (C8, January 16, 1970); Army Reg. 635-100, Personnel Separations, Officer Personnel, para. 5-5 [also referred to as AR 635-100]; quoted in Davis, "Military Policy Towards Homosexuals," p. 76.

67. Ibid., p. 77.

68. Ibid.

69. Every history of gay men and women in the 1960s has its own version of what happened at Stonewall. This particular bar had a clientele that was among the most disenfranchised of the gay community, including transvestites, the young, and people of color. Unlike many of the city's gay men or women, they had little to lose in terms of social position or respectability.

For longer accounts of the riots, see D'Emilio, *Sexual Politics, Sexual Communities,* pp. 231–233; Randy Shilts, *The Mayor of Castro Street: The Life and Times of Harvey Milk* (New York, N.Y.: St. Martin's Press, 1982), pp. 42–43; Bayer, *Homosexuality and American Psychiatry,* pp. 92–93; Marotta, *The Politics of Homosexuality,* pp. 76–79. For the most complete account of the riots, see Martin Duberman, *Stonewall* (New York, N.Y.: Dutton, 1993), pp. 190–209.

70. Bayer, *Homosexuality and American Psychiatry,* pp. 101–154.

71. Shilts's *The Mayor of Castro Street* remains the best examination of a particular community. For an examination of the emergent gay male role in the late 1970s, see p. 86. For a discussion of lesbian imagery in the 1970s, see Lillian Faderman, *Odd Girls and Twilight Lovers: A History of Lesbian Life in Twentieth-Century America* (New York, N.Y.: Penguin, 1991), pp. 215–245. For an examination of the sexual practices of the "gay clone" see Martin P. Levine, "The Life and Death of Gay Clones," in *Gay Culture in America: Essays from the Field,* Gilbert Herdt, ed. (Boston, Mass.: Beacon Press, 1992), pp. 68–86.

72. In *Conduct Unbecoming,* Shilts illustrates the policies of the U.S. armed forces toward homosexual personnel by weaving these stories into his narrative; both Berg and Matlovich become major characters in this book. For a brief examination of the legal questions called into play, see Davis, "Military Policy Towards Homosexuals," pp. 77–79. For further examinations of their individual stories, see E. Lawrence Gibson, *Get Off My Ship:* Ensign Berg vs. the U.S. Navy (New York, N.Y.: Avon Books, 1976) and Mike Hippler, *Matlovich: The Good Soldier* (Boston, Mass.: Alyson Publications, 1989).

73. For an overview of earlier court cases concerning military separations on the basis of homosexuality, see Rhonda R. Rivera, "Our Straight-Laced Judges: The Legal Position of Homosexual Persons in the United States," *Hastings Law Journal* 30 (1979): 841–848.

74. Ibid., p. 851.

75. Shilts, *Conduct Unbecoming,* p. 642.

76. Shilts, *Conduct Unbecoming,* p. 380; see also Davis, "Military Policy Towards Homosexuals," p. 79.

77. The development of a military subculture of gay men and lesbians is one of the primary themes of Shilts, *Conduct Unbecoming*. For example, see his discussion of "The Family," pp. 402–403 and 531–532.

78. These figures have been calculated from the compilations published in "Defense Force Management: DoD's Policy on Homosexuality" (Washington, D.C.: General Accounting Office, 1992). The figures are found on page 13 of the report's supplement, "Statistics Related to DoD's Policy on Homosexuality."

79. Shilts, *Conduct Unbecoming*, p. 549.

80. United States General Accounting Office, "Defense Force Management: DoD's Policy on Homosexuality," pp. 46–47.

81. Ibid., pp. 48–49.

82. Ibid., pp. 50–51. See also Joseph Steffan, *Honor Bound: A Gay American Fights for the Right to Serve His Country* (New York, N.Y.: Villard Books, 1992).

83. United States General Accounting Office, "Defense Force Management: DoD's Policy on Homosexuality," pp. 47–48. See also Shilts, *Conduct Unbecoming*, p. 549.

84. "Review of Guidance on Homosexuality Research," attached to a memorandum from Carson K. Eoyang to the Deputy Undersecretary of Defense, January 30, 1989.

85. Memorandum from Craig Alderman Jr. to Peter Nelson, "PERSEREC Draft Report: 'Nonconforming Sexual Orientations,'" February 10, 1989.

86. The Crittenden Report, for example, concluded that homosexuals did not pose a greater risk than heterosexual adulterers or people engaged in substance-abusing behaviors.

87. For a review of legal doctrine pertaining to national security clearances through the 1970s, see Jerel McCrary and Lewis Gutierrez, "The Homosexual Person in the Military and in National Security Employment," *Journal of Homosexuality* 5 (fall-winter 1979–1980): 115–146.

88. Theodore R. Sarbin, Ph.D., and Kenneth E. Karols, M.D., Ph.D., "Nonconforming Sexual Orientations and Military Suitability," released by Carson K. Eoyang (Monterey, Calif.: PERSEREC, December 1988), p. 6.

89. Ibid., p. 24.

90. Ibid., p. 25.

91. For an examination of some of the issues surrounding security clearances and civilian employees, see Gregory M. Herek, "Gay People and Government Security Clearances," *American Psychologist* (September 1990): 1035–1042.

92. The release of the PERSEREC documents is recounted in Steffan, *Honor Bound*, pp. 214–220. Kate Dyer, a congressional staffer, later released the reports as part of the edited volume *Gays in Uniform: The Pentagon's Secret Reports* (Boston, Mass.: Alyson Publications, 1990).

93. Michael A. McDaniel, "Preservice Adjustment of Homosexual and Heterosexual Military Accessions: Implications for Security Clearance Suitability" (Monterey, Calif.: PERSEREC, January 1989), p. iii.

94. Ibid.

3

Does the Gay Ban Preserve Soldiers' Privacy?

THE "DON'T ASK, DON'T TELL" POLICY IS ALMOST TEN YEARS OLD, BUT THE military's history of sanctioning same-sex behavior dates back to the earliest days of the republic, when Lieutenant Gotthold Frederick Enslin became the first soldier drummed out of the Continental Army for sodomy on March 11, 1778. Regulations prohibiting sodomy were first formalized during the codification of the Articles of War in 1917 and, as historian Timothy Haggerty explains in the previous chapter, military understandings of homosexuality have reflected larger societal understandings, even as actions taken by the military have influenced society. Haggerty shows that military regulations of same-sex behavior and homosexual identity have changed on numerous occasions, and that the rationales that justified various regulatory approaches have fluctuated as well. For example, during World War II, military psychologists justified the discharge of gay soldiers by considering homosexuality a mental illness. During the 1950s, military leaders said that gays and lesbians were particularly vulnerable to blackmail and hence a threat to national security. And when President Clinton attempted to force the Pentagon to allow known gays and lesbians to serve, military officials argued that gays and lesbians would undermine the cohesion of their units.

Recently, some officials and experts have argued that the armed forces must exclude known gays and lesbians in order to protect the privacy rights of heterosexuals. In 1992, for example, Professor Charles Moskos said, "Nowhere in our society are the sexes forced to endure situations of undress in front of each other. . . . If feelings of privacy for women are respected regarding privacy from men, then we must respect those of straights with regard to gays."[1] Moskos and others claim that the "Don't Ask, Don't Tell" policy is necessary for preserving the modesty rights of heterosexual service members who would be exposed in showers and living quarters if the armed forces allowed known gays and lesbians to serve. As we discuss below, the privacy rationale has assumed such a prominent role in the debate over the gay ban that we devote our first panel to its analysis.

The privacy rationale depends on two premises. First, service members deserve to maintain at least partial control over the exposure of their bodies and intimate bodily functions. Service in the military entails numerous personal sacrifices and responsibilities that restrict speech, appearance, and behavior. Although members of the armed forces are not entitled to many prerogatives of civilian life, at least they deserve a degree of control over who sees their naked bodies. In addition, the privacy rationale assumes that observation of same-sex nudity arouses sexual desire when the observer is homosexual and *only* when the observer is homosexual. According to Melissa Wells-Petry of the Family Research Council, the exposure of bodies and intimate bodily functions does not violate privacy rights when heterosexuals are segregated in all-male or all-female settings. When homosexuals observe naked bodies or intimate bodily functions, however, they violate the privacy rights of heterosexuals. Wells-Petry says that the homosexual gaze expresses sexual yearning and that heterosexuals do not want to be the objects of homosexuals' sexual desire. She concludes that soldiers should not be "stripped unwittingly of their right to choose to whom they reveal themselves in a sexual context. Once this happens, the harm is done. As a matter of law, the privacy violation does not depend on any acting out of sexual attraction toward others. It is complete the moment privacy is breached."[2] In other words, the injury takes place the moment that a homosexual sees the naked body of a heterosexual peer.

Concerns for heterosexual privacy are widespread among opponents of gays and lesbians in the military. A search of the Lexis/Nexis database reveals that during the debate over Bill Clinton's proposal to lift the gay ban, 179 newspaper articles and fifty television transcripts addressed the privacy issue in the context of the shower.[3] A 1993 letter to the editor of the *Seattle Times* typified the items in our search results:

> The exposure of your nude body, in circumstances you have no control over while serving in the military, could occur on a daily basis; people in the armed forces take showers regularly, and private dressing rooms are not provided to most enlistees . . . It is not farfetched to think that a homosexual could be attracted to someone of the same sex who is not homosexual and that that attraction or potential attraction could make a heterosexual feel embarrassed and vulnerable while nude.[4]

Analysis of the privacy argument is important because it serves as one of the fundamental justifications for the U.S. military's gay ban. In addition to its prominence in popular discourse, the privacy rationale appears frequently in official debates and regulations. In 1991, District of Columbia circuit justice Oliver Gasch invoked the privacy rationale to justify his unwillingness to reinstate a gay midshipman, Joseph Steffan, whom the military discharged after he acknowledged his homosexuality. Gasch said, "With no one present who has a homosexual orientation, men and women alike can undress, sleep, bathe, and use the bathroom without fear or embarrassment that they are being viewed as sexual objects."[5] Indeed, the congressional statute that codifies the "Don't Ask, Don't Tell" policy reflects a concern for heterosexual privacy in noting that "members of the armed forces [often must] involuntarily . . . accept living conditions and working conditions that are often spartan, primitive, and characterized by forced intimacy with little or no privacy."[6] As former chairman of the Joint Chiefs of Staff Colin Powell explained in 1992, "To introduce a group of individuals who—proud, brave, loyal, good Americans—but who favor a homosexual life-style, and put them in with heterosexuals who would prefer not to have somebody of the same sex find them sexually attractive, put them in close proximity, ask them to share the most private of their facilities together, the bedroom, the barracks, latrines, the showers, I think that's a very difficult problem to give the military."[7] Although the privacy rationale is not the only justification for the gay ban, it is an important element of official and popular explanations as to why known gay and lesbian service members must be excluded from the military.

Does "Don't Ask, Don't Tell" protect the privacy of heterosexual service members in the U.S. military? Following the cost-benefit framework that we described in our introductory chapter, our intent throughout the volume is to address the advantages and disadvantages of the "Don't Ask, Don't Tell" policy. In this chapter, the first of three discussions of the advantages of the policy, participants discuss whether "Don't Ask, Don't Tell" benefits heterosexual service members by protecting their privacy. Hence, in the transcript that follows, conference participants debate the plausibility of the privacy rationale. On one side of the issue, some conference participants argue that the gay ban does benefit heterosexual service members by protecting their privacy and that lifting the ban would undermine privacy. On the other hand, other participants argue that heterosexual service members already shower with known gays and lesbians and that the number of known homosexuals is unlikely to increase significantly after the lifting of the ban.[8]

Melissa Sheridan Embser-Herbert: At one point in history, as I think has been suggested, much of the argument over gays and lesbians in the military rested on the assumption that there could not actually be any gays and lesbians in the military. Oh, some argued, some might have found their way in, but certainly they would have been summarily tossed out. Surely nobody managed to stay in.

I think we have evidence in the room that gays and lesbians have served in the military. Even those most strident in their opposition to gays and lesbians have conceded this fact. Whether through the scholarship of Allan Bérubé on World War II, the autobiographical work of those like Joseph Steffan, Margarethe Cammermeyer, and others, or the continuing work of the Servicemembers Legal Defense Network, we all—as opposed to just some of us—now know without question that gays and lesbians have served in the U.S. military and that they continue to serve.[9]

However, since the codification of "Don't Ask, Don't Tell" in 1993, the argument has somewhat shifted, from whether or not there are gays and lesbians in the military at all, to whether or not there are open gays and lesbians in the military. And that is the point I have been asked to speak on. I am sorely disappointed that Charlie Moskos is not with us today, for he has said, "Open gays do not serve in the American military." He is wrong. There is no question that we have less data on this point, but we do have data. Now before we go on, I have got to tell you that I am thoroughly dumbfounded on many levels by the belief that there are no open gays and lesbians in the military. As Professor Moskos has said, "I should not be forced to shower with a woman. I should not be forced to shower with an open gay." My question on that point, do those who share his view really find it preferable to shower with a closeted gay? Some of these things just really confuse me.

Nonetheless, the central question remains: Is it true that there are few to no open gays and lesbians in the U.S. military? And I think we can bracket what might be a quick comeback from some—"Oh, of course, they are open to each other"—I think we can agree on that response and put it aside. So the question differently stated becomes: Are there gays and lesbians in the U.S. military who acknowledge their sexual orientation to heterosexual co-workers and supervisors? And perhaps more importantly, can we prove it?

I want to share with you a personal anecdote from 1978, which seems like centuries ago. I had completed basic training and had started my advanced training with the military police, a program in which you continued with the same sex-integrated unit, a topic deserving its own day of discussion. Once we began Advanced Individual Training (AIT), we were permitted to leave post on the weekends, and given the means to do so, I can guarantee, we did. But one day my drill sergeant called me into his office. And he called me in with another woman in my unit, whom I had been dating on the weekends. He said, and this is as good a quote as I have been able to remember over the years, "I know what's going on. This is the army, and you two have got to be more discreet." End of conversation. He was not a bleeding heart liberal, and by all accounts he was heterosexual, as well. But he knew. As did most of the women in Bravo Company, Tenth Battalion. They might not have liked it—that is a different question—but they knew.

I could tell you about many of my peers and supervisors who knew of my sexual orientation, when I was both an enlisted person and later an officer on active duty and on reserve. But let me turn to more than my own anecdotal data.

In the early 1990s, I collected survey data from 394 women, who were either still on active military service or were veterans in the U.S. military.[10] I asked women who identified as heterosexual for any part of their military career to respond to the statement, "I knew military women who were lesbian or bisexual." Seventy-nine percent of the women responded "yes." That is, of those who identified as heterosexual at some point in their career, eight out of ten said that they knew military women who were recognized as lesbian or bisexual. In John Bicknell's study of attitudes toward gays and lesbians in the military, specifically among navy and marine personnel, 21 percent of his respondents answered affirmatively to the statement, "I personally know a homosexual service member."[11] And if you look just at naval enlisted personnel, 39 percent said "yes."

In my research, I asked additional questions of respondents who identified as lesbian or bisexual during any part of their active duty career. I want to add quickly that I used this "anytime" phrase, because I asked them to indicate their identity when they entered the military, when they got out, and when they completed the survey. I asked respondents who identified as lesbian or bisexual during any part of their career to indicate "definitely not true," "probably not true," "uncertain," "probably true," or "definitely true" to these statements:

1. Women, whom I believe were heterosexual, knew that I was lesbian or bisexual.
2. Men, whom I believe were heterosexual, knew that I was lesbian or bisexual.
3. Some of my supervisors knew that I was lesbian or bisexual.

Of the 111 women who responded to those items, 64 percent indicated that it was "definitely true" or "probably true" that women whom they recognized as heterosexual knew that the respondent was lesbian or bisexual. Fifty-one percent indicated "definitely true" or "probably true" that men they believed heterosexual recognized them to be lesbian or bisexual. And 56 percent indicated "definitely true" or "probably true" with regard to their supervisors. And I should add that I did not ask for a distinction on the sexual orientation of the supervisor because that question opens up the additional issue of how they would know, on what grounds they might speculate, and so forth.

I then asked, if you answered "probably true" or "definitely true" to any of the three items—those I just mentioned—what led you to believe that others thought you were lesbian or bisexual? The respondents believed that their peers knew about their sexual orientation, but I was also trying to capture what allowed them to draw this conclusion. I received eighty-six open-ended responses to that item. Just over half were some variation of very simply, "I told them." The others gave a range of examples for how their co-workers or supervisors came to know that they were lesbian or bisexual. And I want to take a few minutes to give you some of their exact words. They range, as I suggest, from the simple "I told them" to responses like, "There was an implied understanding with some of my heterosexual co-workers. They accepted my 'friend' stories and didn't try to fix me up with dates." One private first class wrote, "Some just outright asked and I told. Others just had gay-dar I guess." Some wrote about assessments that were made because of their personal activities or what they characterized as style, including the lack of heterosexual dating or the lack of people knowing about their sexual relationships. For example, and these are quotes, "Many of the heterosexuals suspected I was lesbian because I did not date any of the men and did not go to the post club. I never mentioned boyfriends. I choose not to play the role of a heterosexual." Another wrote, "Because I didn't date guys. I lived with a woman." And this is one of my personal favorites, "Some I told, others assumed so from the way I acted, dressed, and played shortstop." And I should add, there were lots of references to being involved in sports and how that immediately made you suspect. In fact some came out to co-workers and supervisors who were trying to date them—yet again another whole topic. Rather than continually rebuff the advances, coming out allowed them to provide a reason for their lack of interest. One respondent wrote quite plainly, "I told a supervisor who was trying to get me to date him."

A number of women alluded to the difficulty of maintaining the lie. An enlisted woman in the Coast Guard wrote, "We lived in close quarters. I came out to some. Others figured it out." An enlisted member of the army wrote, "Rumor control, innuendo." In short, it is hard to lie when you live and work so closely with others. I should note here that I am well aware of the fact that this is one of the reasons why people argue against lesbians and gays—"Oh you're so close." We may get to that in the next session. Again, a thorough response to that argument would be a completely separate topic. But in brief, I take the position of not excluding a minority class because of the prejudices of the dominant class.

Some women made reference to the need to be honest with supervisors if they needed their help. An enlisted woman in the army wrote, "I told my supervisor because I was breaking up an eight-year relationship with my lover. I needed time off and he supported me a hundred percent." And an army captain offered, "Due to a difficult situation which arose I informed my commander because I needed his help."

Many of the women wrote about simply telling because they had been asked—not by supervisors, though some were, and not during an official inquiry, although some wrote of that, too. For many, it was simply that living and working side by side with people they liked and trusted, they could not lie to friends and co-workers. They did not want to lie about an important part of their life, about which they did not feel they should have to lie. One enlisted woman wrote, "When I knew about my sexuality, I was not ashamed of it. And if I was to be true to myself, I had to be true to the people I was close to, whether they were heterosexual or homosexual. I wanted them to accept me for who I was and not for who I slept with." Another woman wrote, "I had co-workers and friends in the military whom I trusted and told that I was a lesbian."

Perhaps we should think about these concerns and create policies that engender trust among service members rather than the current policy, which asks people to lie to each other and to avoid becoming close enough to trust one another. Regardless of whether they told, were asked outright, or figured out that others had figured it out, there is no doubt that many lesbian and bisexual women in the military have been open about their lives to the heterosexual service members with whom they live and work.

Does the gay ban preserve soldiers' privacy? Of course it might for some individual soldiers. If "Don't Ask, Don't Tell" means that even one soldier remains in the closet successfully—and I say soldier because I was army—then one could argue that his or her roommate's "privacy" is preserved. But overall, does the ban ensure that gay and lesbian service members remain in the closet? Hardly. Yes, some gays and lesbians have served while successfully hiding who they are. Many have even made it to retirement. But it is clear that large numbers do not, whether by choice or through discovery. I would argue that in most cases—and this was certainly my experience—there is an unstated agreement among service members to ignore the private lives of individuals as long as they are performing their duties as expected. In sum, people know.

In closing, I have to say that I think we are misguided in even raising the question of privacy. Since when is the military concerned about privacy? In basic training when I slept in a bunk in a row of a dozen or so with four rows to the bay, was anyone concerned about my privacy? During a three-week field exercise, when I had the guy with whom I was riding a twelve-hour jeep patrol hold a poncho around me, so I could go to the bathroom and be somewhat shielded because there were no trees, bushes, or convenience stores—this was in Europe, so there were no McDonald's on the corner—did anyone ask about my privacy? No. You did what you had to do. The military as a rule has no concerns about privacy, and well they should not, I would argue. The primary concern is the accomplishment of the mission, plain and simple. At one time the big debate about inclusion was focused on people of color. Next it was, and I think fair to say to a great extent still is, women. At the moment, it is lesbians and gays. I maintain that only when it can be used as a device for exclusion is privacy held up as an issue of military concern. But for those who insist on arguing that privacy concerns are paramount, the fact remains that gays and lesbians have served and continue to serve proudly, and many do so openly. To argue that we need the ban to prevent the presence of open gays and lesbians rests the debate about gays and lesbians in the military on a premise that simply has no basis in fact. Thank you.

Aaron Belkin: I would like to explain his [Charlie Moskos's] argument. Some of the opponents of gays and lesbians in the military say that the reason for the ban is to preserve soldiers' privacy. If the ban is lifted, then many gays and lesbians would come out of the closet, and there would be a lack of privacy in the shower. Could Laura Miller or someone who knows Charlie very well say a few words about his privacy argument? . . .

Laura Miller: Basically, Charlie Moskos argues that the military does try to preserve privacy between men and women. Obviously, there are exceptions in the field, but even they upset a lot of people, as would your story, Melissa. Generally speaking, the military does not make men and women shower together, share sleeping bags, or undertake any of the intimate functions that are sometimes required of soldiers. Partly because they do not ensure privacy for everyone, they at least try to maintain privacy between men and women. Charlie always argues that if women do not have to shower with men, then why should straight men have to shower with gay men? And it does matter to him whether the person is out or not. It is a useful fiction to presume that everyone in the locker room or shower is straight. Since we do preserve privacy for women, Charlie argues that we should also preserve this privacy for straight men. (And it is predominately straight men who are worried about this problem.) He also emphasizes the complicated problems of logistics. Raising the question of gay men rooming and showering together, Charlie also argues that this arrangement is not fair because straight men cannot room or shower with straight women. How are you going to arrange logistics for sleeping arrangements, showers, and bathrooms? He argues that everyone would have to have his or her own shower, bathroom, and bed, which is very impractical in the military. . . .

Lawrence Korb: I have one question on this issue of privacy in Melissa Embser-Herbert's commentary. Do the data show that in the military women accept lesbians much more than men accept gay men? In other words, are there any data to show that it is easier for women to accommodate homosexuality than men?

Embser-Herbert: My study only looked at women, so the only way I can answer that question is through my own experience. I think there is no question that it is much easier for women. We have data from far outside the military that look at how men and women deal with issues of sexuality, sexual orientation, their friends, and so forth. It makes perfect sense to me that it would be very different. Gay men I knew when I was in the military were out in a much more limited way to other men. They had gotten to know them first, which I think makes a big difference, but my own scholarly work did not look at men's experiences. . . .

Jay Williams: I really like the work that Melissa Embser-Herbert did. In fact, what you found out with your squishy statistics is similar to what I found out doing hard anecdotes—and you actually talked to military people. The joke is Charlie's, but the point is mine. You have a chance to talk to people who serve in the military if you have served yourself. Everyone in the military knows a number of people who are gay. Perhaps they did not "know" know, but they kind of "knew" knew and by and large they are comfortable with it. In fact, for most of us "Don't Ask, Don't Tell" is simply an official version of the "live and let live" policy that most people in the military have had for a long time. Senior personnel, by which I mean 0–5 and 0–6, agree with "Don't Ask, Don't Tell," but they are not yet ready to go beyond it.[12] Perhaps the military ought to use more constructively the time that "Don't Ask, Don't Tell" provides and try to prepare for the inevitable inclusion of gays and lesbians, for I do think it is inevitable. If it happens suddenly or if they do not do something to prepare for it, the military will not likely be ready for it. I do think some things are being put in place. I wonder . . . if I may share a communication that Charlie Moskos sent? . . . [He] offers the following comments. [Jay Williams reads Charles Moskos's e-mail.]

"I have only four points to offer for your attention. As you know, my primary argument for 'Don't Ask, Don't Tell' has been one of privacy rights. (1) What is your own university's policy in freshmen dorms, if a gay student and a straight student are randomly assigned to be roommates and one wants out? Universities love to keep it a secret, but in all cases I know, they will quietly separate the roommates. Why? (2) What accounts for the fact that white males are twice as likely to be discharged for homosexuality than black males in the army? White females three times more than black females? Is the army profiling whites? Is the homosexuality rate exponentially greater among whites than blacks? Or is it that homosexuality has a greater stigma among blacks than whites, even if telling is the quickest way to get out of the service with an honorable discharge? (3) If open gays were allowed in the military, would you favor affirmative action for gays? After all, they are discriminated against more than any other minority. And finally, a generation or more ago, I bought a girl's bike in Germany. My fellow soldiers teased me for a couple of days about my sexual orientation. Today this same behavior would be cause for disciplinary action. Is this a step forward? Or is it political correctness carried to an extreme? Regards, Charlie Moskos." . . .

David Segal: To respond to Larry Korb's question, interestingly, we do not have a lot of data on people in the military that would allow us to distinguish gender differences in terms of tolerance for homosexuality; interestingly, because we collect mountains of survey data on everything else that becomes at all controversial in the personnel area. We have piles of data on gender integration. We have piles of data on soldiers' attitudes toward participation in peacekeeping. We have piles of data on soldiers' attitudes about what influences the quality of life. And there has basically been a ban on collecting data in the services on sexual orientation. However, we have an awful lot of data on American society generally that suggests a very strong gender difference. Yes, it is the case that women are more tolerant of homosexuality than men. And there is no reason to believe that women in the military are any different than their civilian counterparts.

Korb: Does that extend to privacy as well?

D. Segal: Well, that is an interesting issue. And I do not know that we know. Of course, it is only recently that decency and privacy have replaced cohesion as the major reason for keeping people out of the military. Through the whole gender issue, the closure mechanism was cohesion. The argument against including women in the military boiled down to the claim that it would reduce cohesion. I think even Charlie Moskos is now arguing that decency and privacy have replaced cohesion as reasons for keeping people out of the military. And I agree with Melissa that given the nature of the military it is ludicrous. Last summer I was asked to prepare testimony for a case in England involving a woman who wanted to join the Royal Marines as a cook. The Royal Marines said she could not, and among the reasons that they put forward was their inability to provide decency and privacy on the battlefield for women. I have never known decency and privacy to be characteristics of any battlefield, regardless of who was there. This argument is a new construction, but it serves the same purpose. Institutions try to reproduce themselves by confining their personnel to the kinds of people who have traditionally served and keeping other people out. I have a sense that there is a link between the institutional resistance to collecting data on how soldiers feel about gays in the military and the position that soldiers are happier if they do not know that their barracks-mates are gay. It is an "ignorance is bliss" position at both the individual and the institutional level. As an academic, I find it hard to justify finding anything functional about ignorance, because I am in the business of trying to alleviate it.

I do have one last point I want to make. Charlie Moskos and I have had the dorm discussion several times. I am sure that he is right that at Northwestern University if two roommates find themselves of the same gender but opposite sexual orientations that the university will allow them to separate. But that is not a universal position. I raised the issue at my university, the University of Maryland, and the policy at the University of Maryland clearly states that freshmen coming into the dormitories are told that they will be assigned a roommate and that they cannot get rid of that roommate based on differences in things like religion, politics, or sexual orientation. And my students have told me that the policy is followed. One semester three of my female students each said they had gotten bisexual roommates in their freshman years. I asked if it was a problem. "No," they said, "I was not her type." There was no question that they were not going to be allowed out of their residence hall contract. That was the policy. It was university policy. They accepted it. It has not created any problems. . . .

Dixon Osburn: There actually is an area where my organization agrees with Charlie Moskos. We have tried very hard to get the armed forces to allow some form of privacy for service members, so they could go to psychotherapists, for example, and be able to report harassment or deal with the stress of having to live in the closet. And they should be able to go to doctors without fear. Lesbians who go to the doctor may need to disclose their sexual orientation as part of medical treatment, but under the current regime if you do that you will be kicked out, if the doctor wants to kick you out. We actually agree with Professor Moskos, and he has written to the Pentagon along with us, trying to encourage them to adopt some privacy measures along those lines.

My second observation is about something that troubles me, for which I do not have a quick answer. I think the privacy argument is a ruse. I think that "privacy" is a benign term that actually covers up a deep-seated and insidious prejudice. And Moskos's shower argument reflects that prejudice. It assumes that if a heterosexual male and a gay male are in a shower together, then there is a predator relationship between the gay male and the heterosexual male. This deep-seated prejudice exists not only in relation to Professor Moskos's argument, but is also shared, I think, by a great many Americans, even Americans who say that gays should be allowed to serve in the military. When people advance this privacy argument or this shower argument, it becomes very difficult in a sound-bite context to try and find a way to discuss the prejudiced assumption behind the arguments. I would welcome anybody's observations or comments on how to address this problem. . . .

Mady Segal: First I want to deal with the issue of the differences between men and women in the military and their acceptance or their lack of acceptance of gays and lesbians. Even though I cannot produce the data, there was a survey done in the heat of the public discourse around President Clinton's proposal to remove the ban by executive order. This survey showed that it was not only civilian women but military women as well who were much more accepting of homosexual men and women in the military than the men.[13] I believe that there is a very strong gender difference with regard to accepting homosexuality both in the military as well as in civilian society.

But I want to come back to this privacy issue, since it is what our panel is supposed to address. And I think we can agree that eventually this ban is going to go away. We will not have "Don't Ask, Don't Tell." We will have integration of homosexuals in the military, both gay men and lesbian women. Having studied racial and gender integration, I would ask how do we accomplish the integration most smoothly? We have a tendency in the U.S. military to make a big policy change and tell people, "This is the way it is and you're just going to have to do it." In other nations, they prepare their military personnel for such changes. You cannot simply change the policy and expect personnel to accept this previously excluded group and treat them without bias. There is a process that helps smooth the interpersonal integration. Looking ahead, I think we have to address this policy concern.

I was also going to comment on the fear of predatory behavior in the shower—the threat of somebody finding you sexually attractive and acting or not acting on this attraction. Although I do not have hard data on this either, I actually feel that some of the men who are most vociferous in their opposition to having gay men serve in the military are the ones who are most predatory themselves in their behavior toward women. They are the ones who are responsible for a lot of the sexual harassment of women, and they think that harassing someone you are attracted to is the way you behave toward people with whom you might have a potential sexual relationship. Although frankly I think that most of that behavior does not come from any sort of sexual attraction whatsoever; it comes from their desire to force women out of the military. That is, women are invading their territory and they want them out of it.

I think we have to face the basis for this concern about privacy. Although it has been raised in public discourse primarily as a mechanism for opposing the integration of gay men, it is a serious issue for some men. The question remains, when we integrate openly gay men into the military, how do we deal with the concerns about showering and privacy? One of the solutions is to provide as much privacy as possible, except in training and field situations where it cannot be helped. The air force does provide service members with a lot more privacy than other service branches. Air force personnel get their own rooms and such. It is one possible solution. The other way is to define appropriate and inappropriate behavior. Any kind of predatory sexual behavior, whether toward someone of the same sex or someone of the opposite sex, is inappropriate behavior. Standards of not sexually harassing other people can be applied regardless of sex, and frankly would do a lot toward improving the treatment of women as well as gay men, both of which can be dealt with in some of the same ways. Our failure to eliminate sexual harassment of women in the military is an indication of how carefully we need to design this process of integration. As social scientists, we can help in understanding how you actually get people to change their behavior, if not their attitudes. From the research I have seen, people's attitudes actually do follow along from their behavior. If you force them to behave in a certain way, eventually they start to actually change their attitudes. But we are not interested in attitudes; we are interested in behavior. So what kind of behavior? We will have regulations on shower behavior, unfortunately. But it should come within a much wider framework of respect for others. . . .

Christopher Dandeker: I am a bit surprised by some of the discussions of privacy. Leaving aside the question of sexual orientation, most military services in modern industrial democracies are aware that in order to recruit and retain key quality personnel, they are going to have to take very seriously the desires for privacy within a service context. It has nothing to do with sexual orientation. Privacy is a big issue for service members, one that is not going to go away and has nothing to do with sexual orientation. . . .

In the debate we had at the Royal United Service Institute, an independent military think-tank in London, a year or so ago, one of the litigants in the European Court of Human Rights Decision, Duncan Lustig-Prean, made it very clear that the concern of heterosexual males about predatory behavior in the showers is a deep-seated concern that must be respected and looked at very carefully.[14] It should not be automatically responded to as homophobia. However, to get around this particular problem and to lessen its significance, if not to make it go away entirely, he argued that we should translate the abstract fear of the predatory homosexual into a very concrete personal issue. Service members need to know that someone who is gay is someone they know in a professional context who they think is good at their job and thus know that this person is a member of the team first and gay second. Then the abstract predatory fear begins to dissolve. And that is how you get over this issue. The abstract fear is there, and getting over it is not getting over it abstractly, but getting over it in a concrete way.

And that raises a question of what do we mean when we talk about open integration? There is a hell of a difference between integrating personnel who are known professionally and come out as gay, and integrating personnel who are not yet known for their professional competence and are gay. It is a different issue altogether. . . .

Williams: I do not think the issue is so much one of predatory behavior. There are so many effective ways to deal with that kind of behavior in the military, whether it involves two men, two women, or a man and a woman. But a large number of straight individuals in the service do not wish to be the object of unwanted sexual interest. I know they may be fooling themselves that they are attractive to anybody, but nonetheless their concerns are real. We need to do more studies like Melissa Embser-Herbert's to find out how these attitudes are distributed and to learn more about their foundations. We do not need to worry so much about predatory behavior, but the concern is there and does affect how people feel about the presence of gays in the military. . . .

D. Segal: Responding both to Christopher Dandeker and to Jay Williams, I think that the perception of predatory males is a very real phenomenon that has to be dealt with, but one that is not particularly widespread, nor present for all generations. In 1993 when I, Larry Korb, Charlie Moskos, and many other people testified to the Congress on gays in the military, one of the major issues that members of both the House and the Senate committees raised with me was this image of the predatory gay male in the shower.[15] Interestingly the younger staff members would say offline, "My boss is really worried about this, but my boss is too old to serve." What they were basically saying was that they and their peers did not regard it as an issue.

Secondly, since Christopher Dandeker was looking across the table at me when he was talking about the privacy issue, I want to be clear that I raised it in the context of the battlefield. Very clearly the issue of privacy is very different in the barracks than the battlefield, but anyone who aspires to provide privacy and decency on the battlefield, even if they run the Ministry of Defense, knows hardly anything about military operations. . . .

Robert MacCoun: To add a slightly different angle, in the RAND study, we looked at twelve different police and fire departments that have non-discrimination policies, as well as various foreign militaries.[16] Based on experiences in these organizations, we estimated that it would be rare for any unit to actually have an openly gay or lesbian service member, particularly among gay male service people. Among fifty-person platoons, we estimated that 5 percent would have an openly gay man in the unit. With twenty-person crews and teams, it is only about 1 percent. These numbers reflect the current social risks that a gay person faces by coming out in similar organizations that are more tolerant than the U.S. military with respect to this issue. Statistically speaking the privacy issue is not trivial, but it is a very rare and small problem. Few gays come out in police and fire departments and in foreign militaries because they face enormous professional risk, even in a legal regime that allows them to do so.

From that perspective, the concern that one person in a fifty-person platoon will behave in a predatory manner, despite being greatly outnumbered by people hostile to homosexuality, seems implausible. Charlie

Moskos's college dorm example strikes me as a very weak example, because what he is talking about is the exception that proves the rule. The fact of the matter is that there are gays and straights sharing showers all over campuses every day. Occasionally there is a problem, and a college administrator uses discretion to deal with it. Military leaders would have similar discretion in these rare instances. So I have trouble taking this argument very seriously as a significant part of the issue. . . .

Miller: From my research with army soldiers, the fear of predatory gay men in the shower is not so much about gay men being predators. Rather, it is based on their own knowledge and experience of how straight men act. Basically they have fears of being overpowered physically or of being taking advantage of when they are drunk. There is a mythical story around called the "ether bunny story" about a gay soldier who knocks out one of his fellow soldiers with ether and takes advantage of him. And knowing how women are treated in such situations when they register complaints—a he-said/she-said incidence—they are afraid of being in the same situation as straight women and being at the same disadvantage in preventing it. . . .

Michael Desch: I will raise [the issue of expediency] now and go into more detail in my own presentation. I think expediency is the key. We need to understand that the professional military mind-set focuses almost night and day on questions of expediency. What will be the effect of any change, whether it is operational, doctrinal, or personnel, on the effectiveness of the unit? We may not agree with it, but in order to debate seriously whether various policies are likely to be accepted, we cannot dismiss such questions. We have to understand that efficiency and expediency are very important for the audience to whom you are trying to pitch a fundamental change. . . .

Paul Gade[17]: My point is one of clarification in reference to the issue that Mady Segal raised about the survey showing that women tend to be more accepting of homosexuality than men. I think that survey was the one that was done by the *Los Angeles Times* in 1993.[18] . . .

Belkin: Aside from thanking everyone for a wonderful discussion, I have to be frank and say that I am partly dissatisfied, because we did not answer the empirical question, "Does the ban preserve privacy?" And to my mind I think the answer lies somewhere between Rob Mac-Coun's finding that very few open gays serve in police and fire departments and Melissa Embser-Herbert's finding that there are many open gays and lesbians in some units. For me, the answer to the question, "Does the ban preserve soldiers' privacy?" is "no." Based on my studies of foreign militaries, my sense is that if the American ban is lifted, very few gays and lesbians will come out of the closet. Some will, but not too many more will, because as Rob MacCoun says, it is not safe to come out in some units. In those units where it is safe to come out of the closet, we already find many open gays and lesbians. In other words, whether or not the ban is in place has little to do with how many people come out of the closet. Hence, my own sense is that the ban does not preserve privacy in units where gays and lesbians already reveal their orientation. And lifting the ban will not change conditions in the shower because very few additional gays and lesbians will come out of the closet even after they are allowed to do so.

NOTES

1. Lois Shawver, *And the Flag Was Still There: Straight People, Gay People, and Sexuality in the U.S. Military* (New York, N.Y.: Harrington Park Press, 1995), p. 158.

2. Melissa Wells-Petry, *Exclusion: Homosexuals and the Right to Serve* (Washington, D.C.: Regnery Gateway, 1993).

3. More specifically, we searched to determine the number of articles in which the word "shower" occurred in close proximity to the words "military" and "gay." Our search terms were (gay! or homosex!) w/25 (military or soldier!) w/15 (shower!) and our search period was late 1992 through the end of 1994.

4. Linda Jordan, "Letter to the Editor," *Seattle Times* (March 21, 1993), p. 5.

5. Shawver, *And the Flag Was Still There*, p. 158.

6. U.S. Congress, *10 United States Code 654* (Washington, D.C.: Government Printing Office, 1993), Pub. L. 103-160 571, 107 Stat., 1547.

7. Shawver, *And the Flag Was Still There*, p. 25.

8. This section as well as the discussion on pp. 55–58 are based on Aaron Belkin and Melissa S. Embser-Herbert, "A Modest Proposal: Privacy as a Flawed Rationale for Excluding Gays and Lesbians from the U.S. Military," *International Security* 27, no. 2 (fall 2002); and Aaron Belkin, "Gays and Lesbians in the Military," *Oxford Companion to American Military History* (New York: Oxford University Press, 2000).

9. See Allan Bérubé, *Coming out Under Fire: The History of Gay Men and Women in World War Two* (New York, N.Y.: The Free Press, 1990); Joseph Steffan, *Honor Bound: A Gay American Fights for the Right to Serve His Country* (New York, N.Y.: Villard Books, 1992); Margarethe Cammermeyer, with C. Fisher, *Serving in Silence* (New York, N.Y.: Viking, 1994); and S. L. Sobel, J. M. Cleghorn, and C. D. Osburn, *Conduct Unbecoming: The Seventh Annual Report on "Don't Ask, Don't Tell, Don't Pursue, Don't Harass"* (Washington, D.C.: Servicemembers Legal Defense Network, 2001), available at: http://www.sldn.org.

10. Melissa S. Herbert, *Camouflage Isn't Only for Combat: Gender, Sexuality, and Women in the Military* (New York, N.Y.: New York University Press, 1998).

11. John W. Bicknell Jr., "Study of Naval Officers' Attitudes Toward Homosexuals in the Military" (Monterey, Calif.: Naval Postgraduate School, 2000).

12. "O-5" and "O-6" refer to the ranks of lieutenant colonel and colonel, respectively.

13. Melissa Healy, "The Times Poll: 74% of Military Enlistees Oppose Lifting Gay Ban," *Los Angeles Times* (February 28, 1993), p. A1.

14. Lustig-Prean is one of four service members discharged from the British armed forces for homosexuality who began a legal challenge against the British ban in 1994. The European Court of Human Rights ruled in favor of the plaintiffs in 1999 and the British ban was lifted in January 2000.

15. U.S. Senate Committee on Armed Services, *Policy Concerning Homosexuality in the Armed Forces,* 103d Congress, 2d Session (Washington, D.C.: Government Printing Office, 1993).

16. National Defense Research Institute, *Sexual Orientation and U.S. Military Personnel Policy: Options and Assessment* (Santa Monica, Calif.: RAND, 1993).

17. The views, opinions, and/or findings expressed by Paul Gade in this book are solely his own and should not be construed as an official Department of the Army or Department of Defense position, policy, or decision, unless so designated by documentation.

18. Healy, "The Times Poll," p. A1.

4

Does "Don't Ask, Don't Tell" Preserve Unit Cohesion?

WHEN FORMER PRESIDENT BILL CLINTON ATTEMPTED TO COMPEL THE PENTA-gon to allow known gays and lesbians to serve in the military at the beginning of his administration, Congress reacted by including a new policy on homosexual soldiers in the 1994 National Defense Authorization Act. According to the compromise referred to as "Don't Ask, Don't Tell," known homosexuals are not allowed to serve in the U.S. armed forces. Military recruiters no longer are supposed to ask enlistees if they are gay, but any service members who disclose that they are homosexual are subject to dismissal.

The official justification for the "Don't Ask, Don't Tell" policy is the unit cohesion rationale, the notion that military performance would decline if known gay and lesbian soldiers were permitted to serve in uniform. According to the 1994 National Defense Authorization Act, "The presence in the armed forces of persons who demonstrate a propensity or intent to engage in homosexual acts would create an unacceptable risk to the high standards of morale, good order and discipline, and unit cohesion that are the essence of military capability."[1]

The unit cohesion rationale is premised on the assumption that heterosexual soldiers dislike gays and lesbians and cannot trust them with their lives. As a result, if gays and lesbians revealed their sexual orientation, then units no longer would be able to function. As Lieutenant Colonel Robert McGinnis of the Family Research Council explains, "Cohesion is the glue that holds small units together. In Ranger school we would wrap a poncho liner around us when we were cold. So you're sharing body heat. If there is any perception of inappropriate behavior that you think might result from that, you have to have total trust that not only are they going to pull your wounded body off the battlefield but that they won't do anything untoward."[2]

Does the gay ban preserve unit cohesion? And would lifting the ban undermine cohesion? Throughout the volume, we discuss the advantages and disadvantages of the "Don't Ask, Don't Tell" policy in order to determine whether its benefits outweigh its costs. In this chapter, the second of three discussions of the advantages of the policy, participants discuss whether "Don't Ask, Don't Tell" benefits the military by preserving combat effectiveness and unit cohesion. On one side of the issue, experts who oppose allowing known gays and lesbians to serve in the military point to numerous surveys that show that heterosexual service members do not like their gay and lesbian peers and favor preserving the ban by an overwhelming majority. These experts equate straight soldiers' dislike of gay soldiers with the deterioration of unit cohesion. In other words, since heterosexual service members do not like gays and lesbians, units will not be able to develop cohesion and trust if the gay ban is lifted.

Experts who favor lifting the gay ban argue that hundreds of studies show that a group's performance does not depend on whether group members like each other. According to this perspective, group performance depends on whether group members are committed to the same goals or tasks. But whether a unit's members like each other has no impact on its performance. Hence, even though heterosexual service members might not like their gay and lesbian peers, as long as they are committed to military effectiveness their units will perform well. In addition, experts who favor lifting the gay ban argue that since unit cohesion has not deteriorated in police and fire departments and in foreign militaries that allow known gays to serve, it will not deteriorate in the U.S. military if the "Don't Ask, Don't Tell" policy is rescinded. Finally, experts note that the U.S. military itself allows known gays and lesbians to serve during wartime. If known homosexuals undermined cohesion, they argue that gay discharges would increase during wartime.

In the transcript that follows, experts debate whether the gay ban preserves unit cohesion and whether lifting the ban would undermine cohesion.[3]

Aaron Belkin: Today's conference has been structured, at least theoretically, in terms of a cost-benefit framework. In order to evaluate whether or not the ban should remain in place, it is important to determine whether the benefits of the ban outweigh its costs. Hence, the morning panels are designed to ask if there are benefits to the "Don't Ask, Don't Tell" policy. More specifically, many people who oppose allowing known gays and lesbians to serve in the military claim that the gay ban preserves unit cohesion. In other words, many experts argue that the ban preserves military effectiveness and combat capacity. Unit cohesion refers to these sets of ideas, and this panel is designed to ask if these claims are valid. Does the ban preserve cohesion? . . .

Jay Williams: I very much appreciate the opportunity to be here . . . because this conference is important to the individuals involved regardless of their sexual orientation. An important question for the military, this issue is also important to the rest of society as it weighs claims of fairness and effectiveness, both of which are values appropriate for society to pursue.

I will begin by passing out some statistics from our project. These statistics are from the Triangle Institute for Security Studies Project on the Gap Between the Military and Civilian Society coordinated by Peter Feaver and Richard Kohn.[4] Because you can read the tables, I will not recite all the statistics to you. Rather, I will refer to them as I make my remarks.

In other contexts, the topic of gays and lesbians in the military often produces more heat than light, but hopefully not in this one here today. It is important to begin with a common set of facts. People disagree. There are several explanations for why they do so: bad intentions, that is, evil people; inadequate cognitive capacities, that is, stupid people; and different information, that is, uninformed people. Hopefully we can deal with the information issue. I do think people are entitled to their own values and conclusions on a topic like this one, but people are not entitled to their own facts. At the same time, facts do not speak for themselves; they must be interpreted through ethical lenses, which we provide. I would like to begin by addressing the gap between the perceptions and views of civilians and the military on the issue of gays in the military. If you look at Table 4.1, you will see that slightly more than half of both civilian groups (the mass public and the decisionmaking elite) supported gay men and lesbians serving openly in the military,[5] while some three-quarters of military leaders opposed it. These data suggest that the views of civilian leaders are not significantly more supportive than those of civilians at large, but that military leaders are substantially more conservative on this issue than either category of civilians. We did a multivariate analysis, not recorded here, which shows that those most likely to oppose openly gay men and lesbians in the military are current or past members of the military. Those most likely to support the change included women, both women in general and women serving in the military, less religious individuals, and those

Table 4.1 Do you think gay men and lesbians should be allowed to serve openly in the military?

	General Public (%; n = 1001)	Civilian Elite (%; n = 904)	Military Elite (%; n = 713)
Yes	56.4	54.3	18.1
No	36.7	35.6	72.8
No opinion	6.9	10.1	9.1

Notes: n = 2618; Pearson's chi-square = 317.09; significance = .000.

with higher levels of education. Throughout the study, we found that the attitudes of reserve officers tended to be much more consistent with military than civilian attitudes. Reserve officers tracked right along with the active military personnel when they answered our questions.

If you look at Tables 4.2 and 4.3, you will note the presence of a gap between military and civilian leaders over sexual orientation and military service. Military elites more strongly oppose accepting openly gay soldiers than they do accepting women commanders, or women serving in ground combat units. Table 4.2 conveys the percentage of respondents who reported that they would leave the military if either women were allowed to serve in ground combat units or if open homosexuals were allowed to serve in the military. . . .

Again, our civilian respondents were asked to consider this question in hypothetical terms, and military elites expressed sentiments based on their actual careers. Civilian leaders were twice as likely as military leaders to say that they would leave military service if combat units included women. In contrast, military elites were twice as likely as civilian leaders to say they would leave the armed forces if open gays were allowed to serve. These responses show the increasing comfort that military people have with women serving in the military, which is in itself an interesting development.

In contrast, military leaders were four times as likely to want to leave if open homosexuals were permitted to serve than they would if women were permitted to serve in ground combat. These items do vary by gender. From further analysis, we concluded that men were more likely than women to say that they would leave the military in response to the proposed changes. Elite civilian women were more likely than military women to say that they would hypothetically leave the military following either policy change. I am uncertain about how much credence you can put on the hypothetical civilian response, but it is interesting to note that there are some differences at least in the abstract.

Table 4.2 I would leave military service if

	Civilian Elite (%; n = 166)	Military Elite (%; n = 644)	Pearson's Chi-Square
Women were allowed to serve in ground combat units	13.9	6.5	9.62[a]
Homosexuals were allowed to serve openly in the military	15.1	27.5	10.88[a]

Notes: n = 810.
a. p < .01.

Table 4.3 If, under present standards, your commander was female/gay, how would you feel?

	Civilian Elite (%; n = 903)	Military Elite (%; n = 707)		Civilian Elite (%; n = 903)	Military Elite (%; n = 704)
More confident with male commander	24.9	22.3	More confident with straight commander	34.6	65.3
Equally confident with male or female commander	58.7	67.8	Equally confident with straight or gay commander	49.9	20.2
More confident with female commander	1.8	.6	More confident with gay commander	.3	0
No opinion	14.6	9.3	No opinion	15.2	14.5

Notes: n = 1610; Pearson's chi-square = 19.93; significance = .000.

Notes: n = 1607; Pearson's chi-square = 175.56; significance = .000.

Table 4.3 shows that military elites are more comfortable than civilian leaders about the prospect of women serving in military leadership roles, which is an interesting development. Twenty-two percent of military leaders and 25 percent of civilians would feel more comfortable with a male commander than a female. Among all respondents, however, the number who expressed more confidence in a female commander than a male was negligible. Table 4.3 asks how, under present circumstances, which I think is an important qualification, respondents theoretically would feel if the policy was changed to allow open homosexuals to serve. Part of the problem might be the fact that they cannot serve openly and not that they are gay. The problem might be that they are serving under someone who has to keep an important part of their being private, which might affect their ability to serve effectively.

Now, when a similar question compared a gay with a straight commander, civilians were the more supportive group, although both civilians and military leaders were much less comfortable with the idea of working under a gay commander than a female one. As was the case with female commanders, almost no one would prefer a gay commander to a straight one. On this issue, civilian and military women responded similarly. In sum, Tables 4.2 and 4.3 reveal that although military leaders often are depicted as chauvinists as compared with civilians, and although they are less likely to support allowing women to volunteer for combat jobs, they are more accepting than civilians of women in command and less likely to want to leave military service if combat units were to include women. However, they were much more opposed to allowing open gays into the armed forces than either the general public or civilian leaders.

Change the issue a bit. Are these just homophobic bigots? Civilian and military leaders have diametrically opposed opinions about sexual orientation in military service, but other questions need to be asked. Tables 4.4 and 4.5 apply. Both military and civilian leaders answered similarly to a question about book banning: "Would you ban a book favoring homosexuality from a public library?" You can read the statistics for yourself. The multivariate analysis confirmed that there is a lack of association between military service and censorship, when you control for other factors. Highly educated and less religious individuals are even more likely to oppose censorship. In terms of attitudes towards gay teachers in the public schools, military leaders are a little more conservative than civilians.

Finally, I think we need more information from inside the military, which as others have pointed out is hard to get. What is the number and distribution of homosexual service members? What is the extent and basis of opposition to allowing them to serve openly? Until we know this information, we will not know what the military needs to do for the inevitable transition to open integration. . . .

Laura Miller: Because Jay Williams spoke about the gap between civilian and military elites, I will discuss the military perspective in more detail. Given that most admit that they not only know of gays and lesbians serving openly in the military, but also recognize they are quite capable of carrying out their job, why do they still think that the gay ban is important? Privacy is part of the issue, but it is not separate from cohesion.

Rather, they consider privacy to be linked to cohesion. Mostly what they are concerned about are the values, perspectives, and comfort levels of straight men, who comprise the majority of service members. Only about 15 percent of the military are women, so even though we

Table 4.4 Would you support removing a book in favor of homosexuality from your public library?

	Civilian Elite (%; n = 918)	Military Elite (%; n = 720)
Favor removing	10.2	13.8
Not favor removing	84.7	81.7
Don't know	5.0	4.6

Notes: n = 1638; Pearson's chi-square = 4.83; significance = .089.

Table 4.5 Indicate your position on barring homosexuals from teaching in public schools

	Civilian Elite (%; n = 914)	Military Elite (%; n = 722)
Agree strongly	10.5	20.1
Agree somewhat	10.7	22.2
Disagree somewhat	21.3	29.4
Disagree strongly	52.8	21.1
No opinion	4.6	7.3

Notes: n =1636; Pearson's chi-square = 179.32; significance = .000.

find that women are more open and accepting of gays, in its practical concerns the military is concerned with the majority of its members, which for many people are the more valued soldiers. The military justifies the ban because it feels it knows its own troops well. And, they have overwhelming evidence, which our surveys and interviews confirm, that shows the majority of military men are strongly opposed to working with gays in the military, especially open gays. And it does matter to them whether the person is out or not. Not knowing if a peer is gay allows a heterosexual service member to be more comfortable in an intimate environment and share private facilities. If they knew about their peers' sexual orientation, these would be significantly different psychological experiences. Because so many straight military men are upset by, opposed to, and have hostile feelings against openly gay men serving—their primary concern is openly gay men, not lesbians—commanders will have to worry about cohesion problems. If gay men serve openly, they argue they will have to worry about straights getting along with gays, trusting gays, trying to control hate crimes and violence against gays. Even those people who are sympathetic toward gays in the military are concerned about lifting the ban, because of the possible disciplinary actions and problems that military commanders will have to deal with.

Ultimately, the gay ban keeps some people in the closet. For straight men opposed to gays in the military, the ban allows them to keep gays closeted and to feel more comfortable about this situation. Again we must remember there is a difference between lifting the ban and gays coming out of the closet. If we were to lift the ban, then soldiers who I have interviewed say that they would have their own ways of keeping gays in the closet or keeping them out of the military entirely. Gays and lesbians face violence and harassment not only in the service, a topic I hope we will hear more about from the Servicemembers Legal Defense Network, but in the civilian world as well. In either context, coming out is always a negotiating process. When gays and lesbians come out, they always face potential violence or negative reactions from others. Jay Williams's work, a study on the marines by Armando Estrada, and some of the survey data I have collected with Charlie Moskos all show a high negative reaction and hostile opinions among military men toward gays serving openly in the military.[6]

Using studies of civilian workplaces presents certain challenges, even in police and fire departments where people do have to share long hours and intimate situations together, because military leaders argue that these are not combat situations.[7] Currently we do not have enough data about what happens to cohesion in combat when units include open gays. Although we have a few studies, we do not have the type of comprehensive data that we have on civilian workplaces. We are uncertain if combat is a situation in which differences fall away and members bond together to save their lives and preserve one another. Or is it such a dire circumstance that suspicions and mistrusts come out more than ever? Do people feel they need to know the other person and share similarities and bonds with their fellow soldiers? We simply do not know specifically what happens in combat.

Critics of civilian-based studies also raise the question of whether older civilians in large cities can be taken to represent the behaviors of most military personnel, who are for the most part male, young, and more likely to come from the American South.[8] There is some self-selection as to who joins the military, and military leaders argue that the demographics of the people who serve in the military and their values are not adequately represented in studies of civilian workplaces.

We know that military personnel harbor many hostile attitudes toward gays. They argue that military life is different from civilian situations. Service members come from different backgrounds, which affects their attitudes toward the issue of privacy. To establish unit cohesion, they argue, people cannot feel hostile to one another, repulse each other, or act violently against one another. And despite Mady Segal's suggestion, such inappropriate behavior cannot simply be taken care of by a rule or regulation that will cover every contingency. With women, we have already seen how easily the military can undermine its own rules and regulations. Commanders can always look the other way. Soldiers have told me many times how commanders say, "Well, if you're going to take care of that gay guy just make sure you don't do it on post. Make sure you take care of it off post." There are many ways to harass gays and undermine policies that we cannot control by laws or regulations.

Military leaders worry that lifting the ban will encourage gays to come out of the closet, perhaps even in environments where it might be dangerous for them. Pragmatically, the military has to accommodate the values, beliefs, or prejudices of so many straight soldiers, because their reactions to open gays will cause a number of personnel and disciplinary problems. Their reactions will possibly put some lives at risk through hate crimes or violent actions, or even out in the battlefield, where people can actually choose to allow certain people to be killed, or arrange for them to be killed accidentally if they feel that their mission or their lives are threatened. . . .

Robert MacCoun: I am a social psychologist by training and I study small-group behavior. Prior to working on this project, I had published various experimental studies of the effects of gender composition and gender role attitudes on small-group task performance. So even though I had not worked on military personnel issues, I got drafted to work on the RAND study.[9] To put that study in context, I think that President Clinton made an important political choice when he called for the secretary of defense to draft a plan that would allow ending discrimination "in a practical and realistic manner, as well as being consistent with the high standards of combat effectiveness and unit cohesion that our armed forces must maintain." Those caveats framed it as an empirical question, rather than a matter of principle. At great political risk, the president could have acted on principle alone. By framing the issue as an empirical question, he set up the secretary of defense to commission two task forces to study gays in the military, thus putting the administration in a position in which it could not speak out on the issue while the study was still pending during the Senate Armed Services Committee hearings.[10] If you call for a study, you have to wait for the study to be done. The administration commissioned two study teams: a civilian team, mostly located at the RAND Corporation, which produced a 518-page peer-reviewed report, and a Pentagon team, which produced a 15-page double-spaced memorandum. One of the reports was more influential than the other one, and I helped prepare the less influential study.

After the Clinton administration announced its policy, there were a lot of theories about a cover-up of the RAND study. In truth, our findings were presented to the president and leaked to the *New York Times.* Well before "Don't Ask, Don't Tell" was announced, our conclusions were reported in the *New York Times, Washington Times,* and on the *McNeil-Lehrer Report.* Although dramatic and suggestive of intrigue, the cover-up issue is not a serious one.

Today I will talk about one part of the project, the chapter on unit cohesion.[11] To prepare this chapter, I interviewed all the leading military experts on cohesion, participated in focus groups with military personnel, including closeted gays and lesbians, and studied foreign militaries and police and fire departments. There is an enormous amount of literature on cohesion. I read every available empirical study, something I would not wish on anyone. I read unpublished master's theses and military reports. I interviewed major experts.

And as far as I can tell, there is no single thing called cohesion in the cohesion literature. There are clear theoretical measurement criteria for trying to establish a construct like cohesion, and when the appropriate statistical procedures are used, what is quite clear from independent research in sports literature, organizational behavior literature, and military literature is that there are several different types of cohesion. In attempts to measure cohesion, two key dimensions appear again and again. In our report, we refer to them as social cohesion and task cohesion. Basically, social cohesion is how much members of a group like each other. Task cohesion refers to a shared commitment to the group's goal.

It is important to distinguish these two notions of cohesion. In studies that fail to distinguish between them and simply measure overall cohesion, there is a correlation between cohesion and performance. Cohesion is a real phenomenon. But even though cohesion is related to performance, it is not a large correlation. It ranges from 0.25 to 0.32 to 0.36 in these meta-analyses. So there is some reason to be concerned about the effects of cohesion on military performance. But when you break these studies down, a large part of the correlation is due to the effect of performance on cohesion—the experience of having performed well brings a group together. But this effect of performance on cohesion actually appears to be stronger than the effect of cohesion on performance.

When you break the studies down by whether they primarily measured social cohesion or task cohesion, you find that task cohesion is linked to performance. Having a shared sense of mission improves performance. But social cohesion—liking each other—is not correlated with performance. And in fact, for a variety of reasons, high social cohesion is actually detrimental to performance.

There are several factors that promote cohesion, including successful performance, good leadership, proximity, and similarity. Simply being around people tends to make groups bond. Smaller groups are more cohesive, as are more interdependent groups. Many of these factors are operative in a military setting, irrespective of the characteristics of the members of the group. The correlate of cohesion that is most directly relevant to the gays-in-the-military issue is similarity. "Similarity" refers to whether or not members of a group share characteristics such as race, religion, and sexual orientation. Many forms of similarity predict *social* cohesion, but the only type of similarity that is relevant for *task* cohesion is the notion of shared task goals.

Would open homosexuals disrupt cohesion? As I mentioned earlier, given the current attitudes in the U.S. military toward homosexuality very few gays and lesbians in the armed forces are likely to come out of the closet after the lifting of the ban. It is very difficult to argue effectively that open gays would affect task cohesion because task cohesion involves a shared commitment to the group's mission. Anyone who would join the military knowing that they risk facing this kind of prejudice has to believe very strongly in the military's goal.

Social cohesion might be disrupted. By definition if one group member does not like another, social cohesion goes down, a possibility that we took seriously in the report. Consider a five-person unit, in which one person comes out of the closet. Figure 4.1 illustrates the bonds among the members. If one person comes out, it is possible that other members will not speak to each other anymore and that everyone ends up hating each other. But this is not plausible. Factionalism, or when the group splits into factions, is plausible, but we argued that the most likely outcome is ostracism, which is not a trivial outcome, particularly in terms of endangering the ostracized individual. But the social isolation of one individual is very different from tearing a whole group apart. The major problem is one of leadership, of dealing with the possibility of ostracism. But this very concern is exactly why gay and lesbian service members are not likely to come out of the closet. The literature on military attitudes clearly shows the level of hostility among the ranks.[12]

Other areas of social psychology have well established that prejudicial attitudes do not reliably predict behavior (Figure 4.2). Every social-psychology textbook cites the classic studies of attitudes toward ethnic minorities in the 1930s, in which people expressed great antipathy and yet these attitudes did not always predict their behavior. In actual situations, attitudes are only one of many determinants of one's behavior.

Figure 4.1 Disruption of Social Cohesion?

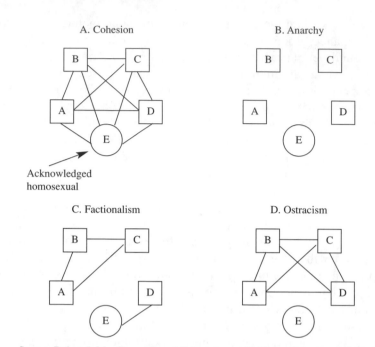

Source: Robert J. MacCoun, "Sexual Orientation and Military Cohesion: A Critical Review of the Evidence," in *Out of Force: Sexual Orientation and the Military,* G. M. Herek, J. B. Jobe, and R. M. Carney, eds. (Chicago: University of Chicago Press, 1996), pp. 157–176.

There are incredible situational pressures on soldiers to perform their duty. The kind of speculation we heard during the Senate Armed Services Committee hearings, when enlisted personnel talked about what they would do if the military would allow gays to serve openly, failed to capture the incredible pressures on them to do their job.

Based on the cohesion literature and other sources of evidence we examined, the RAND study concluded that lifting the ban would have no credible impact on military effectiveness. We recommended the adoption of a conduct-based policy that would hold everyone to high standards of conduct. We did not call for attitude change in the military. We thought that the military's job was to call for certain levels of professional conduct. If people have attitudes that conflict with the conduct that is expected of them, then that is their personal problem. The military's responsibility is to mandate conduct, not attitudes. . . .

Mady Segal: First, I would like to thank Aaron Belkin for organizing this conference and asking me to participate. I will keep my remarks brief,

Figure 4.2   Hostile Attitudes "Overpredict" Hostile Behavior

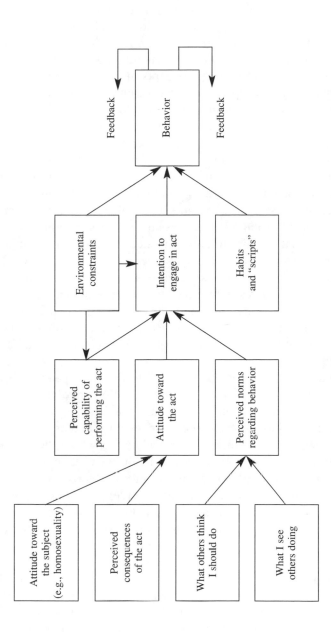

Source: Robert J. MacCoun, "Sexual Orientation and Military Cohesion: A Critical Review of the Evidence," in *Out of Force: Sexual Orientation and the Military*, G. M. Herek, J. B. Jobe, and R. M. Carney, eds. (Chicago: University of Chicago Press, 1996), pp. 157–176.

and expand on some of Rob MacCoun's ideas. . . . I will address three questions: What is unit cohesion? Why is it important? And, does the gay ban preserve unit cohesion in ways that are important for the military?

First, what do we mean by unit cohesion? Traditional definitions of cohesion are not specific. Generally, group cohesion is the social glue that results from all the forces that keep members attached to the group. It is a group property. Traditional concepts of cohesion emphasize peer relationships. Relationships with those in authority were considered parts of leadership, not cohesion. Attempts to measure cohesion have produced multiple definitions and have led to distinctions among different components or types of cohesion. For example, in early conceptualizations, the term "horizontal cohesion" was used to refer to the peer bonding, while "vertical cohesion" referred to bonds between leaders and followers. The latest theoretical and methodological advances distinguish between task cohesion and social cohesion. Task cohesion is the extent to which group members are able to work together to accomplish shared goals. This interdependence is the sort that Emile Durkheim conceptualized as solidarity based on division of labor.[13] Solidarity based on similarity is less functional for the group. Task cohesion includes members' respect for the abilities of fellow group members. For combat situations, it translates into the trust that group members have in each other, including faith that the group can do its job and thereby protect its members from harm. Task cohesion can be horizontal or vertical. Based on task components, vertical cohesion is the respect and confidence that unit members have in their leaders' competence. Involving a more affective dimension, social cohesion involves how well members like each other as individuals and whether they want to spend time together off-duty. Vertical social cohesion includes the extent to which unit members believe that their leaders care about them.

Why is unit cohesion important for the military? Common wisdom says that units with higher cohesion are more effective, especially in combat. My analysis of the accumulated evidence shows that there is sometimes a relationship between cohesion and group effectiveness, but there are three important qualifiers to this relationship. First, the direction of causality is not established. There is evidence that causality works in the opposite direction than what we usually assume. In other words, group success produces cohesion. Second, the evidence for a relationship between cohesion and group performance shows that task cohesion, not social cohesion, relates to success. Indeed, high social cohesion sometimes negatively affects performance.[14] Third, there is evidence that vertical cohesion, or what I would prefer to call effective leadership, affects performance. When members have confidence in their leaders and believe they are competent and care about what happens to them, groups are more likely to be successful in various ways. By definition, good leaders organize task activities within the unit in ways that foster task effectiveness and respect and caring among group members.

So, does the gay ban preserve unit cohesion? If you define unit cohesion as how well members like each other, then perhaps the answer is yes. If we assume that heterosexual members would not like other members if they knew they were homosexual, then arguably the ban helps maintain cohesion, for straight members would not know that they were gay. However, since in the armed forces cohesion matters to the extent that it affects military effectiveness, then the answer is no. Even if task cohesion affected performance, task cohesion is not directly influenced by similarity of personal characteristics that may affect liking or disliking. Were the gay ban to be repealed, and gays allowed to serve openly, I believe that in the short run, issues and processes of integration would arise that would be similar to those encountered in the integration of African-American men in the past and of women of all colors in the past and in the present. The evidence shows that the integration of lesbians would probably be faster than that for gay men, due to military women's more accepting attitudes toward homosexuality and to the less threatening nature of lesbianism to homophobic military men. The evidence suggests that these processes will evolve to smoother and more successful integration as the strangeness wears off and gay service members are seen as competent members and not predators. Many openly gay and lesbian service members, including those who have been discharged for their sexual orientation, have been quite effective. Their outstanding performances have gained them the respect of their peers, leaders, and subordinates. Their continued presence would not have interfered with task cohesion or unit performance. Indeed, for many of these folks, there is no evidence that they interfered with social cohesion even when other unit members knew they were gay.

Overall, in ways that are important to the military, the gay ban does not preserve cohesion.

I would like to end by reading a quote from a speech. I will not tell you initially who said it or when it was said. I have substituted "Group X" for the group whose exclusion is being justified. As I read it, think about whom it refers to and how much it resembles public discourse about excluding gays. When I finish I will tell you who "Group X" actually is and when it was said. Here is the quote: "The army is made up of individual citizens of the United States who have pronounced views with respect to 'Group X' just as they have individual ideas with respect to other matters in their daily walk of life. Military orders, fiat, or dicta will not change their viewpoints. The army then cannot be made the means of engendering conflict among the mass of people because of a stand with respect to 'Group X' that is not compatible with a position obtained by the group in civil life. The army is not a socio-logical laboratory"—I wish I had a dollar for every time I have heard that comment—"To be effective, it must be organized and trained according to the principles which will insure success. Experiments to meet the wishes and demands of the champions of every group for the solution of their problems are a danger to efficiency, discipline, and morale, and would result in ultimate defeat." This statement was made on December 8, 1941, by a representative of the adjutant general of the U.S. Army, and "Group X" is African Americans.[15] . . .

Belkin: For people in the room who might not be familiar with the debate on unit cohesion, statistics, slides, or social-scientific presenta-tions, I will frame the debate briefly. What we are debating here is the unit cohesion rationale and the justification for the gay ban. One justi-fication for the ban is that gays undermine cohesion, and the debate in this room is whether or not that is not true. Those people who oppose gays in the military argue that straight people do not like gay people and that dislike or hatred results in unit cohesion and military effectiveness falling apart. On the other side of the debate, people argue that even if straights and gays do not like each other, cohesion will not fall apart because cohesion and performance depend on commitment to shared goals. Part of the debate centers on whether dislike and hatred are the same thing as unit cohesion falling apart. . . .

Michael Desch: I appreciated Aaron's invitation to come and talk and I will start by saying I primarily view this issue as one the military will have to grapple with as it moves into a fundamentally new operational environment. As I mentioned in my earlier intervention, I see it within the context of military efficiency. That being said, I agree with the find-ings of Mr. MacCoun and the RAND Corporation study and with Beth Kier's terrific article in *International Security,* as well.[16] As they argue, I do not find the wartime unit cohesion argument against ending the ban on open homosexuals within the military to be very persuasive. And as all the previous speakers have mentioned, I think it is crucial to distin-guish between task and social cohesion. I am fully persuaded that a per-son's sexual orientation, race, political affiliation—or whether they root for Notre Dame or not, which I think is one of the big issues in the great cosmos—all of these issues are irrelevant. In wartime and in terms of task cohesion, the gay ban is not tenable.

But everyone, including Beth Kier, concedes that the social-cohesion argument may have more merit to it. The argument I would like to suggest to you is that in peacetime, the context in which the American military currently operates, social cohesion may be as important or maybe even more important than task cohesion. The two basic points I would like to convey today are first, now is not the time to try and make a change of this magnitude. In a minute, I will spell out why I think that is the case. And secondly, there is a time to make this change, but it is in the future. I will tell you exactly when I think that time will be. But the change needs to be made and justified primarily in terms of military efficiency. I believe any other argument will not carry the day.

Let me start by outlining why I think social cohesion is more important for the American military in peacetime. We have already discussed why cohesion might be important for military effectiveness, as well as during wartime why a common threat and a singular mission might bring even disparate people together behind a common task. In fact, in the past the presence of open homosexuals has not affected wartime task cohesion. Allan Bérubé's fine book and Randy Shilts's work provide plenty of anecdotal evidence that during wartime open homosexuality has been relatively well tolerated.[17] Mr. Haggerty referred to the rates of discharge based on homosexuality as having a sort of interesting inverse relationship to our war status. Up until the Reagan period, it is quite close. Discharges for homosexuality go down when we are at war and go up when we are at peace. I think, comrades, that is no accident.

During wartime, unit task cohesion was probably not affected very much at all by open homosexuals. But in peacetime, and especially in the current security environment, task cohesion may be insufficient for insuring cohesion within military units. First of all, today's environment is very different from the environment of ten or eleven years ago. The United States faces no common threat. There are a number of little threats around the world, but not one of the magnitude we faced during the Cold War or that we clearly had during World War II. Likewise, as most everyone knows, the mission of the American military today is up for grabs and in a period of profound flux. Talking about task cohesion in the contemporary American military is fundamentally different than it was even ten or fifteen years ago because within the organization itself, the threat and the mission are under fundamental dispute.

In this particular period, social cohesion has become extremely important, because making a credible task cohesion argument is more difficult today than it was before. If you accept this possibility, then it seems more credible to argue, as many people have, that lifting the gay ban could undermine social cohesion. In fact, there are good reasons for why this may be the case. First of all, without a common threat and an overarching mission, small differences become more important than they might be under fire or in a very intense international security environment. Many examples in everyday life illustrate this point. Without a common threat, little differences that seem relatively insignificant in wartime can become much bigger and much more disruptive. Second, today's American military is much more homogenous than it has been at any time in the past. With an all-volunteer force there are many people, myself included, who are worried because self-selection leads to a much more homogenous and inwardly oriented institution. Throughout history, professional armies, as opposed to mass armies, tended to be relatively homogenous and much different from the rest of society.

Let me suggest some of the ways in which the contemporary military is becoming much more homogenous. First of all: political affiliation. At least within the officer corps, we now have an organization that is largely affiliated with the Republican Party (Figure 4.3). In the Triangle Institute for Security Studies survey, about 67 percent of the officers who responded identified as members of the Republican Party.[18] About 22 percent identified as independent. My hunch is that these people find the Republican Party too liberal. We are dealing with an organization that has become ideologically very homogenous. Second: the regional origins of the officer corps. The military, in particular the army, is predominantly southern. As a transplanted northerner now living in the South, I can tell you that this shift has profound implications (Figure 4.4).

Lynn Eden: Your figures only go back to 1972. What would it look like in the 1950s and 1960s?

Desch: Most people think that the South has been overrepresented historically in the American military for a relatively long period of time, and Janowitz and Huntington confirm this, as well.[19] The U.S. military has been largely a southern institution. I would argue it is becoming even more so, as a result of two other factors. First, more people are spending more time in service, so less people are rotating through the institution, which is making it more of a long-service professional organization (Figure 4.5). You do not have to be a rocket scientist to conclude that the political and regional origins of large numbers of the officer corps correlate closely with negative attitudes about homosexuality. As the American military becomes more of a homogenous and long-term profession force, attitudes on this particular issue are hardening pretty quickly.

Figure 4.3 The Civil-Military Gap in Party Affiliation

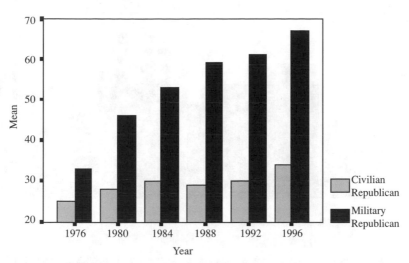

Source: Michael C. Desch, "Explaining the Gap: Vietnam, the Republicanization of the South, and the End of the Mass Army," in *Soldiers and Civilians: The U.S. Military, American Society, and National Security,* Peter Feaver and Richard Kohn, eds. (Cambridge, Mass.: BCSIA-MIT Press, 2001), pp. 289–324.

Why is now not the propitious time to push for change? With the end of the Cold War, the U.S. military is in a period of profound change. Almost everything is up for grabs. In addition to social issues like ending the gay ban or further integrating women into combat, the military is facing fundamental changes in the purpose of the organization, its size, and the amount of money it receives from the federal budget (Figure 4.6). Making a change of this magnitude in an organization that is being pushed on almost every front to make major changes strikes me as a recipe for disaster. Historically speaking, if you look back less than eight years ago to President Clinton's efforts to push this change, there is evidence to support why now may not be the best time. Not only did he fail abjectly, but I think "Don't Ask, Don't Tell" represented more than no change. It actually made things worse in some respects. Clinton's failure set the tone for his relationship with the military from the start, from which he never fully recovered. Even though George W. Bush is unlikely to address this issue, we are faced with the very real possibility that Al Gore might be our commander in chief. Some people take heart that since Al Gore served as an enlisted man in Vietnam and at one point in his career was very centrist on defense issues, he might have a

Figure 4.4 Percentage of Southern Officers

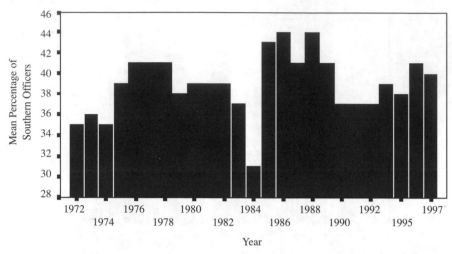

Year

Source: Michael C. Desch, "Explaining the Gap: Vietnam, the Republicanization of the South, and the End of the Mass Army," in *Soldiers and Civilians: The U.S. Military, American Society, and National Security,* Peter Feaver and Richard Kohn, eds. (Cambridge, Mass.: BCSIA-MIT Press, 2001), pp. 289–324.

better relationship with the U.S. military. For those of you who feel confident about this fact, let me make this prediction now: Especially after the Florida absentee ballot mess, Gore's relationship with the American military will be if anything as bad, if not worse, than Clinton's relationship. The issue is not Gore's military service. The issue is that Gore is a Democrat, and the officer corps hates Democrats. I do not use the word "hate" advisedly. I think it is a fair characterization of the situation.

But I do want to end my talk on a positive side, because I do think there is a positive side. I am arguing for prudence here. In my heart of hearts, because I believe that open homosexuals do not affect the military at war, I see no reason to maintain the ban in perpetuity. But if you accept the logic of the argument I am making about the importance of timing, then we ought to think about making this change in wartime or in a period of fairly intense international security threats, rather than doing it in this period of relatively diffuse and amorphous threats. Some people might say that we are at the end of history and that such threats will never return. I assure you they will. Second, if we are to make this change, we have to consider it in terms of military effectiveness. Ultimately, any discussion of principle or political rights will prove unsuccessful in terms of persuading the military leadership.

I leave you with this historical anecdote. Via Executive Order 9981 in 1948, Harry Truman attempted to end segregation in the U.S. armed forces and

Figure 4.5 Increasing Average Term of Service

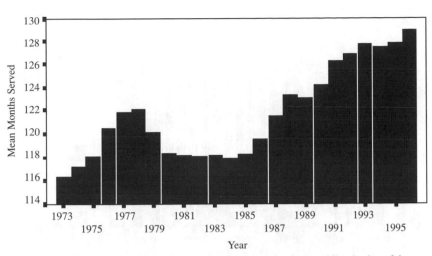

Source: Michael C. Desch, "Explaining the Gap: Vietnam, the Republicanization of the South, and the End of the Mass Army," in *Soldiers and Civilians: The U.S. Military, American Society, and National Security,* Peter Feaver and Richard Kohn, eds. (Cambridge, Mass.: BCSIA-MIT Press, 2001), pp. 289–324.

was not very successful. The real success in ending segregation in combat units came between June and August 1950 during the Korean War. The acute manpower shortages at that time made it clear that we needed every able-bodied soldier who could serve. The Korean War experience and earlier experiences in the Ardennes in World War II were far more effective at integrating African Americans into the military than any executive order. . . .

Eden: Laura, it is clear that you are speaking as a social scientist and reporting on these findings. I do not question what you have found. But having reported on the high hostility and possible dangers that gays face in the military, which we know are not hypothetical, one could arrive at different policy conclusions. One alternative might be that the military should not tolerate bad behavior and should eliminate discrimination of any sort. Another possibility could be that gays and lesbians should not be allowed to serve openly. Could you tell us what policy implications you see following from your findings?

Miller: I think it is negligent, naïve, and simply wrong to conclude that no problems are going to arise. It is also naïve to pass down command rules that bad behavior will not be tolerated, as well as thinking such tactics will be effective given the strength and widespread negative attitudes among soldiers. Repeatedly, I have seen service members build up

Figure 4.6 Decreasing Size of the U.S. Military

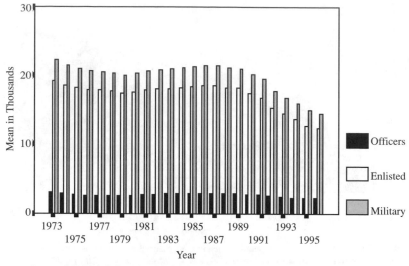

Source: Michael C. Desch, "Explaining the Gap: Vietnam, the Republicanization of the South, and the End of the Mass Army," in *Soldiers and Civilians: The U.S. Military, American Society, and National Security,* Peter Feaver and Richard Kohn, eds. (Cambridge, Mass.: BCSIA-MIT Press, 2001), pp. 289–324.

acceptance among peers in one place. First they let their colleagues get to know them and then they come out as gay. But there is so much transferring among units; deployments change; and people move so often from place to place—gays and lesbians constantly have to prove themselves and face fears or people who fear them. We need to get away from the idea that if we just have the right policy or the right regulation, then we could make service members behave the way we want them to. Much more has to be done. Part of the problem is that military leadership must support this change, and I think we have clear evidence that they do not. The evidence shows that when the leadership fail to support an issue, any change will not be effective. For example, officers could be ordered to discuss tolerance of gays and lesbians with their troops. But they could undermine these orders easily by beginning their remarks to their troops by saying, "Now it's time for the talk on fags." When they argue and believe as many of them strongly do that civilians pushing for this reform do not know what military life is like or how it will impact their missions, then there will be resentment and not the sort of wholehearted enforcement of the policy. It will end up being enforced simply for the sake of appearances. As Jay Williams highlighted earlier, I would argue that we have to think about much more than just policy and regulation. We must deal with how people undermine the policy or harass individuals. We must consider standards of proof and how we will get military leadership to enforce a policy they do not believe in themselves, a policy they believe might cost lives or is being pushed on them by people who they think do not know what they are talking about. . . .

David Segal: Three points. First, very quickly, Executive Order 9981 actually said nothing about desegregation or integration. That was not the language of the executive order. It spoke about equality of opportunity, and back then the accepted legal doctrine of equality of opportunity was *Plessy v. Ferguson.*[20] The standard was separate-but-equal, which was the way the services responded until 1950 when they integrated in the Korean theater of operations.

I have a question for Laura Miller and Jay Williams, to which I do not know the answer. Who are these military elites that this survey talks about? I am old-fashioned. Once upon a time, before I studied soldiers and units, I studied military elites. There may be about four dozen of them: the chairman, the joint chiefs, the chiefs, and perhaps the vice-chiefs, but these are not the people whom you are talking about. I am concerned about this label of military elites, particularly because Jim Dowd at the University of Georgia gave a paper at the American Sociological Association meeting this last summer about his research on a different group of officers, of generals.[21] He reports that from his interviews with these generals he has gotten a very different sense than from what he had read in the press about the military.

My third point addresses the issue of cohesion and performance. Up through 1993 in the U.S. debates on gays in the military, and extending into Britain this year, the argument was made that we did have data on the linkage between cohesion and performance. The main findings came out of research on World War II, and three studies have been cited repeatedly: the Shils-Janowitz study of disintegration in the Wehrmacht, S. L. A. Marshall's study, *Men Against Fire,* and Sam Stouffer's *American Soldier* study.[22] I went back and reread them. They are interesting and, I think, they have some value. However, they have absolutely no value as scientific research.

Shils-Janowitz was one of the denazification studies conducted by the U.S. Army in World War II. American military personnel interviewed German prisoners of war and asked them why they went on fighting. If you happen to be a German POW under Allied control, there is a right answer to this question, and saying you were a Nazi is not the right answer. I think the Shils-Janowitz study proves that there were a lot of smart German soldiers.

S. L. A. Marshall's results reportedly came from after-action interviews with army rifle companies that had come off the line in which
soldiers said that they went on fighting for their buddies. Back in the
1980s there were some inquiries into the nature of this research because
a number of people who served in the infantry in World War II said that
the results of the study did not ring true. Second, they cannot find anybody who was actually interviewed. They looked through the notes,
including those in the Marshall archives, and it may be that those interviews were never conducted. He had a good idea about what was going
on, and he might have been right, but the data do not exist.

With regard to the Stouffer study, we basically misremember a
romantic notion of what his findings were. Stouffer did not ask any
questions about unit cohesion, because that concept did not exist at the
time. He did ask soldiers what kept them going in combat. In no case
was fighting for one's buddies the primary reason for continuing to
fight during a combat situation. In the European theater of operation,
the most common response was that knowing they had to get the job
done kept soldiers going. This is very different from cohesion. Now, it
turns out the second most important reason, the reason picked by the
second largest group of people as to why they kept fighting, was fighting
for their buddies. But that second largest response was only given by 14
percent of the soldiers. In the Pacific theater, when soldiers were asked
what kept them going when the going got tough, the most common
answer was religion, prayer, or belief in God. If Stouffer's data show
anything, it is that there really are not any atheists in foxholes. Again,
fighting for one's buddies turned out to be the second most important
answer. But I think that with respect to all three of these widely cited
studies of unit cohesion, we have data that we have misremembered
from World War II and that do not justify the argument that cohesion is
essential for combat effectiveness. And the research that Roger Little did
on rifle companies in Korea showed nothing of the nature of cohesion
that we like to remember from World War II.[23] And the major finding
that comes out of Vietnam research shows that what you had was a level
of social cohesion rooted primarily in choice of psychoactive substances.
We had primary groups of heads and primary groups of juicers who were
tightly bonded among themselves and unsupportive of the goals of the
army and their country, and that did not function effectively in combat.[24]

Eden: Thank you. Jay, would you respond very briefly to David Segal's
question?

Williams: Yes, I will. We are not referring to general officers. We are
talking about O-5 to O-6 level officers who for the most part participated

in the study while they were at a war college.[25] These are the people most likely to be commanding officers in units. By military elites, we do not mean the very highest. . . .

Desch: On Executive Order 9981, David, the conventional wisdom is that Truman did it to increase electoral support from blacks. Separate-but-equal would not have pushed that through. The standard histories are quite clear in treating this as an effort to further integration, so I do not think that you are correct on that one. . . .

Dixon Osburn: I would like to make an observation about what we call fuzzy math to consider when discussing the data, which addresses one of the polling questions that you asked in your survey.

The first question you asked was do you think gay men and lesbians should be allowed to serve openly in the military? There has been a lot of polling done that asks the question differently, such as, do you think gays should serve in the military? If you look at Gallup's polling data over the past decade, you will see that now over 70 percent of Americans agree that gays should serve in the military. The problem with adding the word "openly" to the question is that it means different things to gay and nongay people. As gay people, we know what "openly" means. It means we can talk to our moms and our dads, psychiatrists, chaplains, confidants, and colleagues whom we trust. Some nongay people do not look at it in the same way. They wonder why gay people have to flaunt it. Does "openly" mean making a grand announcement before the entire unit at the mess hall table? Does it mean running immediately to *Nightline* to declare your sexual orientation? There is a lot of baggage that comes with the term "openly." And when you ask a question using that term without explaining what you mean by it, you will collect data that suppress what people actually believe. If you were to survey the military elite you are discussing and ask them "Should gay people be able to talk to their parents openly about their sexual orientation?" I think your data would be very different. Should gay people be allowed to talk to a psychiatrist about the stresses of the environment? I think your data would be extremely different. I think the data here misrepresent the real opinions of many members in the military.

Williams: But it is more appropriate for the policy change that is being discussed, Dixon.

Miller: Actually, I discovered this difference when Jay Williams and I were coauthoring this chapter and debating what words we could use.

To some degree, I thought of "open" as "known," while Jay interpreted "open" as more of an activist type of—

Williams: Not necessarily activist, but completely out. But we did not write these questions, by the way. This was the Triangle Institute for Security Studies [TISS] survey. We had some input into the wording of the questions, but we took what we got.

Miller: And again, the survey is indicating whether people are aware that that person is gay or not. Because a lot of people say, "I don't care as long as I don't know that they're gay." The language is difficult because for some people "known" means rumored to be gay. But for me, "known" means you know. For some people, "open" means people are aware of it, while for others it is a regular topic of conversation or a major political agenda. There is a problem with the word even in the scholarship and in the surveys. You are exactly right. We should hear more about this issue. . . .

M. Segal: I would like to comment on one of Mike Desch's points. His analysis is very interesting especially since we hear this "the Army is not a sociological laboratory" response all the time. But pitting a change on military effectiveness is not a bad idea. In fact, I think it is a good idea, but I have two caveats. First, during the Cold War there was a known and common threat, but service members spent their time practicing. They did not actually have real missions. They did a lot of training. Now service members are actually being deployed and going on real missions, where there are threats and they do have to rely on each other. Now may be actually a good time, because they have real missions. They may be different missions, and there may be a lot of uncertainty with the missions, but service members are out there in places where there are real threats. It might be a good time, because they will work together and there is commitment to the task at hand.

My second point addresses the kind of recruitment and retention environment that we have currently. All of the services are struggling to maintain a force level of sufficient size both in terms of recruiting new people and retaining the members they have. This is very important for mission effectiveness, so it is a good time to lift the gay ban in that sense. . . .

Williams: I have a very quick comment about Mike Desch's commentary on the increasing Republicanization of the officer corps. Actually there is less of that than meets the eye. A lot of the military has always been very conservative, but people are finally willing to admit they are conservative, and not only conservative, but Republican. . . .

Desch: But the problem . . . is that the TISS data [see Figure 4.3] demonstrate that whereas the military and the general public were roughly comparable in terms of political affiliation in 1976, by 1996 the military officers corps was overwhelmingly Republican.

Williams: I think they are just willing to admit it now. I am not so convinced.

Desch: No, the truth of the matter is you could be a conservative and a Democrat up until the late 1960s. What it means to be a Republican or a Democrat has undergone a big change. Now a conservative Democrat is pretty much extinct. . . .

Deborah Mulliss: I have a general question. We say the military is not a laboratory for social experimentation, but from some of the data that Michael Desch presented, it appears that the U.S. armed forces recruit mainly from the South and that the senior staff reflect one particular political persuasion. But how can the American public feel confident that the senior military will not have a political bias that they will demonstrate through their actions? . . .

Desch: Interestingly, from the TISS surveys, we know that the American public has a great deal of confidence in the American military. On the one hand it is one of the institutions that rates high in public regard, along with a number of other relatively undemocratic institutions in our society. Yet when asked if the military is likely to shirk from obligations that are imposed upon it that it does not want to undertake, that same public thinks that it is quite likely the military will not do what it does not want to, which is a worrisome development. According to the survey they are quite conflicted. Generally the public does not seem to care much about these issues. They get warm and fuzzy about the military, but they are not really thinking about the military's daily purpose. . . .

Larry Korb: I have got one question that I would like to ask any of the researchers to address in their summary remarks if they feel it is appropriate. Is it easier for us, as a multiethnic society, to accommodate different groups than other societies that are much more culturally homogenous? Even if we do not consider gender or sexual orientation, we certainly have integrated a number of other groups.

This idea of polls in the military is not popular. We should not be polling the military about what service members want. We certainly do not ask them where they want to have basic training. If we took a poll, they would not want to go to Bosnia, or they would not want to be in the Gulf. I also tend to agree with what Mady Segal said. During the Cold War there was a lot of practice, other than Vietnam and Korea, obviously. And I do not agree with the argument that now is not the right time. Whenever we deal with a controversial governmental issue, we always hear, "You're right, but now is not the right time.". . .

Miller: In response to your comment about the polls, I would like to bring up a point that Judith Stiehm makes.[26] A political scientist at Florida International University, she has been studying gender integration for decades. One point that she brings up is that you could not survey soldiers about whether we should resegregate by race. The fact that we continue to ask questions of soldiers about policies that already have been implemented—like "Should we take women out of certain units?"—allows the policy to be debated, which tells soldiers they can continue to object to decisions that already have been made. Surveying the troops thus sends the message that policy could be rolled back. The same thing could be said about gays in the military, especially if we lift the ban. If you keep asking soldiers their opinion about whether we should change policy, it suggests that the issue is still up for grabs, rather than stating the policy and expecting service members to accept it.

In response to the question of whether having a multiethnic society makes it easier to address other issues of integration, I would say from my last eight years studying and interviewing army soldiers, they tend to reject any parallels drawn between race and sexuality. They say that people cannot help the race they are born with. So, we should give minorities a break. This reflects a white perspective, but it is the predominant view in the military. But in regards to sexuality, they often say that whether you are born gay or socialized to be gay, you can still choose not to act gay. But blacks cannot choose not to be black, and most soldiers do not see the two as parallel issues.

MacCoun: The RAND report was very wide-eyed in anticipating a wide variety of possible problems with implementation. In fact, we devoted two chapters to that issue. Of course, there will be problems with such a change, and of course they will generate publicity. But again, if we return to the police and fire departments and foreign militaries, which probably understate the hostility toward gays in the U.S. military, then there would be only about a tenth of a percent of active personnel who would be openly gay. It is difficult to seriously argue that such a small percentage would have a measurable impact on military effectiveness. In terms of scale, this problem is trivial for the military. Even if every single time someone came out there were management problems, it would remain a trivial problem relative to the other challenges confronting the military. And recall that foreign militaries and American police and fire departments have not reported management problems after lifting their own bans.

Christopher Dandeker: Two comments. Mady Segal and Mike Desch both made the point earlier that one of the difficulties the United States faces is whether the timing is right for making such a change. We have also been considering the degree to which the armed services have the right to exercise some kind of veto on the change, let alone the timing. It seems to me that Mady Segal said, and I agree with her, that if you are going to make such a change, much time and effort needs to be invested in building a coalition between civilian political leadership and military officers to lay the groundwork for it. As I will discuss later this afternoon, this is one of the lessons of the British experience.

Second, it is important to address the issue of polling, at least topically. It is extremely important to continue polling personnel's views on questions of sexual orientation and other matters. All the evidence I have seen on my side of the Atlantic suggests that the armed services will need to be polling more, not less, and here is my privacy point in another context, because within the objective constraints of service life one thing that personnel want, and this relates to recruitment and retention, is to feel that they are consulted about what is going on in their lives and how their careers are structured. They recognize the realities of service life, but they expect polling to be done seriously and for actions to follow from it, which is still consistent with my point about coalition building that I made earlier. . . .

Melissa Sheridan Embser-Herbert: We need to completely dismiss this notion of being completely out of the closet. There is no such thing. It is an ongoing process. No matter whom you are out to, how out you are, or what you have done publicly, when you encounter new people, you come out all over. It is important to remember that when we think about the terms "open" and "known."

Mostly, I would like to offer a more personal observation about this issue of waiting for the right time. I was sitting here thinking that I enlisted in 1978. This was a time when, for anyone who could sign an X on a dotted line, they found a way to get your body into the military, women included. At that point, can we argue that the military was ready for women? I would say "no." Twenty-two years ago when I arrived at my first permanent duty station, I was given a sleeping bag and shown to a room at the very end of the third floor that had not been cleaned, because I was the second woman to arrive in that unit. They did not quite know what to do with me. We were a nuclear security military police unit, and I was on a squad with three men. When we would go out to the weapons storage site, we would work on-shift/off-shift, but we would stay out there. When we were off-shift, we would share a room with four bunks. Of course, we were fully clothed, waiting for the alarm to go off. One night I remember hearing some commotion and realizing that one of the men was masturbating. And I knew that as a woman in the military you just ignored it. I made some flip remark to him and I ignored it. I was there to do a job. For the most part, I liked my job, so you just learned to live with such things. As I listen to people's stories, what it really comes down to for me is not to limit people's choices in terms of their willingness to serve their country or their employment. The ban did not keep Barry Winchell alive.[27] It does not prevent violence. Maybe we need to move forward and realize that it is not fair to tell a person that you cannot do this job because we are not ready for you. If we had accepted that argument for allowing women into the military, I would never have served. If they had waited until they could have been sure men would not have behaved the way the guys I served with did, there would have been no women there. It is fine to discuss polling, surveys, and data, but I wanted to offer a more personal perspective that for the last however many decades, women have dealt with the kinds of problems we are trying to keep from happening to gays and lesbians. I would like to conclude by saying that gay, lesbian, bisexual, and transgendered people learn how to avoid violence every day. They learn how to make decisions about whom to talk to, whom to come out to, or whether or not to put a picture of their partner up on the wall. We need to give people credit that if they choose to serve in the military, then they will make those decisions. It is not the ACT-UP gay activist or lesbian who joins the military. I think it is time to think about some of these issues in a different fashion. . . .

D. Segal: On the timing issue, earlier this morning I mentioned that institutions tend to reproduce themselves. Organizations tend to move away from that position of reproduction during periods of crisis, which was the case in the United States with regard to race, when we were mobilizing for the Korean War with the generation that grew up during the Depression. We basically needed all the men we could get. We have had two major surges of increased utilization of women in the military. The first actually came during World War II. We brought in hundreds of thousands of women, because we were going through a massive national mobilization. The country needed men for combat and the military felt that women could do the noncombat jobs. By contrast, the attempt to lift the gay ban came on the heels of the collapse of the Soviet Union and the end of the Cold War in Europe. With the downsizing of the American military, we did not need to look for new sources of manpower. It was exactly the wrong time in terms of changing processes of reproduction and closure to say that we have another source of people in the United States that we need to bring into the military. . . .

Paul Gade: I want to comment briefly on and bring together some of the issues vis-à-vis polling military service members. Of course it is one of the things that we might not want to do in studying the issue of gays and lesbians in the military. Larry Korb's comment is well taken for some of the reasons that Rob MacCoun already alluded to. We ask these questions and get some very strong opinions, but they never lead to the kinds of behaviors that we are most concerned about. As we will talk about this afternoon, we have seen this phenomenon over and over again in the foreign militaries that we have studied. If you survey people about gays in the military before the lifting of a ban, they tell you that they will react violently if open gays are allowed to serve. But when the actual ban is lifted, nothing much happens. You might argue that keeping the ban in place and not having a set of rules for implementing the integration of gays and lesbians into the military actually fosters the kinds of violent behaviors and misbehaviors that we are so fearful of when we do these surveys. Interestingly enough, in 1993 when lifting the ban was talked about, and we studied the issue at the Army Research Institute, we were banned from doing a survey by the Department of Defense. At the same time, we thought this response was certainly a less-than-enlightened position. But in retrospect, it was probably a smart choice, because these surveys were generating a lot of heat and not very much light in terms of how to solve these problems. . . .

Tiffany Willoughby-Herard[28]: I have two points. The first might be a bit flip. Since society is becoming more conservative, does that mean we need to have radical people integrate the military and try to infiltrate the officer corps? My second point addresses the need for external foes to integrate major institutions. We have to consider whether that has been the actual historical experience in this country. Does there have to be a moment of incredible focus of social cohesion within the country in order for us to integrate institutions? I do not believe that it is really the case. . . .

Alex Marthews:[29] I would like to speak to this polling issue and the difference between what military people say they would do and what they actually will do. In the British case, before the ban was lifted, many military personnel said they would resign if homosexuals were permitted to serve openly. Since the ban was lifted in February, the data indicate that there have been two resignations, and one of those people was apparently leaving anyway. In terms of why people have resigned since the ban was lifted, the admission of homosexuals has not been a major issue. People are concerned with far more concrete issues of being overstretched, not being able to come home to see their families, or enduring the stress that the army is under. But admitting homosexuals is not a major reason for why people leave. In terms of harassment, after the ban was lifted, anecdotal evidence has suggested that it occurs no more and probably less than before the ban was lifted. . . .

Belkin: I would like to wrap up again by thanking all of you for the discussion, which I found very enlightening and that taught me a great deal. But I found it to be slightly underresponsive to the question of whether the gay ban preserves unit cohesion or not. To my mind, the main point that will determine the answer to that question is Laura Miller's point that violence and harassment cannot be controlled by law, to which I did not hear much of a response. Laura's comments suggest to me that if lifting the ban would lead to more violence and harassment, then perhaps the ban does preserve cohesion. But I would like to conclude by giving a very brief personal opinion. First of all, all of the arguments suggesting that the ban preserves unit cohesion, regardless of what we mean by cohesion, depend on the assumption that if the ban is lifted more soldiers will come out of the closet. I am still not convinced that this is true. Second, I do not understand Laura's point that we cannot control violence and harassment by law. I would think that in a military organization a few dismissals of prominent generals under whose command abuse was taking place might be sufficient to do the trick. But I have never been in the military, so perhaps I am wrong on that point.

NOTES

1. U.S. Congress, *10 United States Code 654* (Washington, D.C.: Government Printing Office, 1993), Pub. L. 103-160 571, 107 Stat., 1547.

2. "Don't Ask, Don't Tell," *Sixty Minutes* (December 12, 1999).

3. This section is based on Aaron Belkin, "The Pentagon's Gay Ban Is Not Based on Military Necessity," *Journal of Homosexuality* 41, no. 1 (2001): 103–119.

4. Peter Feaver and Richard Kohn, eds., *Soldiers and Civilians: The U.S. Military, American Society, and National Security* (Cambridge, Mass.: BCSIA-MIT Press, 2001).

5. Table 4.1 and those that follow are from Laura L. Miller and John Allen Williams, "Do Military Policies on Gender and Sexuality Undermine Combat Effectiveness?" in Peter Feaver and Richard Kohn, eds., *Soldiers and Civilians: The U.S. Military, American Society, and National Security* (Cambridge, Mass.: BCSIA-MIT Press, 2001), pp. 386–429.

6. A. X. Estrada and D. J. Weiss, "Attitudes of Military Personnel Toward Homosexuals," *Journal of Homosexuality* 37 (1999): 83–97; Laura L. Miller, "Fighting for a Just Cause: Soldiers' Attitudes on Gays in the Military," in *Gays and Lesbians in the Military*, W. J. Scott and S. C. Stanley, eds. (New York, N.Y.: Aldine de Gruyter, 1994), pp. 69–85; and Miller and Williams, "Do Military Policies on Gender and Sexuality Undermine Combat Effectiveness?"

7. Paul Koegel, "Lessons Learned from the Experiences of Domestic Police and Fire Departments," in *Out in Force: Sexual Orientation and the Military*, Gregory Herek, Jared Jobe, and Ralph Carney, eds. (Chicago, Ill.: University of Chicago Press, 1996), pp. 131–156.

8. Miller is arguing that even though studies show that known gays and lesbians have not undermined urban police and fire departments, these studies may not be applicable to the military.

9. National Defense Research Institute, *Sexual Orientation and U.S. Military Personnel Policy: Options and Assessment* (Santa Monica, Calif.: RAND, 1993).

10. U.S. Senate Committee on Armed Services, *Policy Concerning Homosexuality in the Armed Forces*, 103d Congress, 2d Session (Washington, D.C.: Government Printing Office, 1993).

11. Robert J. MacCoun, "What Is Known About Unit Cohesion and Military Performance," in National Defense Research Institute, *Sexual Orientation and U.S. Military Personnel Policy: Options and Assessment* (Santa Monica, Calif.: RAND, 1993), pp. 283–331.

12. See Laura L. Miller, "Fighting for a Just Cause," pp. 69–85.

13. Emile Durkheim, *The Division of Labor in Society,* trans. George Simpson (New York, N.Y.: The Free Press, 1933).

14. See Elizabeth Kier, "Homosexuals in the U.S. Military: Open Integration and Combat Effectiveness," *International Security* 23 (1998): 5–39. Kier shows that high social cohesion can undermine group performance when group members conspire to subvert overall organizational goals. She cites several examples such as collective decisions to desert, to disobey orders, and to kill group leaders, a process known as "fragging."

15. See D. A. Bianco, "Echoes of Prejudice: The Debates over Race and Sexuality in the Armed Forces," in *Gay Rights, Military Wrongs: Political Perspectives on Lesbians and Gays in the Military,* C. A. Rimmerman, ed. (New York, N.Y.: Garland Publishing Inc., 1996), pp. 47–70.

16. Kier, "Homosexuals in the U.S. Military," pp. 5–39.

17. Allan Bérubé, *Coming out Under Fire: The History of Gay Men and Women in World War Two* (New York, N.Y.: The Free Press, 1990); Randy Shilts, *Conduct Unbecoming: Gays and Lesbians in the U.S. Military* (New York, N.Y.: Fawcett Columbine, 1993).

18. The Triangle Institute for Security Studies has been engaged in a long-term survey research project to study the gap between the military and American society. See Feaver and Kohn, *Soldiers and Civilians.*

19. See Morris Janowitz, *The Professional Soldier: A Social and Political Portrait* (Glencoe, Ill.: The Free Press, 1960), pp. 211–221; and Samuel P. Huntington, *The Soldier and the State—The Theory of Politics in Civil-Military Relations* (Cambridge, Mass.: Harvard University Press, 1957), pp. 88–89.

20. In its 1896 decision in *Plessy v. Ferguson*, the U.S. Supreme Court upheld the constitutionality of the separate-but-equal doctrine, the notion that separate amenities for whites and African Americans were acceptable if they were equal.

21. Jim J. Dowd, "Connected to Society: The Political Beliefs of the U.S. Army Generals," *Armed Forces and Society* 27 (2001): 343–372.

22. See E. Shils and M. Janowitz, "Cohesion and Disintegration in the Wehrmacht in World War II," *Public Opinion Quarterly* 12 (1948): 280–315; S. L. A. Marshall, *Men Against Fire: The Problem of Battle Command in Future War* (New York, N.Y.: Morrow, 1947); and Samuel Stouffer et al., *The American Soldier* (Princeton, N.J.: Princeton University Press, 1949).

23. See Roger W. Little, "Buddy Relations and Combat Performance," in *The New Military,* Morris Janowitz, ed. (New York, N.Y.: Norton, 1969), pp. 195–223.

24. "Juicers" refers to service members who drank large amounts of alcohol, while "heads" refers to those who were often high on marijuana.

25. "O-5" and "O-6" refer to the ranks of lieutenant colonel and colonel, respectively.

26. Judith H. Stiehm, *Arms and the Enlisted Woman* (Philadelphia, Pa.: Temple University Press, 1989).

27. Private First Class Barry Winchell was beaten to death at Fort Campbell, Kentucky, on July 5, 1999, after facing daily antigay harassment for four months.

28. Tiffany Willoughby-Herard is a doctoral candidate in the Department of Political Science, University of California, Santa Barbara.

29. Alex Marthews is a graduate student in public policy at the University of California, Berkeley.

5

Are Foreign Military Experiences Relevant to the United States?

DURING CONGRESSIONAL HEARINGS THAT CULMINATED IN THE PASSAGE OF "Don't Ask, Don't Tell" and on numerous occasions since that time, scholars and experts have debated whether the experiences of foreign militaries might confirm or falsify the plausibility of the unit cohesion rationale.[1] In other words, twenty-three foreign militaries have lifted their bans on gay and lesbian service members without reporting problems, and experts who advocate allowing known gays and lesbians in the U.S. armed forces often claim that foreign military experiences prove that combat performance and unit cohesion would not decline if the United States lifted its ban.

Opponents of gays in the military often respond that foreign experiences are irrelevant to the U.S. case and do not show that the U.S. military would remain effective if the gay ban were lifted. They raise three arguments to demonstrate that foreign military experiences do not indicate that the United States could lift its ban without problems. First, they argue that even though twenty-three foreign militaries have lifted their bans, there are no known gay and lesbian soldiers in combat or intelligence units of foreign armed forces. During testimony before the Senate Armed Services Committee in 1993, for example, Charles Moskos stated that in Israel known gay soldiers were not assigned to elite combat units, did not work for intelligence units, and did not hold command positions in any branch.[2]

Second, experts who claim that foreign experiences are irrelevant for the U.S. military argue that although many nations have lifted their bans, gay soldiers receive special treatment in these cases. Even if the decision to allow known homosexuals to serve does not harm the military, the special treatment that gays and lesbians receive can undermine cohesion, performance, readiness, and morale. Differential treatment can assume two forms. On the one hand, gay and lesbian service members in foreign militaries may receive special treatment, such as assignment to "open" bases that allow them to commute to and from home and to sleep at their own homes rather than in barracks.[3] On the other hand, gays and lesbians may face various discriminatory obstacles including difficulty of obtaining promotions and security clearances.

Experts opposing gays in the military often invoke a third argument to support their claim that foreign military experiences are irrelevant, maintaining that organizational and cultural differences distinguish the United States from other countries that allow known homosexuals to serve. More specifically, they argue that the U.S. military is a unique institution that cannot be equated with foreign armed forces. In addition, unlike most other countries, the United States is home to powerful gay-rights groups as well as large and highly organized conservative organizations.

Experts who favor gays in the military believe that foreign military experiences are relevant to determining what would happen if the United States lifted its gay ban and argue that known gays do serve in foreign combat units, that gay and lesbian service members are treated the same as their heterosexual peers most of the time, and that although no two cultures or militaries are exactly the same, the fact that twenty-three armed forces have lifted their gay bans without problems suggests that cultural distinctions do not matter.

What is the relationship between the discussion that follows and the cost-benefit framework we described in the introductory chapter to this volume? As noted in previous chapters, our intent throughout the volume is to address whether the advantages of the "Don't Ask, Don't Tell" policy outweigh its disadvantages. Because many experts claim that preservation of unit cohesion constitutes the policy's most significant advantage, determining the relevance of foreign military experiences may be essential for assessing the benefits of "Don't Ask, Don't Tell." In other words, if foreign military experiences are relevant to the U.S. case, then the gay ban may not benefit the military in that it may not be necessary for preserving unit cohesion. In this chapter, the third of three discussions on the potential advantages of the "Don't Ask, Don't Tell" policy, conference participants debate whether lessons from abroad are relevant to the U.S. case.[4]

Aaron Belkin: We are very honored to have with us today representatives from [four] foreign militaries . . . Each of our panelists will address two main points. First, each [one] represents a military where a gay/lesbian ban has been lifted, so we would like to know if there have been any problems following the lifting of your ban. American military leaders often claim that if the gay ban is lifted, then the U.S. military will fall apart. Given that many leaders predicted that the military would fall apart in Britain, Australia, and other countries that eventually lifted their bans, we would like to know what happened in your country after you decided to let open gays and lesbians serve. Second, we would like to know whether the overseas experiences are relevant for the American case. Many people who oppose gays and lesbians raise credible arguments that U.S. culture is different from Israeli culture or British culture. Could your experiences still be relevant? . . .

Deborah Mulliss: My position as the director of Personnel Equity Policy in the New Zealand Defence Force was established as a result of a recommendation from a report on gender integration that was undertaken by the New Zealand Defence Force and published in 1998. The equity director is responsible for insuring that the recommendations from this gender integration report are implemented, monitored, and evaluated. Although the audit focused on gender integration, the recommendations covered a broad range of human-resource issues. When I first arrived, I asked about the situation regarding gays and lesbians in the military. My supervisor told me that it was not an issue, and I asked why not. He said that we have simply decided it will not be. Subsequently, we have not had any problems with the policy, and our policies have focused on inclusive environments and legitimate behavior. We have had a focus on recruiting for success and have been looking at ways to support our commanders with their ability to manage.

In New Zealand, we have a population of almost 4 million, and our military force in total is about 14,000. One of the issues that commanders have to deal with in New Zealand is that a lot of our young people kill themselves, and our high suicide rate has a lot to do with their insecurity about who they are. To deal with this problem, we thought that we should concentrate on educating our commanders on the issues faced by a group of people in the organization who remained invisible. We wanted to equip them with the skills to be able to deal with those issues, because young people enter the military and do not know exactly who they are. As they are trained and develop, they begin to understand who they are. We did not want to create a situation in which a young person had a thought or behaved in a certain way and subsequently was labeled and put into a box. We needed to be able to supply an education process to these commanders, so they would know what they were dealing with and how they might manage it.

Overall, this approach seems to have been very successful. We have
run education sessions for all of our senior commanders, instructing
them to tell their troops what behaviors we expect from them. It is a
professional organization, and we demand that their behavior be legitimate. From our experience, it has been successful. As a whole, the population is reasonably accepting of our broad range of diversity, and this
acceptance comes out in our social policy that the government makes.
The most recent piece of policy that has come out from our government
has been a change in the Matrimonial Property Law Act, which recog-
nizes same-sex couples and gives them the same rights and property
division as they do to married couples. We removed the ban on gays and
lesbians in 1993, and our chief of Defence Force removed the ban on
women in combat in January 2000. We are making a lot of the changes
that we see as a society as reflecting how we as a people are. . . .

Bronwen Grey: I am the director of the Defence Equity Organization,
which was set up three and a half years ago when we had a major structural review within the Australian Defence Force. We brought together
all the equal-opportunity departments in the services and civilian area
and put them together in one organization. Our job is to develop policy
on equity and diversity, develop principles, and insure that they are
implemented throughout the whole defense organization, which includes three services and the civilian component.

Currently, our policy in relation to homosexuality is that we do not
discriminate in line with federal legislation, which means we do not ask
people if they are gay or not. Sexual orientation has nothing to do with
recruitment, promotion, or postings. The change occurred in 1992,
when the government lifted the ban. The service chiefs argued against
it, using all the arguments that we have heard today, but nevertheless
the government decided to conform with legislation and overnight the
ban was lifted. Policy changed, and then nothing happened.

Now I do not have quantifiable data here, but recruitment numbers
did not go down, retention remained the same, and operational effectiveness remained the same. We still did what we had always done. The
Australian Defence Force emphasizes an individual's ability to do the
job. We focus on professionalism and competence. We do not care about
people's sexual activity, as long as it is not unlawful or contrary to the
inherent requirements of the job, which we define as not negatively
impacting operational effectiveness. And there is absolutely no reason
why sexual orientation would. If inappropriate behavior does occur, or
what we would call unacceptable behavior, such as harassment, then the
normal command and management structures deal with it. Sexual orientation is not particularly special.

While there appear to have been no negative outcomes from the change, we have been told by gay people that there were very positive outcomes. They said it has changed the workplace. Gay people do not have to worry about innuendo, rumor, or gossip. Everybody knows, and nobody cares. The emphasis for us is on our workplace, which is open and harassment-free for everybody.

At the time of the change, no specific training was put in place. And in retrospect, maybe it should have been. But in 1992, combat-related positions were opening up to women, so a great deal of training occurred regarding integration. It was quite fortuitous that by covering integration as a whole, gay people were caught up with everybody else in this focus on inclusiveness. Commanders had responsibilities to monitor the situation, and they did. It was up to them to insure that there were no difficulties, and if there were any difficulties, then they had to deal with them through normal management processes. The inclusiveness of the work environment is what we always focus on now.

Commanders have certain responsibilities, which relate to everyone. They are required to develop a fair and inclusive workplace and to take all action to stop or prevent unacceptable behavior, which we define quite specifically. Commanders have to prevent unacceptable behavior, stop it, and deal with it promptly and sensitively. If they do not, they are called to account for it. You will note that my talk about unacceptable behavior is not defined in terms of homosexuality or heterosexuality. The term "unacceptable behavior" means any behavior that offends, humiliates, or intimidates other personnel. It does not matter if it is homosexual or heterosexual.

Obviously some pockets of homophobia still remain. To say that everything is marvelous would not be true. But we do collect statistics of formal complaints of unacceptable behavior for the government and report them every month. Since 1994–1995, there have been 514 complaints of sexual harassment, and twelve of these related to sexual orientation. . . . We have telephone advice-lines that people can phone anonymously and ask what they should do if they feel they have been discriminated against or harassed. The advice-line is also open for commanders and leaders who may want to know how to handle an issue. Perhaps a better statistic to share is the number of calls we have received. Since September 1998, when we began keeping record of them, we have had 2,042 phone calls, 25 of which related to sexual orientation. On that basis, you would have to say that lifting the ban has not been a big problem.

Currently, the issue for our gay members is the recognition of their same-sex partners, which unlike New Zealand, we do not do. We do not recognize same-sex partners for purposes of financial conditions of service, such as accommodation or travel. But there is a groundswell of pressure within the Australian Defence Force to insure that this change will be brought about. However, we have political leaders who wish to address it for the entire government bureaucracy. Notwithstanding this, members can notify their same-sex partner as their next of kin. When they deploy, as we did to East Timor, their same-sex partner can be their next of kin, and the family support center that we set up supports all families. It does not matter what type of families they are.

Our latest initiative is to develop an interactive training package on understanding homosexuality. We want to dispel all the myths that surround homosexuality, and we certainly have found in cases when someone does come out, people want to know how to manage it best. We are putting together this course that will be available shortly, early next year, which we hope will give some assistance to people.

I would like to close by sharing two incidents about what happened when someone did come out. The first one was in an infantry unit, which are not normally known for their liberal attitudes. But there was a young soldier there who felt that he had to come out, because he was denying part of his life. He told his regimental sergeant major (RSM), who was surprised, but the next time everyone was together, the RSM stood everyone up and said, "Now look, Johno wants to tell us something. He's thought about it, and he wants to tell us about it. Now you all know Johno, he's a pretty good bloke"—that is Australian for guy— "You know he's a good mate, and you know he'll stick by you. You know he's a good soldier. Now he wants you to know that he's gay. And quite frankly, we don't care, because we know Johno is a good bloke." This soldier is still serving, and this RSM showed significant leadership in dealing with this issue. This soldier has not had to face any harassment. The second case involved a lieutenant commander who was the executive officer on a ship. He called the ship's company together and said, "I'm gay." The reactions ranged from, "Yeah, well we all knew that," to "Oh, are you?" It created a bit of a stir and a bit of a chat, but that was it. The only way I can conclude is by emphasizing how I started: for us, lifting the ban was a nonevent, despite all the dire predictions. The Australian Defence Force focuses on operational effectiveness and is only concerned with a member's ability to do his or her job professionally. And sexual orientation plays no part in this concern. . . .

Steve Johnston: I am . . . the chairman of the Armed Forces Lesbian and Gay Association in Great Britain. . . . As you are well aware, up until January of this year the United Kingdom maintained a policy banning lesbians and gays from the armed forces. Before this decision, every five years the Armed Forces Select Committee met to talk about armed forces policy. In 1991, Stonewall, another group working for gay rights in Great Britain, was invited to present evidence to the Armed Forces Select Committee. Some years before this meeting, a gentleman had been discharged from the parachute regiment and was invited to present evidence with Stonewall. The evidence powerfully testified to how lesbian and gay men were treated while they served, and this meeting inaugurated an association that was named Rank Outsiders, which Robert Ely started. He then posted a letter in some of the gay press in London, inviting others who had suffered as a victim of the armed forces policy, and a number of people made contact.

Over the next few years, the organization grew, and we started to think about how we could challenge the policy itself. In 1995, we created the group called the Armed Forces Legal Challenge Group, which consisted of solicitors, barristers, members from Stonewall, and members from our association, and decided to create a method through which we could bring about the change in the United Kingdom legally. First the case went to high courts, then to the courts appeal, next to the House of Lords, and finally it was sent to the European Court of Human Rights in Strasbourg. In May of last year, the judges in Strasbourg met to look at the United Kingdom policy. And in the following September, they announced that the United Kingdom government was in breach of some of the articles of the European Convention of Human Rights, mainly Article 8, the right to privacy, and part of the convention called Article 14, the right not to be discriminated against. The United Kingdom government was forced to review its policy. It took very seriously how to change this policy, because on January 12, the secretary of state for defence stood up and literally and quietly said that the United Kingdom no longer had this policy. No fanfare, no fuss. The national press gave a few column inches to announce the fact that lesbians and gays could serve openly.

We have since moved on, and it is now December. At this time, it is too early to establish whether or not there is or has been a problem, or whether or not our current nonpolicy has been effective. But my association runs a help and advice line, which is known by most members of the armed forces and is advertised in most of the gay press throughout the country. To date we have had no reports of any harassment or of any bullying, nor have we had any reports of homophobic bashing. In fact, it appears that the policy is being so well received that my association now has been invited by the Ministry of Defence to speak to them on a regular basis, which we do. To date, it has been a success. I hope our participation in this conference . . . shows that if the United Kingdom lost its policy, perhaps the "Don't Ask, Don't Tell" policy of the United States will fall also. . . .

Belkin: Deborah Mulliss, you are an official in the New Zealand Ministry of Defence and have told us there is no problem with gays and lesbians in your military. Bronwen Grey, you are an official in the Australian Ministry of Defence, and you have told us that there is no problem in Australia. But Steve Johnston, you are a gay activist. Why should we trust you? What evidence do we have that the lifting of the ban has not caused any problems in Britain?

Johnston: As I said before, the British ban was lifted on January 12, 2000. Yes, I would be the first to admit, it is still early. We do not know what will happen next, but we do know that every report we have received from serving members of all three services, be it the navy, the air force, or the army, shows us that a problem has not been caused. In fact, the way I perceive it, Rob Nunn and I were victims of this former policy. The people we have spoken to have actually said they do not have a problem with gays in the military, and they never have. The problem was the policy itself and the mere fact that you could not be a gay man or a lesbian or associate with a gay man or a lesbian. In fact, the policy in the United Kingdom made you guilty by association and guilty by state of mind. But since the ban has been lifted, we have not had one reported problem, either from our own advice-line or more importantly from the government. In November last year prior to the actual announcement by the defence secretary, Simon Langley (the vice-chair of Rank Outsiders) and I were invited to go to Whitehall to discuss the lifting of the ban with the deputy for the Defence Staff in the United Kingdom, our equivalent of a four-star general. We gave them a number of proposals suggesting how we thought the ban could be lifted and accommodate everyone, gay or straight, and we were surprised and quite shocked that we actually thought alike. More importantly, the Ministry of Defence said to us that even though we were this lesbian and gay activist group, we were not going to have a problem, were we? In fact, we were thinking exactly the same thing. As I said before, the policy was lifted on January 12, without fanfare or ceremony, and it has been business as usual.

Belkin: But does the Ministry of Defence agree with you?

Johnston: Well, yes.

Belkin: How do you know?

Johnston: They have told me.

Belkin: At how high a level?

Johnston: As I have said, our main uniform contact is the deputy chief of Defence Staff. There is only one person higher. . . .

Lawrence Korb: Since the European Court of Human Rights told the United Kingdom to drop the policy, will the other members of the European Union also have to change the policy?

Johnston: For those that signed up to the European Convention of Human Rights, most certainly. . . .

Avner Even-Zohar: From 1987 to 1993, I served in the Israeli army as a captain in the education unit. During my military career, I was not out of the closet. Israel lifted the ban against gays in the army in 1993, as I was being honorably discharged from the military. In my unit, though, and when I served in the officer corps, I assumed everyone knew that I was gay. My sexuality did not disturb them much, so much so that at the end of the officer's course I was chosen by the other cadets as the exemplary cadet of the course, despite or maybe because of the fact that they knew I was gay. When I served later as a commander, which was actually my last post in the Israeli army, I served as a commander of a small unit that had more than one hundred soldiers in the upper Galilee in Israel, and again my soldiers knew that I was gay. I remember one staff meeting when I was really upset with them, and at the end of the meeting I left the room. As soon as I left, people began to talk about me. I was standing near the door and heard one of the officers tell another officer, "We must find him a boyfriend." . . .

The Israeli military found a way to place gay people in submarine units because their skills were high and because military leaders believed that gay sailors would get along well with other men. In addition, because most submarines have only two officers who supervise dozens of highly skilled personnel, submarine service requires extensive training as well as the willingness to forgo the possibility of promotion to officer rank. Military leaders thought the gays would be willing to extend their military service to four or five years, and since they would be unlikely to choose the military as a lifelong career, they would be willing to serve for extended periods of time without the possibility of promotion. Many gay people actually served and told Danny Kaplan, the leading researcher of gays and the Israeli military, that even before lifting the ban, it was quite common for gays to serve in a submarine unit. . . .

Why should the United States do what other countries do? First of all, because lifting the ban works, and . . . Israel is a very successful example of lifting the ban and actually very relevant to the United States. First of all, the Israeli army, as is true of the other armies represented on this panel, is very conservative. Because there is no official separation of church and state in Israel, there is a strong religious influence on the government, which is why the religious right in the United States reminds me a lot of some of the religious right that we have in Israel. The religious right might even be more influential in Israel, because these people are actually cabinet members and ministers in the Israeli government. But lifting the ban has still worked in Israel.

The Israeli army is also extremely important to Israeli society, and I think many gay people in this country tend to underestimate the importance of the U.S. Army to this country. In Israel, the army is the melting pot of Israeli society. In this regard, Israel is very similar to the United States. We have waves of Jewish immigrants from all over the world, and the United States was based on immigration, as well. The Israeli army serves to socialize all these people into Israeli society. Many conservatives in the United States dismiss other countries' experiences, arguing that the U.S. military deploys much more often and has a larger role to play than other militaries. But I would argue that Israel does, too. . . . Since 1993, the Israeli army has not had a moment of complete peace with absolutely no fighting going on in the Middle East. The relevance of the Israeli experience lies in the fact that the Israeli army is fighting as we speak and lifting the ban did not hurt it. . . . The Israeli army is doing very well and, to the extent that it is not doing too well, it is not because of the lifting of the gay ban.

As to how the ban was lifted, the decision did not come from the army, and I strongly believe that such direction will never come from any army, because the majority of them are so conservative. Military generals protect their own careers and their own power structures and they would never open the ranks to other people willingly. Pressure has to come from forums like this or from the public, which was the case in Israel. Both the late prime minister, Yitzhak Rabin, who at that time was the minister of defense, and the chief of staff, Ehud Barak, who until this morning was the prime minister of Israel, actually supported the change.[5] But the decision actually came from the parliament, the

Knesset. Yael Dayan, the daughter of General Moshe Dayan, was primarily responsible for pressing for the change, and even though she is not a lesbian herself, she supported the cause. Professor Uzi Evan, who was also very influential in developing the Israeli nuclear bomb, came to the Knesset. He revealed his sexual orientation to the whole nation and explained how he was dishonorably discharged from the army. People realized that we could not afford to lose such a brilliant scientist simply because of his sexual orientation. No country can afford to lose such talent because of sexual orientation.

Belkin: Many people in this country who oppose allowing gays and lesbians in the military argue that other countries may lift their bans, but that no one comes out of the closet in those cases. You spoke about being partially in the closet when you were in uniform, although you thought some people knew you were gay. . . . What do you think about the issue of openness? Are there open gays in combat units now in Israel? Or is everybody in the closet? . . .

Even-Zohar: Danny Kaplan is a leading scholar in this field, and he actually asked soldiers whether they knew of a gay person in their unit. And about 20 percent said they did know gay people in their own units, including combat units. So people do come out of the closet, and even if they do not, their colleagues know about them, and life goes on. We have had at least seven years to look at the situation in Israel and realize it is happening—people do come out of the closet in the Israeli army. We also know at least one high-ranking officer who died. Everyone knew he was gay, and his partner actually got his pension. . . .

Christopher Dandeker: My answer to the question of whether foreign militaries are relevant to the United States is yes, particularly if you look at the case of the United Kingdom, even though I recognize that we do not even speak the same language [laughter]. And there are obviously other political differences about which we will have to think.

Let me make four or five introductory remarks. First, although the British armed forces are modest in size, most people recognize that they have an international reputation as a fighting force. I think that is quite an important issue. Second, we all know from our discussion this morning that gays have always served and will always serve in the armed forces of any nation. The only question is what the circumstances are in which they do so.

Third, we have also been talking this morning about how the armed services need to balance two different imperatives—the functional imperative of preparing efficient war-fighting organizations and the social imperative of responding to the needs of the society that they serve and from which they gain their legitimacy, the society from which they do not simply recruit people and to which they return them. In debates on gays in the military and minority ethnic communities, too often these imperatives are seen as zero-sum relationships. But this assumption is not true. The evidence indicates that it is not always the case that responding to the social imperative necessarily leads to a compromise of operational effectiveness. The classic example is equal opportunities. Equal opportunities in the armed services do not simply involve citizenship equality issues. Rather, providing equal opportunity can actually be part of a business case for sustaining operational effectiveness in terms of widening the recruitment pool of quality people.

Fourth, in the atmosphere of accelerated change that the end of the Cold War has brought about, armed services around the world need to take a proactive view of change and think ahead. For example, we should think about the "Don't Ask, Don't Tell, Don't Pursue" policy not as the end game, but rather as a framework within which to think about what we can live with five or ten years in the future. Last, it seems to me that everyone accepts the need for the military to be unique in some of its cultural and organizational attributes. Personnel in the armed services, civilian or military, but especially those in uniform, need to recognize that although they have a right to a private life, they need to suspend some of their rights in order to conform in a necessary way to the institutional values of the military.

Let me turn to the more specific issues relating to the case of British armed forces. This year the United Kingdom has moved to a position not dissimilar to that of the Australian military. That is to say, the ban has been lifted. In January, a code of conduct was introduced that makes no specific reference to gays, but applies regardless of service, rank, or gender. It is a code of conduct that links existing policies on antibullying and antiharassment, whether on the basis of gender or other criteria. This code of conduct was introduced after the European Court of Human Rights made its ruling on September 27, 2000.[6] It is important to note that in between the ruling and the construction of the policy, which is a very short set of statements, a great deal of work went into building a coalition within the military between senior officers and the civilian side of the Ministry of Defence in order to construct a policy that both sides felt could work.

Crucial in this whole exercise is what is known as the service test, the question that commanding officers throughout the chain of command have to ask when faced with potentially problematic behavior.

The regulation states, "Have the actions or the behavior of an individual adversely impacted or are they likely to impact on the efficiency or the operational effectiveness of the service?" That is it. Now that policy applies whether a service member makes statements about the Aryan Nation, gender, or sexual orientation. The policy has been known colloquially as "Don't Ask, Can Tell," or as I prefer, "Don't fear it, but don't flaunt it," a point to which I will return.

In the material of the code, it is acutely evident that those who constructed it were aware that implementing it successfully means that one should not exaggerate the capacity of regulations on their own to resolve this question. The effectiveness of the system rests on what I would call a social compact among those who have to make this policy work. I use the words "social compact," which I do not think anyone else has in this context. By that I mean officers in the chain of command have to use discretion and make a judgment on whether behavior breaches the service test. Then they have to decide how they will discipline the service member, which could include having a quiet word with the person or a number of other possibilities from a spectrum of potential responses.

On the other hand, . . . what does open integration mean? Gay personnel who can now serve openly in the military without being thrown out have to realize the implications of the service test. It seems to me that two things follow. First, as a minority group living in the service world where the majority feel differently about sexual orientation, gay and lesbian service members must recognize that there will be a need for respect for the majority sentiment, especially in the transitional period. Second, sexual identity is secondary to professional identity. If someone wants to come into the armed services and use it to develop sexual-identity politics first and a professional career second, then the regulations very clearly leave room for that person to be weeded out, either at the training or post-training stage. Importantly, the regulations are short and succinct. A whole volume of regulations could be written, but it would not cover every circumstance. Even more important, the policy will work only on the basis of the goodwill that the parties who are involved generate. If you like, it is a very English pragmatic view. I would say that, would I not?

Let me try and spell out some of the implications of the policy. . . . First of all, after the code of conduct was introduced I was quite surprised by how the press accepted some of the personnel who came out. The most famous one to my knowledge, at least in press coverage, since then has been the case of our navy. As a principal warfare officer on HMS *Northumberland* in his early thirties, Lieutenant-Commander

Craig Davis is on the fast track for a very senior ship-driving position and post–ship driving, as long as he does not crash it, and perhaps for something more senior than that. He not only came out, but his partner was also quite quickly accepted in formal functions. That occurred more swiftly than I thought was going to happen. . . .

I predict that in the infantry battalions of the British army, the pace of openness will be slower, for reasons we might discuss. In the case of Britain, as well as the case of the Netherlands, the degree of openness we can expect is less than we might assume, because it is quite low even in the most liberal and supportive environments of the Netherlands, including the Dutch navy. The real test will not be when people come out who already are well established in the service, but when those who are already out join. This is because it is different to come out in a context where your professional identity and competence are known and trusted, than in a situation where they only know your number and rank and wonder if you can do the job because they know you are gay. It is a different situation entirely. In terms of how well this is going, the test will come when time has gone on a bit longer. . . .

Two days ago, I asked a very senior person who wishes to remain nameless about the bullying statistics. He said that such as they are, the bullying statistics are stable. I said that the global figure is stable, which could mean the gay bashing has increased, while the other stuff has decreased and perpetrators have decided to shift targets. He said that they did not think so. "Anecdata" do not suggest that is the case. I must acknowledge I get the term "anecdata" from Peter Feaver. I like it.

The real question in relation to post–gay policy has less to do with gays in the military and more to do with financial issues and the rights of unmarried partners. . . .

One of the most important results of the policy change is how little impact it has had on operational effectiveness. Before the policy change, senior colonels and brigadiers in the people's side of the army sat around saying, "God, the world might shatter if we make this change." Now when they sit around the table, they realize it did not. This policy has changed their attitude toward what is vital to the armed forces, which is why the gay issue has been so important. On a whole range of military culture issues, a number of which have nothing much to do with sexual orientation, they have to ask, what is the vital ground? What do we have to do to retain personnel and sustain operational effectiveness given that this factor has changed? . . .

Within a few months of this policy change, the British armed services are introducing not only the code of conduct, but a code of moral conduct as well. They are asking service personnel, whatever their orientation, to live up to a standard slightly higher than what is expected in civilian society, for example, on issues like adultery. This moral code is a reassertion of an important component to the British military tradition, which is based on the assumption that it is distinct from society. It is a distinct corporate group that because of its war-fighting needs and for operational reasons, not moral superiority reasons, has to have a code of conduct that separates it from everyone else. It is not a citizen in uniform. . . .

Korb: I can answer the question very briefly. Foreign experiences should matter but they will not. The United States should take into account the experiences of foreign militaries, but our military will find a way to ignore them. Let me elaborate, and then I will end by asking Christopher Dandeker a question based on the article he published in *International Security.*[7] If you are a scholar addicted to accurate data, it is important to keep in mind when dealing with the government that that is the environment in which you operate but it may not be the environment in which government officials operate. I have been appalled many times when people have presented data that were flat-out wrong to secretaries and cabinet officers and even the president of the United States. Not to mention the argument that Michael Desch and Laura Miller alluded to earlier that the data may be correct, but that now is not the right time to lift the ban given the turmoil that would result. This is a common argument that military leaders use to oppose many proposed changes.

Let me give you a couple of examples of what I am referring to. In 1981, the Supreme Court made a decision that military retirement was not retired pay.[8] The Court decided that retirement pay was in fact retainer pay. The Court argued that retired service members theoretically could be called back to service, although most of them would not have fit in their uniforms. Nonetheless, they could be called back in an emergency, and in World War II the military did call some rather elderly folks back into service. The problem was that people who got divorced were not including this pay in their divorce settlements. There are a lot of retired men from the military who go through their mid-life crises, get divorced, and leave nothing to their spouses. . . . When I argued that the length of someone's marriage should be considered in the divorce and retirement pay, the entire Joint Chiefs of Staff went to the secretary of defense and argued that if we did such a thing, we would have to bring back conscription. Recruiting and retention would suffer. If you asked the military leaders "Do you favor your wife getting part of your retirement pay if you were to divorce?" I cannot imagine too many of them saying yes. Officially our department did not support this change. Fortunately we had some enlightened legislators with whom we were able to work and come up with a reasonable solution. But the fact of the matter is that you have to keep these attitudes in mind, which is why I do not pay a great deal of attention to their threats that if certain things change, the military will fall apart, because I hear similar threats about every issue. And by the way, we did make the change, and in fact recruiting and retention increased. . . .

Why should we as social scientists and government officials look at foreign militaries? Because they are the best thing to look at. As the RAND study did, we should look at police and fire departments.[9] Before you make the decision to lift the ban, there is no way to know how it will turn out, so you should look at other militaries and similar organizations. The assistant to one of the flag officers who worked on the fifteen-page study that the military did to justify retaining the ban, which . . . included only about three pages that responded directly to the RAND study, called me one day and asked if I would recommend his boss for membership in the Council on Foreign Relations. I said "no" to this poor O-6 who worked for this flag officer.[10] He said, "Why not?" I said, "Look, your boss signed up to this study that was complete nonsense, knowing the RAND study." He said, "Oh, I better go talk to—" I said, "I'm only kidding. I still will recommend him." But the fact of the matter is that these were intelligent people who threw away the RAND study. They disregarded it. Even if you look at other militaries and argue that lifting the ban worked in Britain, Israel, or Australia, our military will not pay much attention.

But it is ironic, because the military argues that it needs international military contacts. They want to talk to other militaries and share certain information, which is good for diplomacy, so obviously we want to share their experiences. But the first thing the military says when the gay issue is brought up, at least until we had the British decision, is the U.S. military is different. They do not deploy like we do, or they are not as big as we are. Or they have a different culture. But of course, there are Australia and Canada, which have very similar cultures and lifted their bans successfully. Foreign militaries are not as big as we are, but now you have the British. . . . I cannot think of a body more removed from the British military than the European Court of Human Rights. The decision to lift the British ban was made not only by civilians, but civilians in the European Union, about which the British have mixed feelings. But in fact, the new policy seems to have worked well. So, why does everyone worry about whether you have a civilian president or a civilian secretary of defense make the decision in the United States? Christopher, given what you wrote in the discussion you had with Dr. Kier, have any of the things that you predicted in the article come true?[11] It seems to me that it has gone pretty well from this side of the Atlantic. . . .

Dandeker: Insofar as the first point is concerned, any government in the European Union would be bound by the European Court of Human Rights decision. Any government or any political party in the United Kingdom would have been bound to follow the ruling. In any case it is an academic issue now, in the sense that the Charter of Human Rights is incorporated into British law. Any future case on this issue or any other concerning human rights would be resolved within the United Kingdom courts without any need to go to the European Courts of Human Rights because of this incorporation. Complying with the European Court of Human Rights was not related to party politics. Rather, it was something that any government would have done, because previous governments have said they would abide by the charter and abide by the court's decisions. The crucial point was that the government took the opportunity to take some breathing space between announcing what their policy would be and the announcement of the decision by the court. They did some very fancy footwork in and around the Ministry of Defence, both formally and informally. Now when the records are opened in thirty to fifty years, I suspect, suspect and no more, that Charles Guthrie, the chief of the Defence Staff, will, on this and many other issues, be seen as one of the great soldier-diplomats of the post–Cold War military in managing a rather difficult process of change. Even though he has been sniped at as being Blair's poodle on a whole range of questions, he will go down as a figure who was crucial in lubricating this difficult civil-military transformation.[12]

With regard to the article in *International Security,* I hope to have made it clear that we should be cautious in terms of thinking things are going swimmingly well. Yes and no. It is too early to tell. We do not know, as I said. I am aware that there is official concern on the part of policymakers and in-house researchers on how well those who are already known to be gay at the recruitment trainings will be treated. There is concern about what goes on in the navy. As we all know, not only do countries' armed services differ, but so do the various branches of the armed services of any particular country differ, as well. The Royal Navy culture is not the British army culture. Indeed if you were to say that, you might get a very interesting response from the British army. And the army would argue that there is no army culture either; there is regimental culture. Ultimately, I would say we have to be very careful and wait and see.

At the same time that there is publicity about the lieutenant commander I made points about, there is also press about a rather severe and nasty case of an enlisted person getting the crap kicked out of him for being gay and coming out. Let us be cautious. This is a process of change and transition. Again I would argue that the "Don't Flaunt It" is a very significant part of the service test. Most of those involved in the European Court of Human Rights case were aware that the price to be paid for lifting the ban was discretion, even reticence, with regard to sexual orientation until such time as the glacial pace of cultural change shifts the nature of the heterosexual culture in the armed services, not an unreasonable pragmatic conclusion to draw, I might add. An ideologue at either end of the political spectrum of this issue could easily blow apart this delicate compromise. The social compact I referred to could be seriously damaged by an ideologue who tries to get in and to make mischief, but the service test is there. I believe it would get widespread support if it led to the dismissal of a "gay activist" or any other form of activist, if that one activist was bringing collective interest down just for the self-serving interest of one individual. . . .

Paul Gade: If Larry Korb says that foreign experiences should matter but they will not, then I say they can and they will, but under a different set of circumstances. Larry is correct in saying that the military will not pay attention to this information until lifting the ban becomes a fact of life. Then the experiences of the military services in similar cultures will become important. They will pay attention then, in order to know how to implement their policies and avoid some of the pitfalls that other nations have experienced. . . .

I will start my discussion of the importance of studying the experiences of foreign militaries by discussing how the Army Research Institute began to examine this issue in 1993, when lifting the ban first became a possibility. One of the reasons I believe that foreign militaries can and will be relevant is that from the beginning the army asked us to study this issue and come up with recommendations for implementing changes that would be necessary. Initially, we called in Gregory Herek, a well-known social psychologist who had recently published what now is a classic article in the *American Psychologist* on sexual orientation in the military service.[13] In that article, he suggested that there were three areas of study that we ought to examine in regard to this issue. First, we should assess the attitudes of service members. Second, we need to examine the experience of integrating minorities and women in the military services. Third, we should include foreign militaries in our studies of the experiences of other organizations with gay and lesbian personnel. As I mentioned this morning, the Defense Department quickly quashed our attempts to study the attitudes of service members. For many years, the Army Research Institute has studied and continues to study issues surrounding the integration of minorities and women, particularly women more recently. We did complete a few small studies on the integration of gay and lesbian personnel in other organizations, such as police and fire departments, but we focused most of our efforts on foreign militaries. Why? As Larry Korb mentioned earlier, they are appropriate analogues for the U.S. military. In fact, they are the best analogues we have for the U.S. case. To give you a flavor of what we were able to do by studying foreign militaries, let me summarize our conclusions and discuss some of the advantages that are available by studying foreign militaries, as well as suggesting at least one way to do it that fosters the application to the U.S. case.

In the Western cultures that we studied, we noted a trend that suggested a decrease in discrimination against people because of their sexual orientation, which included restrictions on military service. Remember, though, the European Court had yet to rule on this issue. However, tolerance for homosexuality, rather than active integration, appeared to be the cultural norm. One notable exception was in the Netherlands, which had taken a more activist role. In the Western countries we studied, including the Netherlands, most gays and lesbians who served in the military did so without revealing their sexual preferences, which we have heard a number of people talk about today. Heterosexuality is still the cultural norm within these societies, especially within their militaries. Although tolerated, homosexuality is still shunned within Western societies, and again, especially in Western militaries. As a result, homosexual bashing may be a particular problem for military services where bans remain in place or may have only recently been removed. Polls of attitudes of military members that were taken prior to the lifting of gay bans in countries like Canada and the Netherlands indicated that there was a potential for violence and disruption after the removal of the ban, but in fact little such disruption occurred after these countries decided to allow known gays to serve. Dire predictions of lost cohesion, lower morale, poor recruiting, and decreased retention based on surveys of military personnel in these countries simply have not materialized.

If the U.S. services are ever ordered to cease excluding gays and lesbians who actively engage in homosexual behavior, we would expect that they will do so effectively and without major incidents, provided that the leadership institutes policies and implements practices that clearly communicate support for the change. However, the success or failure of such policies and practices would depend in part on gay and lesbian organizations, as well. If such organizations maintain a low profile, as they have done in other countries, the inclusion of gay and lesbian service members would likely proceed without incident. However, even if military leaders are successful at initiating such policies and practices, those in the military are likely to tolerate gays and lesbians, but will be unlikely to accept them fully. I say this because none of the countries we studied, including the most liberal society, the Netherlands, fully accepted homosexuality.

Finally, it seems unlikely that forced inclusion of gays and lesbians in the military services would accelerate the liberalization of American society in this regard. In all of the countries studied, societies liberalized with respect to homosexuals; then the military followed suit and not the reverse.

One of the major advantages to studying foreign militaries as analogues for the U.S. case is that they provide a social-historical context in which to view the issue. The social context provides insights into relationships between the larger culture and the military, for example, the liberalization issue I just mentioned. Historically they provide us with a longitudinal view of the issue as it evolves over time and within and between cultures similar to the United States. We have learned over and over again to examine what people say they will do as opposed to what they actually do, which we continue to rediscover as more and more countries drop their gay bans. A second advantage of studying foreign militaries is that it permitted the collection of large amounts of information over a short period of time in a very cost-effective manner. For example, we were able to collect information on eleven countries in a matter of a few months. Third, it enables insights into the pitfalls that we need to avoid, as well as solutions that have been tried in cultures similar to the United States. I think the Canadian case nicely illustrates the dissimilarity between what people were fearful about and what actually happened, and also the importance of co-opting leadership in making a successful policy change. Finally, it provides a useful context for interpreting the results from the other methods that Gregory Herek suggested, such as the integration of minorities and women in the military. It points to the limitations that Rob MacCoun talked about earlier this morning about attitude assessment and making behavior predictions from those kinds of attitudes and opinions.

I think our study of foreign militaries proved successful, because we collected the information differently from the way most people had in the past. Instead of using a large number of our own social scientists and sending them out to foreign militaries and foreign governments to gather information, we hired a group of savvy military social scientists like Christopher Dandeker to help up us study this issue. We then convened these social scientists as a group several times. This allowed us to focus the issues on the U.S. case and develop common themes and a common approach that we continually checked against one another through the series of meetings. By working in this manner, we obtained information we could not have otherwise, particularly with respect to the differences between the policies and practices of foreign militaries. As everybody knows, policy is not the same as implementation. We saw subtle differences between the two that we would not have seen had we tried to send someone into a culture to immerse him or herself for such a short period of time. Furthermore, we gained access to countries no outsiders had been able to study, France being the most specific example. Finally, our method enabled more in-depth analyses of the information, particularly with respect to the relationship between the society and the military culture and what those differences and similarities might be. In closing, let me say that studying foreign militaries is not only relevant to the U.S. case, but provides essential prescriptive information to both sides of the issues that is simply not available anywhere. . . .

David Segal: Knowing that I have studied the relevance of other countries, every once in a while officials in the defense establishment ask me about them. But the first question they ask me at the end of my explanation is, "Why should we do what they do?" They translate the question of the relevance of what other militaries do into a model of what we should do, which are entirely different questions. Clearly we should not and do not need to feel compelled to imitate other countries simply in the interest of conformity and the notion that all militaries are equivalent. It reminds me of a time earlier in my life when I used to approach my parents and ask permission to do something because my friends were doing it. Frequently, my parents responded by asking if my friends jumped off the Brooklyn Bridge, would I do it? Having a strong superego and a reasonable sense of propriety, I generally said no, if my friends jumped off the Brooklyn Bridge I would not do it. Generally the discussion ended there. It took years to pass for me to realize that my friends had never really thought about jumping off the Brooklyn Bridge. Most of the stuff that I wanted to do with them was reasonable. But my parents imputed a sense of collective stupidity to my friends to keep me from doing things that they did not want me to do. In a very real sense, our senior officials in the defense establishment are imputing that same sense of collective stupidity to the international community, whereas the experience with my friends was one of collective wisdom. They had a sense of what they could do to make life interesting and still not put them at risk. There is a sense of collective wisdom in the international community, as well.

It is important, however, to recognize that there are important differences between the United States and other nations. The United States is one of a very small set of nations that actually expects its armed forces to engage frequently in hostile operations on unfriendly shores. It is a general expectation in the United States, but a rare one in the global community. In the three decades that I have researched military organizations and operations, I have spoken to very few non-American senior military officials, civilian or uniformed, who expected their forces to be engaged in exchanges of fire on their watch. Several were actually horrified at the thought that it might happen. Most nations regard their militaries as fulfilling basically three functions: homeland defense, internal social control, and a symbol of sovereignty. We have higher expectations and more extensive expectations of our military. Given the norms that have prevailed in the global system over the last couple of decades, combat-effectiveness is less important to such nations than it is to those that actually expect to engage in military operations. Early on in the move to bring in new NATO members, senior military officials from one of these countries explained to me that his nation's army was a television army. I had never heard that term before and asked him what he meant. Did they look good marching in parades and showing their flag? No, he meant they actually spent most of their time watching television. We must keep in mind that there is a range of ways in which militaries are organized cross-nationally.

But beyond the issue of simple mimicry, there are very good reasons to attend to the experiences of foreign military forces. We have to recognize that most modern military operations these days are alliance or coalition operations. We are not likely to be alone on our side of the battlefield. Given the trend in the Western world toward greater acceptance and indeed celebration of diversity in populations and in military forces, we will not be the only voice on whether our soldiers fight on battlefields that are integrated on the basis of sexual orientation. As a nation we need to think about this issue whether or not we change our policies, because we are going to be fighting in coalition forces that are integrated on the basis of sexual orientation.

Second, other nations have preceded us in resisting sexual-orientation integration, in forecasting dire consequences if it occurs, and then have gone through the process and found out if their expectations were right or wrong. If nothing else, their experiences provide us with a way to evaluate the hypotheses that we have shared with them on the consequences of integration. More importantly, they also give us an opportunity to learn from their experiences, regarding what works and what does not, should we eventually change the policy. If we in fact lift the ban and make sexual-orientation integration work in the U.S. military, it will not be simply a matter of changing the policy and having it happen. As was the case with racial integration, and as has been the case with gender integration, this process is initially problematic in human-resource management terms and has to be managed. But it can be managed. Many military leaders have said to me that if they have to do it, they will do it and make it work. But we cannot assume that it will happen without being managed, and we should learn from other nations who have gone through the process.

Third, the experiences of other nations serve as a reminder that in democratic nations, armed forces are not only agents of the cultures and populations they defend, but also reflect them. Among the cultural items reflected are the attitudes, values, norms, and behaviors of the society regarding population diversity, including those dealing with areas like gender integration and sexual-orientation integration. Indeed, we have alluded several times today to the importance of cultural consistency. Because both gender integration and sexual orientation are rooted in social values, these two processes tend to co-vary.

I want to share with you briefly some data from a paper that Mady Segal, Bradford Booth, one of our graduate students, and I published last year in a book called *Beyond Zero Tolerance*.[14] Basically our research looked at eighteen nations and developed a small archive dealing with their policies and preferences regarding both gender integration and sexual-orientation integration. Then we made two lists of the eighteen nations, one ranked by tolerance toward women and the other ranked by tolerance toward gays, and determined for each country whether the level of tolerance toward women tended to correspond to the level of tolerance towards gays. Two important points emerge from the data. First, in this set of nations, most of which are fairly democratic, there was indeed some variation in both gender integration and sexual-orientation integration. Second, as I suggested a moment ago, those two dimensions tended to co-vary. Militaries that were fairly well integrated on the basis of gender were also fairly well integrated on the basis of sexual orientation. For some reason, they tended to be fairly cold places, like the Netherlands, Denmark, Canada, and Norway. I am uncertain about the climatic determinants. Things look very different in the Mediterranean region, perhaps a new twist to geopolitics. We also see some intuitive cultural consistency. More traditional cultures, like Turkey, Greece, and Italy, tend to be more resistant. On a number of dimensions, societies that have moved in the direction of modern societies are down here at the higher, that is to say, the lower rankings (Figure 5.1). So these data suggest that at least with regard to these forms of integration, the military does reflect the culture of their host societies. This table represents a snapshot taken right after the major gender integration of the military had taken place, but before the recent decision of the European Court. Being a believer that there are patterns of culture, my expectation would be that over time one would see in this distribution a regression toward the mean, that is, an increasing consistency of culture. Interestingly, the two exceptions are the United States and Great Britain. Since then, there has been movement on the part of Great Britain on the issue of gays in the military, as a result of the European Court decision. If we were to move these points around on the basis of new data, Great Britain would move closer to the regression line. There

Figure 5.1 Plot of Mean Rankings: Gender and Sexual Orientation
(1 = most integrated; 18 = least integrated)

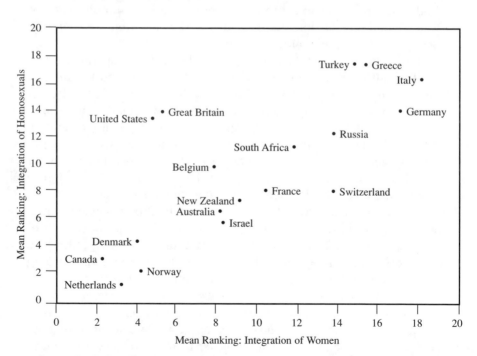

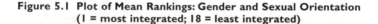

Source: David Segal, Mady Segal, and Bradford Booth, "Gender and Sexual Orientation Diversity in Modern Military Forces: Cross-National Patterns," in *Beyond Zero Tolerance: Discrimination in Military Culture,* Mary Katzenstein and Judith Reppy, eds. (Boulder, Colo.: Rowman and Littlefield, 1999), p. 233.

is currently discussion in the United States not only on the issue of gays in the military, but also on the issue of women in the military. One of the planks of the Republican platform is to resegregate entry-level military training on the basis of gender, which essentially moves away from integration. This development moves the United States closer to the regression line, although on a different plane than Britain is likely to move. . . .

Laura Miller: Paul, you mentioned that there are prescriptive lessons that we could learn from the ways that other militaries integrated gays. I am wondering, what kinds of steps, if any, were taken prior to the lifting of gay bans to educate service members? What, if any, preparatory work did they do? For instance, what are the consequences for making gay jokes or hostile comments, things that do not necessarily cross the line of assault, but obviously create a hostile environment?

Gade: I cannot really answer the last one. My recollection as to the former is that the best information we have on that comes from the Canadian case, in which there were several leadership-training courses implemented and some very stringent policies to communicate to the Canadian leadership that the government was serious about having this integration happen. Once this message is communicated, it is important to establish a kind of "chain-teaching," with the leaders communicating to the subleaders and the subleaders on down the line through the chain of command. Then the procedures are actually taught, as well as the mechanisms concerning how the policies will be implemented. This tactic was an important approach that the Canadians used very successfully.

Miller: Can anyone else discuss what other militaries do?

Rob Nunn: My personal experience in the Royal Navy has been that the other people are far more embarrassed than I am. They have more difficulty when they realize they have said something that may be offensive. They get flustered and find it pretty awkward. Everyone is in hysterics, and then they get quiet and try and rephrase what they said. It is quite satisfying that they have had more of a problem with it than I have.

I would like to return to the point that was raised earlier about bullying and harassment. I know that if someone started harassing me in my service environment, about a hundred other people would jump on that person. They will not tolerate it, because of the way the policy has been implemented in the Royal Navy. There is a code of conduct, and everybody abides by it. It is as simple as that. Harassment is not tolerated whether you are straight, gay, bisexual, or whatever. It is simply not tolerated if you step over that line. At least that has been my personal experience in the last three months. . . .

Dandeker: One of the implementation problems associated not so much with integration of gay personnel, but with a code of conduct, is humor. Most service personnel I talk to recognize that one of the peculiarities of the armed services is the need for humor in the face of having to prepare for death or other unpleasant things. When I spoke with some navy personnel, they said that was a problem. Not so much an insuperable problem, it was something that had to be faced head-on. Everyone recognized that a fighting unit has to have humor as a crucial part of its survival mechanism, and they were constructively playing with how to resolve it. It is not necessarily a huge issue, but it is something that has to be faced.

Nunn: Yes, I would agree with that. . . . I have been asked some weird and wonderful questions. People do not know quite what to say. There are situations in which they have said something, and there is raucous laughter from everybody in the room, because they realize the innuendo in it. They all sit there red-faced trying to ask the question again so I am not offended. But I am not offended. . . . You have to maintain a sense of humor. It does not matter who you are. All walks of life need humor. If you get officious about things, then it all goes wrong.

Mulliss: We have found leadership to be absolutely critical. . . . If you are going to bring about a significant social change, it is very important to have commitment from leadership and accountability of leadership all the way through an organization. We hold our people accountable for implementation of equality and diversity, as well as education and training. We put a tremendous amount of work into providing people with information on what is acceptable, what is not, how to deal with a problem if it does occur, as well as management and leadership and the requirements of dealing with unacceptable behavior. . . .

Jay Williams: It is not only on issues of social policy that the military in this country refuses to learn lessons from others. In 1972, I was teaching at the Naval Academy, and an officer was assigned in from Vietnam. In Saigon he translated the lessons learned from the French warfare in the 1950s as we were preparing to leave Vietnam. It is hard not to wonder if some lives were lost and people hurt because we refused to learn lessons from others' experiences. The attitude of, "After all, they're only French," was a big mistake.

A group of us here addressed another lesson from foreign militaries in a project on the postmodern military, the fruit of which is out there on the display table in the lobby.[15] Since its publication, there have been some changes in some of the countries, but overall the relationship between the military and society after the Cold War is very interesting in several dimensions, gays in the military being one among them. Much of what we think we know about what foreign countries do is actually wrong.

Finally, we cannot forget the importance of leadership and judgment. I like Christopher Dandeker's code of conduct, and my first thought is that we ought . . . to apply the British code to our own country. But the problem with this code is that it is too sensible. It would never work here, for reasons that are difficult to describe exactly. But in a hyperlegalistic society like our own, it is difficult to be moderate. We have interest groups who immediately push people to the extremes, and if you are an extremist, you are fortunate, because only half the lunatics are throwing things at you. If you try to stay in the center and have judgment, someone will question you in every case. And in this society, it is especially difficult to exercise discretion. There are a lot of career-seeking missiles out there for military people and this issue is one of them. Unfortunately, in this society it may be too much to expect people to actually be adults and use judgment. . . .

Belkin: I have debated Charlie Moskos on whether foreign militaries are relevant on several occasions. He argues that American culture is different than other cultures in which gays and lesbians have been allowed to serve. What I think he means relates to what Jay Williams is saying about our very polarized culture. But I want to ask, why does that matter? Because many of the countries that have integrated gays into the military have polarized cultures, especially on gay rights, and other countries that have integrated gays into the military have homophobic and masculinist cultures. And conversely, in the United States, when we have integrated in police or fire departments, we have done it successfully. So I am not so convinced that having a polarized culture means that the U.S. military cannot lift its gay ban successfully.

Williams: Each culture poses particular challenges and opportunities for trying to make changes of this nature. I was not arguing that we should not do it, nor do I think we should do it right now, either. It is a prediction. The ban will be lifted, and to allow it to happen smoothly in the United States, there are certain limitations that the culture poses through the attitudes that exist in the society. . . .

Diane Mazur: What both Jay Williams and Aaron Belkin said is important. It reminds me of a few years ago when allegations of adultery were prosecuted in the U.S. military. I have always thought that the military's biggest problem was its fear of exercising judgment. The British service test and code of conduct are full of judgment, but we have become a military that is so afraid of exercising judgment. What we do instead, as we saw in all these adultery cases, is to career from one unexplained decision to another without explaining the basis for any of them. All these decisions are inconsistent with one another, and the military would be on stronger ground if it was willing to explain itself and to stand on whatever judgment it rendered. We will not be able to move forward from the place where we are now unless the military is willing to risk making judgments.

Williams: You are absolutely right, but Congress and interest groups have to avoid crucifying the military when it does exercise judgment. The military is terrified of Congress and the media. . . .

Miller: I would like to add a bit to Aaron Belkin's description of Charlie Moskos's position. Charlie argues that not only are we polarized, but we have a very active religious-right community and a very active gay and lesbian community. It is not just civilian and military leaders who will be involved in this policy and integration, but there are many different interest groups who actively want to get their hands in things, muck things up, and make things a problem from both sides. He would say that in other societies people are polarized on this issue, but there are not these powerful resources of activists trying to get involved in military policies and use them as an example or a front for social change.

Belkin: Does he think we are more polarized on gay issues now than we were on race in 1948 when President Truman ordered the military to integrate African Americans?

Miller: I do not know.

Mady Segal: The issue of adultery is a good example of how military regulations are interpreted, how the press covers it, and how the public interprets what has happened. When I sat on the Congressional Commission on Military Training and Gender-Related Issues, the ten of us on the committee evaluated components of basic training. We debated whether the military should be gender integrated or segregated, and one of the issues involved personal relationships between members of the military, especially cross-gender relationships, which included frater- nization and adultery. We found the Uniform Code of Military Justice [UCMJ] quite clear and unanimously agreed that there was no reason to muddle around with regulations and policy on adultery. But what peo- ple did not understand was that it was not simply adultery that could be prosecuted. You could not prosecute for just adultery. There had to be proof that there was sexual behavior and that at least one of the partners was married to another person. But it also had to be demonstrated that the behavior was injurious to good order and discipline. Without prov- ing all three of these parts, then the military courts cannot find for adul- tery. The same is true for leaders as they interpret the Uniform Code of Military Justice, which they are all supposed to do. Just as the British code of conduct stipulates that each case will be judged on its own merit and requires that such action should be always proportionate to the seriousness of the misconduct, the same sort of thing is already in place in American military policies on adultery. The UCMJ requires judgment and asks if the actions or behavior of the individual has adversely impacted or is likely to impact operational efficiency of the service. . . .

Dixon Osburn: As part of one of the interest groups that advocates on behalf of people who are or who are perceived to be lesbian, gay, or bisexual, I think it is important to recognize where there is common ground. Since the very beginning, part of the common ground is that the Servicemembers Legal Defense Network has advocated that there needs to be leadership from the top and discretion at the command level. In the seven years under this policy, we have found neither. Part of the problem is that no one wants to deal with the issue. Let me give you an example that suggests possible change, which addresses a question that Laura Miller asked about what kind of standards can be set up to mini- mize harassment that occurs in the field. For any kind of harassment training to work there must be commitment from the top, from the sec- retary of defense to each of the service secretaries and on down the line. They must make clear that harassment will not be tolerated and estab- lish clearly what harassment is, because in the current culture there are different views about what constitutes harassment. Some might see say- ing "dyke," "fag," or "queer" as everyday banter or that the boys are just being boys. It is slowly becoming understood that as the gay ser- vice member who experiences such harassment, you have no ability to respond to it, especially because of the "Don't Tell" policy. Service members also need to be told how to report the harassment, where to report it, what they should say, and what they should not say. For gay service members, reporting abuse is particularly problematic because victims may be investigated if a commander tries to find out information about their orientation. Again, there must be very clear guidelines about what they can report and where to report it. Plus, the leadership has to make clear that there will be consequences for the harassment, consequences not only for the individuals who engage in the harassment, but there will be consequences for the leaders who tolerate and condone that harassment. If an enlisted member has just hit somebody because he is perceived to be gay and the NCO standing by watches it and does nothing, then the NCO needs to be called for that as well. It also needs to be clear what those consequences are. And the consequences need to be commensurate with the type of harassment, the severity of it, the frequency of it, and the rank of those who engage in it. No, we do not believe that somebody should be court-martialed for calling somebody a fag. You can pull somebody aside and verbally counsel them on the spot, informing him it is inappropriate behavior that will not be tolerated. The Pentagon has been struggling a great deal with these questions in the wake of Barry Winchell's murder, and I have been very proud of the steps they have been taking. The story is still unfinished, but even on issues as difficult as harassment, guidelines can be set and the right message can be sent. . . .

Lynn Eden: I have two questions for Christopher. For those people who do not read *International Security* every night before they go to bed or every morning when they wake up, Beth Kier wrote an important recent article based largely on the RAND study.[16] It was very synthetic and pulled in additional material, advocating that there would not be a problem with the integration of gays and lesbians in the U.S. military. A couple of letters came in, one of which was from Christopher Dandeker.[17] In this letter, Christopher, you took quite a strong stand on the issue. As you said today, you wrote that it is very important for the military to have a fighting spirit and a sense of uniqueness. You said that the British military accomplished this by excluding open homosexuals from the military. From the letter, it sounded as if the sky would fall down if this were to change. I would like to know, have you changed your mind? I gather you have. How did you change your mind? What was your process? As a serious academic, how did you deal intellectually with making a prediction that did not come true? . . .

You mentioned the importance of humor. You also said that the proper phrase might be, "Don't fear it, but don't flaunt it." Now I live in the Bay Area, and how one defines "flaunt" might be different in different places. For example, in San Francisco men dressing as women is not flaunting. Even the candidate for mayor has done that. And men marching in the gay pride parade wearing nothing except an American flag is not considered disrespectful. Straight couples at the opera wearing nothing except a tiny bit of modest cover and covered head to toe in tattoos is also not considered flaunting. It is certainly not considered beyond the realm. They were not escorted out. In fact, it was considered only polite not to look at them. It is hard for us to know what flaunting is, because it all seems quite humorous and fun. How do you define flaunting?

Dandeker: On the first question, I suspect I will not be the first or the last to revise one's opinions in the light of evidence, argument, and discussion.

Eden: Most people do not.

Dandeker: Well, there we are. However, one of the issues in dispute, both then and now, and indeed during the discussions today, is what we mean precisely by open integration. In relation to the result of the European Court of Human Rights decision in the British case, I would have been much more cautious and indeed possibly hostile to the code of conduct had it not included levers within those regulations that legally allow the exclusion of ideologues who wish to place gay identity before professional identity. This crucial point distinguishes varieties of open integration. Once I worked out that particular view, then as a citizen as well as an academic, I was able to feel more relaxed about a policy that the core of the armed services could find acceptable. I do not mean they are waving flags saying, "This is great!" The answer to your first question depends on what open integration means, and in the United States the attitudes toward this question will hinge on exactly the same issue.

There are two cross-cutting issues here. The British case showed that you are foolish if you expect a successful policy to be built on regulations or law alone. It is a mistake to do so. If you argue that we have to base our policy on laws and regulations alone, because we are legalistic freaks in the United States, then, fine, but that is your problem. For the moment, the policy in the United Kingdom works because people recognize that commanding officers apply the code with discretion, and gay service members also see the need for discretion or even reticence. If in doubt, do not flaunt it. If in doubt, do not come out. If you do come out, negotiate it successfully, not at the abstract level, but at the concrete level. We are discussing two issues: what we mean precisely by "open," and what the relationship between law and custom is. What we seem to have learned here, although no one has said it, is that the attitudes of "Don't Ask, Don't Tell, Don't Pursue" within the U.S. armed services are not unconnected with a zero-defect mentality that we see in peacekeeping operations. The obsession with force protection and not using judgment—the mentality of "watch your ass, in case someone in the White House questions your decision"—would not happen in the British armed services.

How do I define flaunting? I agree, it is an issue. I do not know the precise roots of "Don't fear it, don't flaunt it." It was a journalistic spin, but it was certainly not a journalistic creation. It came from official sources. "Don't flaunt it" is a colloquial way of saying, if in doubt, do not come out until a service member is certain he or she can negotiate the process at the concrete level of the individual's relationship with the unit members, with whom he has already developed a professional relationship. As I said earlier, in relation to both the sexual-orientation issue and the ethnic-minority issue we have to recognize that a diverse military that lacks a sense of humor will be a less effective military. Having talked to many soldiers, I have learned that they feel very strongly that if you get rid of humor or police it, you will have a serious problem. We can police certain kinds of humor, but a residual level of humor is required, which can pose a problem. It is not an insuperable problem, but it is a problem. . . .

Michael Desch: Lynn asked what the standard for flaunting might be, and I appreciate that in the Bay Area you have one standard. I would propose that Radcliff, Kentucky, is the standard most likely to be accepted within the military. What does that mean? It means absolutely no behavioral differences from anyone else. One of the most striking things you notice any time you visit any military unit is the level of conformity. I overheard an interesting exchange between two Air Force ROTC instructors on our campus. One day one of their cadets showed up with his sleeves rolled up the wrong way. Apparently, in the army sleeves are rolled up one way, and in the air force there is a different way. I laughed until I started thinking more about it. This conformity involves how you roll your sleeves, how you have your hair cut, what sort of glasses frames you use. Aside from prejudice and taste, it functions as the means by which they get their cadets to submerge their individuality to the group identity. An effective way to accomplish this goal is for everybody to wear the same uniform, have the same haircut, and manifest lots of different similarities. Sexual orientation is one of the most individual parts of a person, and reconciling a sexual identity that is very different from the rest of the group not only flies in the face of prejudice, but it also defies this ubiquitous trend toward conformity throughout the military.

Second, intellectually I buy this business of using other militaries as a role model for the United States. But I am not in the military and never have been. My discussions with military officers have left me deeply skeptical. The U.S. military does not believe that any other military is on par with it. I used to think that they must have some respect for the Israeli Defense Forces [IDF], but I had a long conversation with an army colonel who had been an exchange officer for a year with the IDF. He thought they were no better than our National Guard. We can argue that the Canadians, Norwegians, and Dutch were able to lift the ban all we like, but if this attitude is widespread and the American military does not accept them as being peer militaries, then basing the argument on their experience could be as successful as arguing that the Dallas County sheriff can do it, which, as many people in the military have said, is like comparing apples and oranges. . . .

Korb: But I would bet anything that if the other militaries had problems, the U.S. military would be the first to use them as examples. I agree with you. Foreign militaries are relevant, because they are the best examples we can study, but our military will always find a reason to say they are irrelevant, whether because of their size or culture.

Desch: I agree that it is rhetorical, but looking at the foreign cases at least persuaded me that lifting the ban would not undermine military effectiveness. I am convinced, but I am not convinced that military leaders will be persuaded by this argument, given that they do not seem to have much respect for other militaries.

Even-Zohar: But they will not make the change anyway. The change will not come from them. It will have to be imposed upon them.

Desch: Yes, but our success at imposing policies on the American military that it does not want has been mixed at best. A number of people have echoed this point—if we do not get the senior leadership to buy into it, it will not happen.

Robert MacCoun: In response to this last exchange, when the RAND study began to look at six other countries, some military officials told us to just focus on Israel. It was the one country they would pay attention to and take seriously. . . . We were told again and again that there was a key legal problem in the United States, and I am wondering if it is a problem in other countries and how it is handled. The Uniform Code of Military Justice has an antisodomy statute, and we concluded that part of lifting the ban would require adding some language to the code that would limit the UCMJ prohibition against sodomy to just non-consensual sodomy. We were told there would be an immense barrier to making any kind of change to military law. Is this an issue in British or Israeli military law?

Johnston: According to the European Court, what I do outside of my uniform on my own time is my business. It is not your business. I think that answers it in a way. We have never advocated that gay people go to work in uniform and hold hands. . . .

Simon Langley: Given that America has to work with NATO allies, most of whom have now lifted the ban, how on earth will you prevent U.S. soldiers from working with nations that allow openly gay men and lesbians to serve? Either in terms of joint operations, where you may be commanded by gay men or lesbians, or also on a micro level, when you send people on exchange programs, where they spend three or four years in a foreign country under their rules? How is this going to work? . . .

Steve May: The problem is ours. I do not know. You cannot solve the problem.

Grey: It is definitely an American problem. There is a spin on this issue that I think is interesting, that you might be interested in from our perspective. Our Human Rights Act defines sexual orientation as heterosexual, homosexual, lesbian, or bisexual orientation. So, when we lifted our ban, we looked at where we were advantaging heterosexuals over anybody else. We found that we were advantaging heterosexual people over homosexual people, which helped with the development of our policy. If you are focusing on recruiting for success then you want to develop policy to get what you want, not one that avoids what you do not want. Overseas our troops are known for their ability to manage diversity. Often we are deployed overseas because other people cannot manage their diversity. Our strength in this area is an important aspect of why our military is successful. . . .

Belkin: My own perspective about the relevance of foreign militaries is that when the United Kingdom still had a gay ban, many people in the Pentagon cited the British case as evidence for the point that the U.S.

military could not integrate known gays. Now that the British no longer have a ban, people in the Pentagon do not believe that the British case counts as evidence. This leads me to believe that we have an answer to the question that is the title of our conference: "Is the gay ban based on prejudice or military necessity?"

NOTES

1. See U.S. Senate Committee on Armed Services, *Policy Concerning Homosexuality in the Armed Forces*, 103d Congress, 2d Session (Washington, D.C.: Government Printing Office, 1993); "The Connection," *National Public Radio* (December 20, 1999); Charles C. Moskos and Stacey L. Sobel, "Should Gays Serve," *Salon* (June 13, 2000), available at: http://www.salon.com/news/feature/2000/06/13/fight_club/index1.html.

2. U.S. Senate Committee on Armed Services, *Policy Concerning Homosexuality in the Armed Forces*, p. 350.

3. See Charles C. Moskos, "From Citizens' Army to Social Laboratory," in *Gays and Lesbians in the Military: Issues, Concerns, and Contrasts*, W. J. Scott and S. C. Stanley, eds. (New York, N.Y.: Aldine de Gruyter, 1994), p. 64.

4. This section is based on Aaron Belkin and Melissa Levitt, "Homosexuality and the Israel Defense Forces: Did Lifting the Gay Ban Undermine Military Performance?" *Armed Forces and Society* 27, no. 4 (summer 2001): 541–566.

5. Barak resigned on the day of the conference, December 9, 2000.

6. Four service members discharged from the British armed forces for homosexuality began a legal challenge against the British ban in 1994. The European Court of Human Rights ruled in favor of the plaintiffs in September 1999, and the British ban was lifted in January 2000.

7. T. Barkawi and C. Dandeker, "Rights and Fights: Sexual Orientation and Military Effectiveness," *International Security* 24 (summer 1999): 181–186.

8. See *McCarty v. McCarty*, 453 U.S. 210 (1981).

9. See National Defense Research Institute, "Analogous Experience of Domestic Police and Fire Departments," *Sexual Orientation and U.S. Military Personnel Policy: Options and Assessment* (Santa Monica, Calif.: RAND, 1993), pp. 106–157.

10. "O-6" refers to an officer who holds the rank of colonel.

11. See Barkawi and Dandeker, "Rights and Fights," pp. 181–186.

12. General Sir Charles Guthrie served under Tony Blair as chief of Defence Staff of the British armed forces until February 2001.

13. Gregory M. Herek, "Sexual Orientation and Military Service: A Social Science Perspective," *American Psychologist* 48 (1993): 538–547.

14. David Segal, Mady Segal, and Bradford Booth, "Gender and Sexual Orientation Diversity in Modern Military Forces: Cross-National Patterns," in *Beyond Zero Tolerance: Discrimination in Military Culture*, Mary Katzenstein and Judith Reppy, eds. (Boulder, Colo.: Rowman and Littlefield, 1999), pp. 225–250.

15. Charles C. Moskos, John Allen Williams, and David Segal, eds., *The Postmodern Military: Armed Forces After the Cold War* (New York, N.Y.: Oxford University Press, 2000).

16. Elizabeth Kier, "Homosexuals in the U.S. Military: Open Integration and Combat Effectiveness," *International Security* 23 (1998): 5–39.

17. Barkawi and Dandeker, "Rights and Fights," pp. 181–186.

6

What Does
"Don't Ask, Don't Tell" Cost?

THE PREVIOUS THREE CHAPTERS ADDRESS WHETHER THE "DON'T ASK, DON'T Tell" policy has any benefits. Remaining within the framework of a cost-benefit analysis, this chapter switches gears to discuss whether the gay ban has any costs. Experts who oppose allowing gays and lesbians to serve openly in the armed forces argue that the "Don't Ask, Don't Tell" policy has very few costs associated with it. According to this perspective, although about one thousand service members per year are discharged for homosexuality, most of these cases involve "tell discharges" in which service members are fired after they come out of the closet (or "tell"). Since most people who are separated from the armed forces have the choice to remain in the military if they do not reveal their sexual orientation, opponents of gays in the military suggest that many gays are taking advantage of the "Don't Ask, Don't Tell" policy as a free pass to avoid their obligation to serve. In addition, these experts suggest that the financial and other costs associated with the ban are minimal.

Experts who favor lifting the gay ban respond that even though most discharges are in fact "tell discharges," such discharges are not voluntary. They claim that service members reveal their orientation because they see leaving the military as their only option for avoiding antigay abuse. In addition, supporters of gays in the military point to financial costs, talent loss, and a culture of fear and mistrust as results of the "Don't Ask, Don't Tell" policy. According to this perspective, the military would strengthen itself and increase cohesion and performance by lifting the gay ban.

In the preface to this volume, we note that although our deliberations include a critical mass of scholars from the left and the right, we were not able to achieve an even balance of views. Perhaps nowhere in the volume is this imbalance more noticeable than in this chapter, given that we were unable to locate any expert who would deliver a presentation arguing that the "Don't Ask, Don't Tell" policy entails minimal costs. At the risk of appearing overly defensive, we repeat the point we raised originally in the preface that many conservatives declined our invitation to participate in the sessions. Following a presentation on the costs of the "Don't Ask, Don't Tell" policy, scholars discuss some of the legal issues surrounding the gay ban, in particular the courts' tradition of deferring to military judgment.[1]

Aaron Belkin: [In this session our] focus will be whether the gay ban has any costs. First, we should discuss whether the gay ban has any costs for the military. Many people believe that the ban benefits the military, and we have dedicated three panels to the question of benefits. In this panel I hope we can consider whether the ban imposes any cost on military performance and combat effectiveness. The second cost that we may or may not associate with the ban is the impact on gay and lesbian soldiers' civil rights. A debate I had with Elaine Donnelly, who runs the Center for Military Readiness, on Catholic Family Radio illustrates this question well. When I mentioned that I thought that the ban did involve some costs in terms of causing violence, Donnelly said, "No, that's just a few whining lesbians who are complaining about that." After our debate I read a Pentagon survey that reported that 4 percent of all soldiers last year witnessed a violent attack against a gay or lesbian service member, which translates roughly into 60,000 accounts of violent attacks. Of course, this figure does not answer the question of whether those beatings are the result of the gay ban or of something else. Hopefully this discussion will help us address whether the policy is partially responsible for some of these costs. . . .

Dixon Osburn: What does "Don't Ask, Don't Tell" cost? It costs approximately $30 million every single year, or $82,000 every day, or $3,400 per hour. Since 1950, "Don't Ask, Don't Tell" and its predecessors have cost the American taxpayer approximately $1.5 billion. That ends my presentation. Thank you. [Laughter.]

But that is just the beginning of the costs. First, how did I derive these numbers? These numbers come from a formula established by the General Accounting Office [GAO] in 1992 when it was asked to produce a report on the costs of the gay ban.[2] The General Accounting Office only calculated the total costs of training replacements for each service member discharged for being gay. The GAO determined that in 1992, it cost the government on average $28,000 to train replacements for the enlisted members booted under the gay ban and on average $121,000 to train officer replacements. Then, as now, the vast majority of those kicked out for being gay were enlisted members.

There are some problems with the GAO numbers, in that they severely undercount the actual cost of the gay ban. The numbers I have calculated since the 1992 GAO report are not adjusted for inflation. The numbers do not take into account the current economy, job market, or recent increases in military pay. The GAO did not calculate the cost of gay investigations, the cost of administrative discharge boards, the time spent by commanders at all levels dealing with gay investigations and issues related to "Don't Ask, Don't Tell, Don't Pursue, Don't Harass," the time spent by service and Department of Defense lawyers, or federal litigation costs.

Let me give you some examples from our own cases that give you an idea of how these costs can pile up. Marine Corporal Craig Haack's nightmare started when a criminal investigator knocked on his door, entered his barracks room, overturned his bed, and took his computer, computer disks, personal journals, and address books, looking for information about his sexual orientation. Technical Sergeant Daryl Gandy was one of seventeen service members caught in a witch-hunt that originated at Hickam Air Force Base several years back and that ultimately spread into the army and the navy, as well. Criminal investigators entered his workplace and handcuffed him in front of his co-workers, saying he was under investigation for being gay. They proceeded to question dozens of his colleagues, asking questions such as, "Does Technical Sergeant like girls the way that other guys like girls?" How did Gandy find himself in this kind of predicament? It was because prosecutors entered into a pretrial agreement, a plea bargain, with another airman who was charged for male-male rape and promised him that they would reduce his sentence if he coughed up names of gay colleagues. He was facing life in prison on that charge and others, but they said they would reduce his sentence to twelve months. He coughed up seventeen names, and the prosecutors went after them.

West Point cadet Nicole Gavin found herself the subject of an investigation in retaliation for reporting her commander for misconduct. The commander had asked her point-blank if she was a lesbian. She said that question was inappropriate and reported him. He then ordered that her personal diary be taken, as well as 250 pages of e-mail, to try and verify her sexual orientation.

It is not uncommon for investigators to seize and analyze diaries, computers, computer disks, address books, and e-mail looking for information about a suspect's sexual orientation or conduct. It is not uncommon for commanders and inquiry officers to ask dozens of service members about their private lives in an attempt to determine if someone is gay. It is not uncommon for inquiry officers to ask 90 to 150 questions about someone's personal life to gather data to punish the interviewee. And it is not uncommon for investigative officer reports to be 200–500 pages long and several inches thick. And I know, because I have been through enough of them.[3] These investigative costs—the costs of gay investigations, discharge boards, command time, lawyer time, and federal litigation—all are calculable. But none of those costs have been calculated and included in any cost estimates for the current policy.

The costs of training replacements for those kicked out under the gay ban also fail to measure the silent casualties of the policy, like Commander Jill Szymanski, who decided to resign her commission and abandon a very promising career solely because of "Don't Ask, Don't Tell, Don't Pursue, Don't Harass." She was tired of living in the closet, tired of looking over her shoulder every single day. And I would suggest to you that there are hundreds of service members who leave the military every year because of the gay ban.

There are other costs that are not as easily calculated as these. They are the human costs of this policy. First, think of the human costs to the individual lesbian, gay, or bisexual service members. Imagine the cost of being forced to live a lie twenty-four hours a day, seven days a week. Your friends and colleagues ask you, Why aren't you married? Who was that on the phone? With whom did you share your vacation? Who's this in the photo? With every question you have to lie, evade, and dissemble. If you were heterosexual, you would not have to think twice about those questions. But as a gay man, lesbian, or bisexual, you have to be on guard twenty-four hours a day, because if you let the truth slip, you may lose your job. "Don't Ask" is a myth.

Imagine the plight of some of our clients. One man's partner of twelve years had a degenerative illness that required care around the clock. There were no other family members who could provide the care. Our client, a sailor, was ordered to go to sea for a six-month deployment. Under any reading of the navy regulations, he would have qualified for a hardship discharge. But there was only one catch. He had to be heterosexual, and his partner had to be his wife. Imagine not being able to talk to your loved ones while away on missions at times when heterosexual service members are able to stay in touch. Being unable to list them as an emergency contact. Or being unable to meet your partner when your ship returns to home port after a mission to the Persian Gulf. Imagine being afraid to send or receive e-mails or letters for fear they would become evidence against you. Imagine living under a law that denies the three most powerful words in the world—the ability to say openly, "I love you." As Elizabeth Kier pointed out in her article in *International Security,* "The lack of support for the families of gay and lesbian personnel has a negative effect on homosexual service members; the military cannot support the families of homosexuals if they cannot serve openly."[4]

Imagine fearing that every click on your phone is CID or NCIS or OSI listening in to your conversations.[5] Or wondering whose car is parked across the street from your apartment building. Imagine living with a permanent knot in your stomach, as your commander calls you in, not knowing if you are going to get a commendation for your great work or be told that you are now under investigation for being gay. Imagine what it is like to live, work, command, and serve in an environment in which it is commonplace for your colleagues, superiors, and subordinates to say "fag," "faggot," "dyke," "queer," "die fag." This year the Pentagon's inspector general did a survey of 75,000 service members and found that 80 percent of them heard antigay comments in their unit.[6] In the vast majority of these cases, the commanders heard the comments and took no steps to stop them. Imagine being told in an antigay harassment briefing that the first principle is that homosexual conduct is incompatible with military service. That you are not worthy, that you are second-class citizens. Second-class status is not based on your abilities or on your merit, but because of who you are and what you say. Imagine knowing that the full weight of the law and the full resources of the U.S. military will be brought to bear against you if anyone knows the truth.

"Don't Ask, Don't Tell" is the only law in the land that allows an employer to fire somebody for being gay. There is no other law like it at the federal, state, or local level. Imagine having to choose between your job and your life, as you decide whether or not to report the antigay harassment you have experienced, knowing that the command could ultimately turn the investigation against you. And understand that a service member not only loses his or her job for being gay, he or she loses his or her livelihood, his or her chosen career, and his or her military family. It is rejection at every turn.

What psychological costs does "Don't Ask, Don't Tell, Don't Pursue" impose? Researchers could look at any of the issues that I have just raised and perhaps quantify the costs of the closet and the costs of the hostility. I would submit to you that the price would be staggering.

Let me reshift the focus briefly from the individual lesbian, gay, bisexual service members to the costs to our armed forces as a whole.

I would argue that productivity is hurt by bigotry. Productivity is hurt by harassment. Productivity is hurt when a service member has to look over his or her shoulder every single day for Uncle Sam. Productivity is hurt when a valued member of a team is removed from a unit for being lesbian, gay, or bisexual. Bigotry and harassment not only hurt the individual gay service member, they also hurt everyone else. I would submit that double standards do not advance unit cohesion. The haves and the have-nots, us versus them, these models do not advance unit cohesion. One need only remember the famous blue-eyed/brown-eyed study to understand the deep divisions caused by double standards.[7]

One of the many chilling moments in a court-martial that followed the murder of Barry Winchell was when an NCO took the stand and said, "I thought the army was a band of brothers, but no longer." At the court-martial, soldier after soldier took the stand and testified that Barry Winchell faced daily antigay harassment for four months prior to his murder and that his commanders did absolutely nothing to stop it. Last year on July 5, one soldier took a baseball bat and crushed Barry Winchell's head in while another goaded him, because they perceived Winchell as gay. Policies that treat people as second-class citizens suggest that you can treat them violently. "Don't Ask, Don't Tell" does not create a band of brothers. It creates, I would submit, a band of thugs.

I would suggest to you that "Don't Ask, Don't Tell, Don't Pursue, Don't Harass" is also costing us leadership. The current generation of young adults entering the military, our future leaders, sharply disagree with this policy. And many are packing their bags and leaving the armed forces rather than staying in an organization that is out of touch with the American people. The latest Gallup polls have found that more than 70 percent of Americans support gays in the military. I think it is time for the Pentagon to catch up.

President Truman did the right thing in 1948. As Beth Kier pointed out, the decision to desegregate the armed forces was "a political decision to address"—and I underline—"a costly policy that violated the civil rights of American citizens."[8] Courage is another human value that is hard to equate with a dollar. And, I would conclude, that if Master-Card were to do the pitch for the Pentagon, "What is the cost for doing the right thing? It is priceless." . . .

Diane Mazur: Today I will speak about judicial deference and "Don't Ask, Don't Tell." Being a lawyer, I believe the most significant factor that prevents any revision or repeal of "Don't Ask, Don't Tell" is the extraordinary deference that courts afford to military decisionmaking. Today the military makes decisions with the assured understanding in almost all instances that its decisions will not be second-guessed by courts. As well, Congress legislates on the same basis with an almost surety that its decisions will not be second-guessed by courts.

More generally, let me first discuss the general nature of judicial deference. Constitutional lawyers speak in terms of levels of review, which means how closely courts are going to scrutinize decisions that are made by other government agencies. There is a strict scrutiny level of review that is applied with reference to laws that are drawn on the basis of race. There is an intermediate level of scrutiny that is given to classifications that are drawn on the basis of sex. And almost every other remaining government act on any general social or economic ground is usually reviewed on a rational-basis level, which means a court will ask, Is this government decision rationally related to any legitimate government purpose? Interestingly, for the last twenty-five years the courts have reviewed constitutional questions that arise in a military context by what is essentially a fourth level of review, a sub-rational basis level. In effect since the Vietnam War, this fourth level of review corresponds to the all-volunteer military. Let me give you two examples of the language of this subrational-basis level of review. First, in *Gilligan v. Morgan*, the court writes, "It is difficult to conceive of an area of governmental activity in which the courts have less competence. The complex, subtle, and professional decisions as to the composition, training, equipping, and control of military force are essentially professional military judgments, subject always to civilian control of the Legislative and Executive Branches."[9] Second, in *Parker v. Levy,* the Supreme Court writes, "This court has long recognized that the military is, by necessity, a specialized society separate from civilian society. . . . Military society has been a society apart from civilian society."[10]

Today federal courts no longer consider themselves obligated to determine whether military decisionmaking is in accord with the Constitution, or whether the military's decisions are even rational under rational-basis review. Instead, they simply determine whether the military itself believes it is acting rationally. If so, the courts will defer to the military's belief.

In general, "Don't Ask, Don't Tell" cases have not seriously questioned the application of this fourth level of judicial review, and the plaintiffs in those cases have instead tried to carefully explain why the policy is constitutionally irrational. The problem with this strategy is that this fourth level of review, this subrational-basis level of review, tolerates a certain level of irrationality. This tolerance of irrationality is the primary reason that several circuit courts of appeal have considered "Don't Ask, Don't Tell" to be constitutional. But today I would like to look at the history of this idea of judicial deference and see where it comes from. Its most prominent applications are in two areas: we see judicial deference to military policies that concern women and gay citizens. But the origins of judicial deference are actually from something quite different, and I believe that judicial deference was never intended to apply to the situations that it is most commonly applied to today.

To begin with, where does this language come from that states that courts are without competence to make professional military judgments? This statement is a very serious one, and interestingly enough this language comes from the Kent State case, *Gilligan v. Morgan.* In response to the shootings, a class of Kent State students filed suit against the Ohio National Guard, and they asked the court to establish standards for the training of the Ohio National Guard, to choose what weapons they would be entitled to carry, and to limit the scope of the orders they would be permitted to carry out. The plaintiffs further asked that the court be assigned a continuing supervisory jurisdiction over the Ohio National Guard to insure they carried out these determinations with respect to training and weaponry and scope of orders. There was no particular constitutional right at issue with this case, and as most people would say, it was not surprising that the Supreme Court declined to accept this responsibility. It believed that a day-to-day supervisory role in the core operational aspect of the Ohio National Guard was not a court's role and should not be carried out by the federal judiciary.

Second, where does this language come from that establishes the military as a separate society apart from civilian society? Until more recently when broad challenges have been made to policies that exclude people from the military or limit a person's opportunities within the military, most constitutional claims against the military came up in two contexts. The first was whether an individual could be forced to serve in the military, and the second was whether an individual's court-martial violated some constitutional right. A case from 1953 illustrates the first context, *Orloff v. Willoughby.*[11] The plaintiff in that case, Mr. Orloff, was inducted into the army as a physician against his wishes, but he refused to sign the loyalty certificate that was required at that time, denying any involvement in subversive organizations. This refusal made him ineligible for a commission. The army attempted to place him as an enlisted man in the medical field. Mr. Orloff sued, arguing that the army had to discharge him, because they were not using him in the capacity that made him eligible for the draft, which was as a physician. The Supreme Court looked at this case and said, "It is not within the power of this court to determine whether specific assignments to duty fall within the basic classification of this petitioner. . . . Judges are not given the task of running the army. The responsibility for setting up channels through which such grievances can be considered and fairly settled rests upon Congress and upon the president. *The military constitutes a specialized community governed by a separate discipline from that of the civilian.*"

This decision by the Supreme Court is perfectly consistent with the Constitution. The Constitution gives Congress the power to make rules for the government and regulation of the land and naval forces, otherwise known today as the Uniform Code of Military Justice. The Court declined to get into the middle of a contest between Mr. Orloff and the military about whether he was going to serve as an enlisted man or as a commissioned officer. The court did not consider that its role. It is one thing to defer to the military's choice with respect to internal discipline of an individual, but it is quite another to defer to it with respect to broad policy initiatives that more generally affect the relationship of civilian society to military society. Deference to a particular disciplinary decision within a separate system of military justice is not the same thing as deference to an across-the-board disqualification of citizens from service.

There has been one justice who has been primarily responsible for this interpretation of law. Justice William Rehnquist has been intent on making these two very disparate situations one and the same, these individual disciplinary decisions and these much more broad policy decisions that the military or Congress might make. Interestingly, Justice Rehnquist was a law clerk to the justice who wrote *Orloff v. Willoughby* in 1953. And twenty-one years later, he took certain language from the *Orloff v. Willoughby* opinion, which he may have actually written himself as a clerk, and recharacterized it in a way that was much more friendly to the direction he wanted the Court to take. He took the language stating that the military constituted a "specialized community governed by a separate discipline" (the Uniform Code of Military Justice) and misrepresented it. He changed the language of "separate discipline" to claim that the military is a "specialized society separate from civilian society" and a "society apart from civilian society." He used this separateness to justify extraordinary judicial deference. Over the years, he has since used that same misrepresentation of language to justify a series of decisions that he has written. For Justice Rehnquist, it is a culture war, which he gets ahead in by characterizing military society as being separate from civilian society.

Let me give you three examples of what has happened between 1974 and today. In *Parker v. Levy,* he used the language of a separate society to uphold the court-martial of a physician who expressed his opposition to the Vietnam War. In *Rostker v. Goldberg,* he upheld Congress's belief that women would be of so little use to the military in times of war that they need not register for the draft.[12] And in *Goldman v. Weinberger,* he upheld the military's refusal to allow a military psychologist who was an Orthodox Jew to wear a yarmulke indoors.[13]

In the pre-Rehnquist era, the Supreme Court decided military cases in a different manner, the best example of which is the draft card–burning case of the *United States v. O'Brien* in 1968.[14] Can draft cards be burned in protest? The ultimate answer of the court was "no," but the analysis they went through was exactly the same First Amendment analysis they would have gone through in a nonmilitary context. Moving to *Rostker v. Goldberg* in 1981, this standard has changed. In the decision that women are of insufficient utility to the military to be asked to register for the draft, Justice Rehnquist writes, "Judicial deference to such congressional exercise of authority is at its apogee when legislative action under the congressional authority to raise and support armies and make rules and regulations for their governance is challenged." At the beginning of my talk, I said classifications on the basis of sex normally are evaluated under an intermediate level of scrutiny. They have to be justified in some significant way. Significantly, in this decision Justice Rehnquist was able to evaluate the draft law under the fourth-level, subrational-basis review, instead of the intermediate scrutiny that it otherwise would have required.

Why is this significant today? Only two justices are still on the Court who joined the Court's most recent opinion that sets out this idea of judicial deference to all military decisionmaking, Justice Rehnquist and Justice Stevens. One is eighty, and the other is seventy-four. They are the two oldest members of the Court. Rehnquist's misrepresentation of precedent has facilitated the much larger problem that has developed in civilian-military relations, the separatism that he celebrates in these judicial opinions. Today we see this separatism in a number of incidents, for example, in what happened with the Florida absentee balloting and all of the allegations that were traded back and forth. We see the effect of this separatism in "Don't Ask, Don't Tell" and in the difficulty we have trying to make it work. We ought to examine much more closely this idea of judicial deference to the military, this idea that there is a military exception to the Constitution, because there is no basis for it under the Constitution. If you look at the way it has been set out through Supreme Court law, it is clear that it is based on misrepresentation alone. It feeds this separatism that is very corrosive to the military and its place within society. Thank you.

Lynn Eden: Does anyone want to argue some other position for him or herself or on behalf of someone else who might not be here? Ask us to consider that the costs are less? Or argue that there are other costs to lifting the ban that have not been considered? Or perhaps there are benefits that outweigh the costs, like the employment of lawyers?

Jay Williams: As long as people can get out of jail free simply by playing the homosexual card, whether they are gay or not, the gay ban will always be a problem for the military, because it has an enormous cost to the military. People who get a great deal of training, find they do not like military life, and then decide to leave the armed forces have a quick vehicle to do so.

Michael Desch: I have a question for Mr. Osburn, which involves the implication of his argument that the current policies encourage violence against gays in the military. Off the top of your head, do you know what the rate of violence against gays or lesbians is in general society, and whether the rates in the military are any different or more or less about the same? It would seem to me that to prove your point, you would have to demonstrate that the rates of violence in the military are significantly higher.

Osburn: I do not have hard data for you. Gregory Herek may actually have some of that information, if we were to enlist his assistance. I do know of one study, which I have not seen, so I cannot say exactly, that shows in cases where there has been an antigay initiative that has passed or a progay law that has been repealed that the instance of antigay harassment in those cities has escalated. I do not know if that is probative for the question that you are asking. But I will go back to my comment, which was stated somewhat cautiously, and repeat that when a law treats people as second-class citizens it does invite harassment. . . .

Laura Miller: We have not discussed fully the cost to straight women. . . .

Melissa Sheridan Embser-Herbert: In setting us up for this discussion, Aaron Belkin mentioned the cost to gays and lesbians, and personally I have to say thank you to Dixon Osburn. I thought your presentation pulled together a number of different pieces that I often try to argue with people. But usually my emotions are too high, so I thank you for that. You used the expression that the gay ban hurts everyone, which reminded me of a book that has been around for a long time called

Homophobia: How We All Pay the Price by Warren Blumenfeld.[15] And I wanted to say that by setting up the costs solely in terms of gays and lesbians, we completely ignore the cost to heterosexual women and even men, as well. Because of the link between gender and sexuality in our culture, we cannot look at this issue as one that has a negative impact exclusively on gays and lesbians who are in the military. Without going into too much detail, I would simply argue that as long as we have the ban, we cannot move forward in eliminating sexism, to the degree that it is at all possible in our culture. I will leave you with one observation that was incredibly sobering to me when I worked through my data. Focusing on what people did to negotiate issues of gender, I asked women a series of questions about how they emphasize or de-emphasize masculinity and femininity. I was shocked at the people who voluntarily responded to a question specifically about femininity by saying that they act feminine in order to be seen as heterosexual. It is amazing how these two issues are linked. But what almost had me in tears were the surveys in which women wrote about their choices to engage in unwanted sexual relationships because they sent a message that took suspicion off of them. This experience was true for women who identified as heterosexual as well as lesbian. I want to emphasize that we have not attended well enough to the fact that there is an incredible price or cost paid by service members who are heterosexual, as well as gays and lesbians. . . .

David Segal: This instance might be one in which I am willing to accept your invitation to represent somebody else, that somebody else being Charlie Moskos, although I am not certain that Charlie would accept what I am about to say as representative of his views. It also might serve as a basis to begin to answer a question that Rob MacCoun raised earlier. It has not been historically unusual, sociologically if not legally, for the military to be regarded as a separate society. And in legal terms, military forces have had their own bodies of law, in our case the UCMJ, their own legal labor forces, and their own court systems, systems of courts-martial. When Charlie made his very important conceptual contribution to military sociology back in the 1970s, he suggested that the military was shifting from an institutional model to an occupational model and becoming more like a civilian job.[16] One of the dimensions that he thought was likely to change was a reduced autonomy of military justice and the integration of the military justice system into the broader national justice system. And indeed on that basis, as the Cold War in Europe ended and national security concerns became less paramount, courts may in fact have become more willing to intervene in military cases, particularly military personnel issues, rather than deferring to the military. I thought, perhaps incorrectly, that the courts' deference was rooted largely in knowledge of military technology that was frequently classified. And in fact, American courts have remained quite deferential to the military. But things have changed in Europe. We have seen not only increased interventions of civilian courts in military issues, but also the intervention of transnational courts, the European Court, which has breached not only the boundary between the military and civilian sectors, but also national sovereignty, in a sense. Whereas in the United States we continue to regard the military as a separate entity, and, for example, UCMJ applies to the activities of military personnel whether they are off or on duty or in or out of uniform, the European courts increasingly have been very explicit in regarding military service as a form of employment. This shift is exactly what Charlie said would happen with the transition to an occupational model. It has imposed employment law on the way that the European militaries raise and maintain their forces. The difference between the maintenance of a separate legal system and the incorporation of employment law as governing military forces is one of the important differences we have to attend to. . . .

Lawrence Korb: I have a few questions for Dixon Osburn. Would you have preferred we stay with the old Claytor policy rather than the Clinton policy?[17] Under the earlier policy, if you answered honestly when they asked you whether or not you were a homosexual, then you were not allowed to enter service. The second question refers back to a comment of Jay Williams. While it is true that a lot of people are ferreted out of the military through no fault of their own, there are cases in which people come out of the closet in order to get out of their obligation to the armed forces. I have seen a couple of service members with medical training in some of the service academies in which there was no evidence that anyone came after them. They simply decided that they did not want to fulfill their obligation. In your research and with the people that you serve, have you come across any of those situations, because they make it very difficult to deal with the points that you are making? I also have a question for Diane Mazur. Since Congress enacted the UCMJ and as it presumably changes based on the statistics we saw earlier, is there any reason why it would not intervene and change some of these archaic provisions about adultery and sodomy?

Mazur: The fundamental point I would make is, whether you have a majority in Congress of one nature or another, constitutional rights are not supposed to be subject to majority control, regardless of which majority is in control. If you have a Supreme Court that takes the position that there is a military exception to the Constitution, then that goes against the idea that constitutional rights are supposed to be independent of Congress's majority.

Osburn: To answer the first question: Do I prefer "Don't Ask, Don't Tell" or the prior policy? The answer is neither. I think former representative Gerry Studds put it best when he said that if "Don't Ask, Don't Tell" had been implemented the way it was intended, then it would be slightly less awful.

To the second question, we have had 2,500 clients in seven years, and in our research we find that clients who decide to come out to their commanders do so for two primary reasons. Those who experience harassment reveal their sexual orientation because they feel like there is nothing else they can do to stop the abuse. When you hear people calling you or other people in your unit fag and faggot and dyke and queer every single day, it makes for a very difficult environment. We also find that there are service members who come out for reasons of integrity, especially those of the younger generation, kids who are eighteen, nineteen, or twenty years old. These younger people who serve have just come to terms with their sexual orientation, and as a part of a generation familiar with *Ellen* and *Will and Grace*, they do not want to live in the closet. They want to serve, but they are not willing to do so at the price of their own integrity, and indeed they also see it as very much part and parcel of the core values of each of the services, which say you need to have honor, integrity, candor, and truth. They recognize the unfortunate consequence that they may lose their careers.

That is not to say that Jay Williams is not right. There are probably some people who use this tactic as a way to get out. We have not seen that in our research, but let me give you an example of what we have seen. Two years ago, my codirector Michelle Benecke and I were invited down to Lackland Air Force Base. Lackland was experiencing a phenomenal rate of gay discharges at the base, and the secretary of the air force invited us to go down there and see if we could figure out what was going on. Their data showed that the vast majority of the trainees were being kicked out in the first couple of weeks. It is possible that some straight people were using the policy to get out, but we found a very different situation there. For example, we talked to one of the trainees who was being kicked out at the time, who read through his military training manual and equated "Don't Ask, Don't Tell" with the Uniform Code of Military Justice. He asked the leader in his flight,

"Does this mean that because I am gay you are going to throw me in jail?" And instead of cautioning him from making such a comment and getting him a defense attorney so he would know what the policy said, they immediately shunted him over into the discharge process. They had not even trained him on the policy yet. We said that we needed to put a pause on these discharges, and they needed to teach the trainees what the law was. Then they could make the decision, because they could not expect people to know the law in advance of teaching them. They have since instituted a sort of break. If someone says something, they respond by taking him or her to a defense attorney who explains the law, so he or she can decide what will happen. The result has been that the gay discharges of that base have decreased 600 percent, which is a phenomenal decrease. It may be that some of the straight service members realized that this policy did not apply to them. But it is also true that there are many gay service members who understand the rules better and have to suck it up and go through with it or say no and get discharged. . . .

Dandeker: What strikes me as an interesting point to pursue, as David Segal said earlier, is despite everything we have heard about judicial deference, the U.S. military's involvement with other nations undermines the workability of "Don't Ask." I suspect, and obviously this rests upon what the next commander in chief might wish to do, if the United States continues to become more closely involved in peacekeeping operations with its friends and allies, then there will be a wave effect as a result of its personnel serving with other personnel with different social and legal traditions. The policy may actually be forced to change. For example, Germany, as you know, has changed its policy on women in the military following a ruling of the European Court of Justice, not the European Court of Human Rights, [but] the European Union Court of Justice. Interestingly, a Bundeswehr officer in command of a Dutch-German unit asked his own service commanders, What do I do? This was because the Bundeswehr has a rather more restrictive view on gays in the military than the Dutch do, and he asked how to run a policy when people from different traditions work together. The interesting question to ask is, When will that occasion happen with the U.S. forces? . . .

Belkin: If we consider the violence directed toward gays and lesbians in the U.S. military, then we have to ask whether that violence is a result of "Don't Ask, Don't Tell" or of broader American culture. To determine the answer, we need to compare the rates of violence within the military to those outside of it. Assuming we can find the resources,

154   *Don't Ask, Don't Tell*

I would like to make a commitment that my center will sponsor a study on this issue, because I think it is an important question.

As today's conference concludes, I keep returning to a finding from a Pentagon survey, in which 4 percent of military personnel witnessed a violent attack directed against a gay or lesbian person last year. This percent translates into 60,000 witness accounts. It is possible that each violent attack was witnessed by ten people at once, which would mean that there were only 6,000 violent gay bashings and not 64,000, but I wonder if the rates are that high even in civilian society. But before we collect the data to answer the question, I think we can turn to evidence from foreign militaries for a provisional answer. Tonight representatives from foreign militaries will present data that suggest that after the lifting of a ban, violence against gays and lesbians tends to disappear. I believe that in the three years after Australia lifted its ban, the rate of phone calls to a sexual harassment hot line that concerned sexual orientation was something like 1.5 percent of all calls—

Bronwen Grey: Yes, the rates are infinitesimal. We have advice lines that people can phone and ask advice if they feel they have been discriminated against or harassed. I have the figures, and the number of calls in relation to same-sex issues is really infinitesimal.

Belkin: My understanding of what happens once a ban is lifted is that people who are attacked can report their attacker, and attackers know they will be reported, so they do not carry on with their violence. My sense is the gay ban itself is responsible for much of the violence by making it difficult if not impossible for victims to report abuse.

NOTES

1. This section is based on Aaron Belkin, "The Gay Ban Isn't Based on Military Necessity," *Journal of Homosexuality* 41, no. 1 (2001): 103–119.

2. U.S. General Accounting Office, *Defense Force Management: Statistics Related to DoD's Policy on Homosexuality* (Washington, D.C.: Government Printing Office, 1992).

3. As of December 2000, the Servicemembers Legal Defense Network has provided legal assistance to approximately 2,500 service members.

4. Elizabeth Kier, "Homosexuals in the U.S. Military: Open Integration and Combat Effectiveness," *International Security* 23 (1998): 5–39.

5. These organizations are investigative branches of the military. "CID" is the Army Criminal Investigations Division; "OSI" is the Air Force Office of Special Investigations; and "NCIS" is the Naval Criminal Investigative Service.

6. U.S. Department of Defense, *Military Environment with Respect to the Homosexual Conduct Policy,* Report No. D-2000-101 (Washington, D.C.: Department of Defense, March 2000).

7. The discussion refers to a 1968 experiment by third-grade teacher Jane Elliott that was first described in the 1969 film *Eye of the Storm.* See William Peters, *A Class Divided* (Garden City, N.Y.: Doubleday, 1971); and Susan Hogan-Albach, "A Hard Lesson," *Minneapolis Star Tribune* (January 18, 1999), p. EI.

8. Kier, "Homosexuals in the U.S. Military," pp. 5–39.

9. *Gilligan v. Morgan,* 413 U.S. 1 (1973).

10. *Parker v. Levy,* 417 U.S. 733 (1974).

11. *Orloff v. Willoughby,* 345 U.S. 83 (1953).

12. *Rostker v. Goldberg,* 453 U.S. 57 (1981).

13. *Goldman v. Weibberger,* 475 U.S. 503 (1986).

14. *United States v. O'Brien,* 391 U.S. 367 (1968).

15. Warren J. Blumenfeld, ed., *Homophobia: How We All Pay the Price* (Boston, Mass.: Beacon Press, 1992).

16. See Charles C. Moskos, *The American Enlisted Man: The Rank and File in Today's Military* (New York, N.Y.: Russell Sage Foundation, 1970).

17. The version of the gay ban that "Don't Ask, Don't Tell" replaced was issued in 1981 by W. Graham Claytor Jr., deputy secretary of defense under President Carter.

7

Openly Gay Service Members Tell Their Stories: Steve May and Rob Nunn

STEVE MAY: TONIGHT I WOULD LIKE TO SHARE WITH YOU MY STORY, NOT AS an academic, because I am not one, but rather as a soldier and as a state policymaker. I joined ROTC [Reserve Officers Training Corps] in 1989 when I was seventeen years old, because military service was part of my American dream. It is one of the things I have wanted to do since I was a very young boy and something that I felt obligated to do. Because this country had given me and my family so much, in many ways, I felt it was my obligation to repay our nation through military service and a willingness to defend the country, should it ever become endangered. For four years, I was a member of ROTC at Claremont-McKenna College . . . , and then in 1993 I was commissioned as an officer at about the same time that "Don't Ask, Don't Tell" was first being implemented. I spent two and a half years at Fort Riley, Kansas, in the First Infantry Division and loved my job. I loved the opportunity that the army gave me to wear the uniform and lead American troops. I was proud to be part of the great institution of the U.S. Army. In 1995, for a number of reasons, I left, but the primary reason was simply I was tired of living a lie.

I left partially because "Don't Ask, Don't Tell" forced me out. I was no longer willing to live the immorality that it required me to live. I went on in life and decided that I could serve the public in another way, through the state legislature. In 1996 I ran for the state legislature as an openly gay Republican. Even though I lost the election that year, the newspapers and the media were rather interested to know about this creature called an openly gay Republican running for the Arizona state legislature. As a result, my sexual orientation became widely known. Since I had been out of the army for a year and a half, I thought it really did not matter. In 1998, I ran for public office again as an openly gay Republican, but I won that year.

After being sworn in the next year, I engaged one of my colleagues in a debate that became very high-profile. Karen Johnson, my colleague who represents an area of Mesa, Arizona, submitted legislation that would have prohibited counties and cities from offering domestic partnership benefits to their employees. . . . She is a Republican, as am I, so we had a lot in common. She is a . . . practicing Mormon, and I am a recovering Mormon. I tried to discuss this issue with her with some amount of logic, but I figured out it would not get me very far. I went up to the committee hearing at which she was testifying and was making a number of comments that I felt were untrue and were extremely hurtful toward gay and lesbian people. I went before the committee and said, "I know many of you expected me to sit quietly in my office, but I cannot sit quietly in my office when another member attacks my family and attempts to steal my freedom. And furthermore if this legislature intends to take my gay tax dollars, which work just as well as your straight tax dollars, then treat me fairly under the law." This concept, I must say, was revolutionary to Republicans in the Arizona state legislature. Gay people actually paid taxes, too! It surprised them that we did not exist in some twilight zone, but we were part of the community in which everyone lived and also paid taxes. Maybe this concept of the social compact, which we learn about in high school government classes from the Federalist Papers, should apply to gay people, too. This concept was revolutionary in 1999 in the state of Arizona.

I made these comments on February 3, and two days later a computer in the bowels of the Army Reserve Personnel Command building in St. Louis, Missouri, spit out a little piece of paper calling First Lieutenant Steve May back into the active reserves. Strange coincidence it was, and three weeks later, I received a notice in the mail, one of those little certified letters you get that includes a green postcard that requires you to go to the post office and pick up the letter. It said it was from the Army Reserve Personnel Command. Remember at that time the nation was preparing for a major ground conflict in Kosovo. My partner picked up the card and said, "Honey, I don't think you should go get this letter." My mother, who had also heard about it, called and said, "Maybe you don't want to go get that letter." But I said to them both, "That's not the honorable thing to do." I picked up the letter and found that indeed I was called back into an active reserve status. I thought I would have to resign my position in the legislature, leave my position at my company, and serve my country again in uniform. And, I believed that I very well might end up in Kosovo.

As you can imagine, I felt conflicted considering that there was a policy called "Don't Ask, Don't Tell." I was obviously openly gay on the front pages of the newspapers and had been for two and a half years. I had been out of the army for three and a half years and openly gay for two and a half years, and the army called me back into service. I reported for duty in April of 1999, half-thinking I would be kicked out within an hour. Instead of being kicked out, my commander called me into his office and said, "You are now the executive officer of this two-hundred-soldier transportation company, and here is what I want you to do." Okay. The reality was that many people in my unit knew exactly who I was, because my unit was based in my district. A month later, a weekly newsmagazine did a front-cover story with the headline, "Gay Right Wing Mormon Steve May is a Walking Talking Contradiction." I am gay, but I do not think I am right-wing. I am a recovering Mormon, but as you know, the liberal media does not really care about accuracy. Interestingly, the article was published the day before my next drill. You can imagine how I felt, when I got to drill. All my soldiers were passing this magazine out to each other and talking about it, and my supply sergeant came to me and said, "Hey sir, this looks like you! In fact, this guy spells his name just like you do." And I said, "Sergeant, let's go to the motor pool and get back to work." And we did.

Three months later, my battalion commander called me up to her office and said, "I want to talk to you about two things. First, will you take command of a detachment?" "Okay. What's the second thing ma'am?" "Second, we have to conduct an investigation into allegations of your homosexuality." She brought in the investigating officer and told me that she would conduct the investigation. I said, "Well, ma'am, my private life has been public record for three years, so this investigation should be very short."

Six months later, the army concluded in its one-hundred-page investigation that indeed I might be a homosexual. They should have asked my boyfriend, but they did not. On the day the report was completed, I was sent in for psychiatric and physical evaluations at the Veterans Administration hospital to make sure that I was mentally fit to be involuntarily separated. I met with a psychiatrist. I was okay with the physical evaluation part because I had maintained myself in relatively good health since leaving the military, but being a gay Republican I had a lot of concerns about passing the psychiatric evaluation. In fact, the psychiatrist knew exactly who I was, because he had read all the stories. The Arizona newspapers had followed the story rather closely, on the front page, no less. He said, "So, Lieutenant May, I understand that your homosexuality is the cause of all your problems." I said, "Actually, sir, the policy has caused me some discomfort, but otherwise I'm okay." He proceeded to do an hour-and-a-half-long interview, asking me a number of questions about my childhood and whether I had been molested or abused. At the end he gave me the copy of the report that he was submitting as part of my packet for involuntary separation, and as only the army can do, he checked the box that said I was mentally unremarkable. Now, that is a good thing in the army. He also found that I was mentally responsible for my actions, so I could not argue that I was homosexual by reason of insanity or anything else. For some reason they felt it necessary to anticipate and block that legal defense so that I could not use it.

This incident occurred in December of 1999, and in January I went back to my drill and continued my business through February and March, as well. In March I sent eighteen kids to Kosovo, and when I came home from getting them prepared, I received another letter in the mail. The army asked me to resign, and they said if I resigned all the problems would go away. They would not attempt to recoup any moneys they might have given me for college. In fact, they were so kind that they actually wrote my resignation letter for me. I called Servicemembers Legal Defense Network and asked if this was normal. They said that sometimes the military gives people the option to resign, but never before had they seen the army actually give someone a resignation letter that required only a signature. I decided I would not resign, because I felt that it would be inappropriate considering that when the army called me back into duty in February the year before, I was willing to give my life for my country. But because the army discovered that I was in love with a person of the same gender, my life was no longer worthy to give. I could not give the military the satisfaction of discharging me on that basis.

In April I went back to work, and in May I did it again and in June, as well. In July of 2000, I was made the acting commander for my annual training period. Me, the homosexual, who was undermining morale and cohesion. We had a terrific annual training period. In August, I served again, and in September I also served again. Almost a year and a half later, I continued to serve in my capacity as an officer in my army reserve unit. On September 16, of this year, I was finally brought to a separation hearing, where for twelve hours government attorneys maligned my character, fabricated lies, and created stories about my record of service, all of which were completely untrue. Throughout the hearing, it became clear that what upset them most was my perseverance in telling my story to the American public. They played tapes of my appearance on a variety of shows, including *Larry King* and *Good Morning America,* trying to prejudice the board and convince them that I was pursuing a personal political agenda and not being a loyal soldier to the U.S. Army. Never before that day had my loyalty or my conduct been questioned, nor my performance, leadership, sense of duty, or service. There I sat for twelve hours, while the government attorneys made up lies about my character simply because I had made a statement in the legislature that I was gay.

On that day I was ashamed that my country would treat one of its soldiers that way. I was ashamed for my army. I was ashamed for the fellow officers who would treat another officer in that way, which was completely unnecessary. We went into the hearing saying we stipulate to the facts and agree that I am gay. We agreed that I said that I am gay. But what we should discuss was whether or not I should have been discharged under the provisions of the "Don't Ask, Don't Tell" policy as written by Congress. But the government attorneys refused to stipulate to the facts. They said, "No, we want to prove that you are gay and that you said that you are gay." Only in the army. The next morning, we had the opportunity to present the evidence to the contrary. Within a matter of minutes, we responded to every one of their allegations. Then the board deliberated for an hour and voted to give me an honorable discharge. They felt they had no other option than to discharge me, but they felt that because of my eleven-year record of service, I deserved the honorable discharge.

But I did not think it was an acceptable resolution to the problem. My country had recalled me into service, and I went, because it was the honorable thing to do. Now they wanted to kick me out, and not because of my performance, but because of my speech? I appealed to my commanding general, who last month rejected my appeal. Currently, my appeal sits on the desk of the secretary of the army, who will make supposedly a final decision as to whether to accept the findings of the lower board or to overturn them. If he decides to accept the findings of the board, then I have the option of filing suit in civilian court, where we can advance the legal arguments we have not been able to advance before.[1]

In spite of this experience, my service in the army has been a wonderful experience on the whole. Serving as an openly gay man for nearly a year and a half has presented certain obstacles, but every time I come up to an obstacle I think back to when I was a second lieutenant at Fort Riley, Kansas. There I was a platoon leader for a chemical smoke company, and my first job was to integrate women into an all-male platoon. And I will tell you, it was not easy. Up until October of 1994, smoke platoons had been reserved for men only, because we fight. Well, we do not fight exactly, but we serve on the front lines with the forward armor and mechanized infantry units. I cannot emphasize how little the men wanted to integrate women into the platoon. Some of the women wanted to get in, because it was a prime spot for them. But none of the men wanted the women to come in, and I got calls from the men, and even from the men's wives, because they opposed women coming into the unit. Many people also argue that gays should not be allowed in the military, simply because of the opposition that individual members and military leadership feel.

But we have this little secret weapon in the military that we use to deal with these types of problems. It is called leadership. It is command leadership, and this leadership is what we learn in ROTC and at the service academies. We also have problems in the military. We have problems when we take people from disparate backgrounds and bring them together. We will always have problems. We continue to have racial problems today. Some soldiers do not want to follow the orders that a black commander gives them, or ones that a white commander gives them. We still have problems with gender relations in the military, and we still have race-based gangs. We still have violence in military units. In 1993 in my own barracks at my infantry unit, we had race-based killing. Such incidents happen, but it is the charge of military commanders and leaders to overcome these obstacles.

Some critics also have alleged that now is not the time to make a change in military policy about gays and lesbians, simply because we are not at war. Does that make sense? For some reason the cohesion argument is more applicable during times of peace, because we do not know what we are doing, have no common mission, or do not know who our enemy is. The reality is that missions for soldiers in the field, for soldiers at the battalion level and lower, have not changed. And it does not change between times of peace and war. The sense of who we are as a military might be muddled at the Pentagon level for those people who are planning our strategic front, but our mission at the company level remains the same. We train to fight, and whether we are shooting live rounds at a live enemy or shooting live rounds at a target down the range, our mission does not change. We do the same tasks and train the same.

To solve the problem of integrating women into my unit, I took everyone into the field. The more I could take my unit into the field, the more they were forced to work together and overcome adverse scenarios. The great change in acceptance for these new people I had brought into the unit occurred when I took them to the National Training Center in Barstow, California. For four weeks we lived in a field environment and effectively played war games. At the end of this time, our unit came out stronger than it was before. It was cohesive, and they were proud of what they had accomplished. They had overcome significant adversity in a terrible environment. We were stuck out in the desert for four weeks with no shower facilities or anything else, eating MREs twice a day, and the men and the women learned to respect each other.[2] That is leadership.

Where do we go from here? What should the policy be? I will have a chance to talk a little bit more on the panel, but let me leave you with this concept. When I spoke with Senator John McCain about this policy, he said that when he was in the Naval Academy about forty years ago, everybody knew there were gay people there and nobody cared. But for some reason he thinks that today these southern boys, eighteen and nineteen years old, care more than he or his peers did forty years ago. I do not think it is true. The policy that today we call "Don't Ask, Don't Tell, Don't Pursue" should become, "Everybody knows, nobody cares, so let's get back to work."

Of course there are those who say we will never convince military leadership that they should accept this change in policy. The reality is that military leadership will always oppose significant change. They have done so in the past and will continue to do so in the future. Those people who are in positions of leadership today have been told for twenty years or more that homosexuals are unfit for military service. They have been told this so often that whether or not it is true, they believe it and will not change. The American people will have to demand change, because they will recognize this policy is unfair and unjust. The arguments about military readiness are simply untrue. Perhaps most importantly, they will recognize this policy does not reflect the values of the American Founding Fathers and it conflicts with who we are as an American people, who pride themselves on equality and justice for all. Congress will change the law eventually, and although our military leaders will still object, they will have to do what those of us in the army have done for a long time, "suck it up and drive on." They will have an opportunity to salute smartly and say, "Yes, sir," or "I resign." As well, the civilian leadership will have to demand change from them, which they will, because the American public will require it. I will close by saying that what has frustrated the army with my case more than anything else is that I just will not sit down and shut up, because I believe I have an obligation to the American people to share my story with the public. I am not really fighting the policy. Some of you here are fighting the policy. The Servicemembers Legal Defense Network is fighting the policy. I am simply telling my story. But my story is so absurd that the policy is fighting itself. As long as people are willing to listen to my story, I will continue to tell it to the American public, and I will never surrender. . . .

Rob Nunn: I am a serving member of Her Majesty's Royal Navy. You cannot believe how much it means to me to be here this evening, and I would like to take you back in time and explain the circumstances as to why I am here.

I joined the navy in 1972, and was drafted to submarines very quickly after my basic training. Because the navy was short of manpower, I was part of one of the first groups of people to go directly to submarines. At that stage of my life, I was not aware of my sexuality. Joining the navy was the best thing I ever did and away I went with my career. I served on a couple of World War II submarines, which really does date me, and then I moved on to nuclear submarines, building a career over twenty years. In the eighteenth year of my career I came back after an extended time at sea, and I began to find out about my sexuality. I could not quite put my finger on it, but something was bothering me. I moved into the base and lived there for about two years, at which point I came out to my parents. I told them I was gay and waited for the thunderbolt to hit. But Dad said, "Well, you're our eldest son and we love you, as long as you're happy." I thought that was a good start.

Two years later, I received a phone call and was asked to report to the base, because they needed to talk to me. I went back to the base and was cautioned that I was being investigated for being gay, or homosexual—they did not know "gay" in those days. Because of my position at the time, which was chief petty officer coxswain, or chief of the boat on your submarines in U.S. terms, I was treated with kid gloves. Because part of my responsibility on board the submarines was discipline, I knew how they would handle me. I knew how the process worked and what the questions and restrictions were. They asked me if I would like to go to the police headquarters for the evening until the service police turned up to do my interview. So I sat and watched television and had a meal. Half past ten at night, I was taken back to my cabin and the service police searched through my personal belongings. They took away my diary, my Filofax, my photographs, and some letters. I was told that I could go until eight o'clock the following morning, at which time I had to be back to start my interview. The following morning I came back and went into an interview room with two service investigators, and we started. About eleven minutes into the interview, I mentioned I was gay.

Eleven hours and forty-something minutes later, over two days, the interview finished. I was asked forty-three specific questions about my sexuality and with whom I did what, questions that were very personal, very degrading, and very painful at times. I was then told to go away to Edinburgh and that I would be called when they needed to talk with me. Seventeen days later, I was thrown out of the navy. I had not been charged with anything, except for the mere fact that I was gay. My captain told me he could not afford to lose me, but his hands were tied. That was it, and there I was with twenty years of a career gone.

I then spent the next eight years trying to build a new career from scratch, at first earning nothing and then finally achieving a reasonable wage. Eventually I joined Rank Outsiders and moved on from there.[3] At the moment, I have a legal challenge under way for compensation, and part of the discussion in the legal case involved the question of whether I would return to military service if asked. I said, "Yes, of course I would," because it was my career before they took it away. I needed to get back, and I have never lost the urge to be back in the services. In January of this year, the lifting of the ban facilitated my return to service. . . .

In September, I went back into the navy, and upon my arrival at the establishment I kept thinking, what will happen, what will this be like? My main fear was my peers, the people who knew me eight years ago when I was thrown out. But I have been dumbstruck by the support and the overwhelming question of why the hell did it happen in the first place? Now that I am in a training establishment, there are women in my mess, which is quite different for a submariner. When I returned, I found out that one of my biggest supporters at the base when I was thrown out was a service policewoman, who was there at the moment when I was taken in for my discharge interview. She said she did not understand why it all happened, this comment coming from the people who actually enforce the law. Everyone else whom I knew or have met since I have returned say it is great to have me back. I have even received phone calls from people like this one guy who spent an hour on the phone with me from Scotland. I had met him twice about ten years ago, and he could not understand the fact that I had been thrown out in the first place. What was the point? That has been my reception. . . .

I went back in through the gates of our training establishment, and the first brief I was given stated that no sort of harassment, whether related to sexual orientation, gender, race, creed, or color, would be tolerated. Anybody who was found doing it would be thrown straight out of the navy.

And here I am. Forty-five years old. I am here with my partner. You have paid for me to come and talk to you. I am talking about gay rights.

I am in San Francisco. And I am a serving member of the Royal Navy. I could not be prouder at this moment.

NOTES

1. Shortly after the December 2000 delivery of these remarks, the U.S. Army terminated discharge proceedings against May in January 2001, thus allowing him to complete his full term of service.

2. "MREs" (meal, ready-to-eat) are military rations.

3. Rank Outsiders was a British activist group designed to support gay veterans and to pressure the British Ministry of Defence to lift the gay ban. Recently the group changed its name to the Armed Forces Lesbian and Gay Association.

8

What Have We Learned?
The Future of "Don't Ask, Don't Tell"

LAURA MILLER: TO BEGIN, WE SEEM TO HAVE A GREAT DEAL OF AGREEMENT on the fact that gays and lesbians have served in the military throughout American history, and the evidence tends to support this view. Today we have not questioned whether they can perform their job. The questions about harassment, gay bashing, and hate crimes are an issue, and there has been little agreement about how problematic these questions will be. Generally, we have agreed that some reckoning will have to take place with hostile attitudes of American military personnel, who are predominately male.

We first addressed the issue of privacy and tried to answer the question of whether the gay ban preserves privacy. The answer I heard suggests that on the one hand, no, nothing really preserves privacy in the military, but on the other hand some moderate adaptations could be made in peacetimes in the barracks. There is no reason why we could not have shower-curtain dividers or increase other aspects in the daily routine living environment that would help with recruitment, retention, and morale. In certain situations, the military could recognize that people actually like to have some privacy. But in the field we cannot guarantee privacy for anyone, straight men, women, or gays. There will always have to be some adaptations in those situations. Yet even in the field, people use field ponchos or dividers or go behind the tank instead of right next to everyone. People will find ways to accommodate their need for privacy where they can. Where they cannot, they adjust accordingly.

On the issue of cohesion, many of us seemed to accept the idea that task cohesion and social cohesion are two different animals. There is no evidence that task cohesion, the ability of units to perform their work, would fall apart if gays were to come out, and we also need to remember that the lifting of the ban would not necessarily guarantee that more gays would come out. But we still have dissent over the role of social cohesion and whether or not we can apply studies based in civilian workplaces like fire departments or other militaries to the U.S. military environment. We still have not reached consensus whether social cohesion matters more in the military than task cohesion, how it affects combat-effectiveness, or how important it might be in peacetime.

There is evidence that in some situations there will be some degree of social conflict when some gays come out. Again, even when people choose to come out to people who know them well and trust them, the problem remains that the out gay or lesbian service member still has to interact with new personnel who come to the unit and deal with people in other units. Rumor and gossip abound throughout the military, so it is difficult to know how these stories will be twisted and how people will find out about someone's orientation. Given the amount of conflict that already exists, based both in civilian society and on the negative attitudes of military personnel, there is evidence that social conflict will occur. What we do not know is to what degree negative attitudes will translate into negative behavior. In my opinion, of the large majority of military personnel who oppose gays in the military, the majority of them are not people who would pick up a baseball bat and beat people. A great deal of them base their ideas and attitudes about gays in the military or gays in general on stereotypical images from television or movies and not from direct experience with gay and lesbian people. Their negative attitudes may not necessarily translate into hostility toward gays, because they are based on abstract impressions that come from out-of-context situations about people they do not know. *Will and Grace* may offer some positive images, but it also presents some negative images as well. It is possible to use whichever image you want to adopt for a variety of purposes.

We have also raised the question of whether we should make policy based on military attitudes. For the most part, people have agreed that there is no precedent for doing so. Polling people and asking their opinions is not how you run a military. But the importance of polls, interviews, and attitudes involves finding out what kinds of issues will have to be dealt with if integration occurs. If the ban is lifted, we need to know what issues we will have to deal with, what we will have to educate people about, and what types of elements we should put in a code of conduct. It has more to do with learning about the type of people in the military and their responses to the issue, which I firmly believe you need to respect. I do not mean you have to agree with them or you have to like them, but you cannot dismiss them. We have plenty of evidence that there will be some problems, and we need to better predict what they will be and plan for them.

The question of timing is related, but there has been little agreement about this issue. On the one hand, it has been argued that right now is the best time to lift the ban. Because of the chaos and the many issues that we currently face, this issue will be just one of many, and rather than waiting until everything is straightened out and this problem becomes the one social issue that everyone latches onto, make the change now. By making the change during peacetime, we start the transition before a major conflict, so when wartime comes, people will have already adjusted to it and worked out the kinks in policies. On the other hand, we have argued that in wartime or combat, soldiers have to focus on an enemy and have to worry about living or dying, which will diminish the importance of other soldiers' sexual orientations. The added pressure would make wartime the best time to successfully integrate gays and lesbians into the military.

In spite of our disagreements, much of our focus today has been on implementation. Most of us presume that lifting the ban is inevitable. But perhaps we should ask whether a Bush presidency makes it seem less inevitable or if anyone believes there might be a rollback from "Don't Ask, Don't Tell" to make the policy even stricter, especially given the composition of Congress and the Supreme Court. We may want to discuss this question further and examine how we have been operating under the presumption of the inevitability of the ban being lifted. Is it inevitable?

But this point is where the foreign military example comes into play. If people want to use the foreign-military example, then they will. If they do not they can dismiss it as irrelevant. But when we think about planning and preparing for implementation, the lessons from other militaries seem to emphasize education against stereotypical views and attitudes and they may have something to say about exactly how the policy should be implemented. Other militaries' experiences show us to some degree how to codify what behaviors should or should not be accepted or what kinds of jokes should or should not be considered offensive. We will need to find a balance between discretion and codifying everything. When discretion is allowed, then people are allowed to take into account individual circumstances, the record of the person, and the spirit in which a joke was meant, which allows for a lot of fairness. But one problem with discretion is that it does allow for discrimination, which also applies to other minorities, like the promotion of women. If we allow for discretion, then we can make sensible decisions, but this discretion can also allow people to discriminate unfairly. A commander could say that by coming out, a service member would be engaging in behavior that is detrimental to his unit and cite the disclosure of sexual orientation as a violation of the code of conduct. But if everything is codified, a ridiculous adherence to standards is created. People can become too exact and say this issue was not in the code. But again, too much discretion raises the possibility of using discretion for discrimination.

We also discussed the point of a behavior code. One possible course of action could be for us to lobby against harassment, bullying, and other forms of behaviors that are allowed currently and used against women. The current problems that women in the military face are excellent examples of what we might face. They demonstrate how people can undermine leaders or policies or how military leaders can undermine civilian directives. This issue offers us many lessons, and addressing them could lay the foundation for integrating open gays. Advice-lines are also important. They have proven to be so for women dealing with sexual harassment. They allow more choices than keeping it to yourself and saying nothing or having a formal complaint, going to the media, and making a federal case of it. Especially if we were to allow for more discretion, we need advice-lines so people can find out the best way to work out this new ground.

One of the problems that we face in the military is that when military personnel talk to chaplains, doctors, psychiatrists, or even lawyers, they do not have the same kind of client privileges that civilians do. A commander can call up and ask for a service member's psychological records, and the doctor has to share them and even disclose what he or she has said in a session. The same is true with chaplains. Anything can be disclosed. Obviously, this issue is very problematic for gay and lesbian service members. Mady Segal might have a comment on this issue.

To return to the larger question of the ban, we have to make clear that lifting the ban is not the same thing as people coming out of the closet. The lessons from foreign militaries and civilian organizations suggest that people out themselves in environments in which they feel that it is safe to do so, so there is no reason to think that lifting the ban will result in mass outings. But people will continue to come out, and even if it is only a small percent of people who are bashed, ostracized, held back in their career, or beat to death, any number is too many. We should take the opinions of military personnel seriously, not to decide policy but to understand their fears, beliefs, and understandings about what it means to be gay or what it means to be openly gay. This understanding is crucial and will be key to carrying out successful integration on the ground, a successful integration that does not just look good on paper or to a politician, but one that will actually work and protect lives.

From my research, I can absolutely affirm that winning over military leaders will be an essential part in the success of the implementation of the policy, but to win them over, we will need to stress the cost to the military of training and personnel. The costs are much more convincing. They will not get behind the arguments of civil rights. Even though much of the population is behind lifting the gay ban on the basis of civil rights and opposition to discrimination, military personnel regularly give up rights and privileges. They are taught repeatedly that the army's needs come before the birth of children or family wishes. Even the highest-ranking officers give up some of their personal rights and privileges. In the case of minorities and women, we have seen that people are integrated when the military thinks it can fill a need or when these new groups can serve a purpose. The problem of retaining quality personnel will also become a compelling argument, which has already worked to a great degree. Not only does the military need bodies, but it is also having a hard time getting skilled bodies. In terms of winning over military personnel and getting the type of backing to make the real-life integration work, we will have to talk to them in their language and convince them that integration actually makes sense. . . .

Lynn Eden: Aaron Belkin ended the last session by suggesting critical areas of research. Mike Desch raised a comment during the last session about the comparative rate of violence in the military and civilian spheres and what should follow logically. If people have other suggestions about important areas of research, not only in terms of implementation, but also in terms of determining who is right and who is wrong on this whole issue, then please comment. . . .

Robert MacCoun: Anyone who does compare the rates of antigay violence in the military and civilian sectors should take into account the base rate percentage of gays in the military compared to the base rate percentage of gays in the civilian sector. In other words, we do not know how many gays there are in the military, and if you do not know the base rates, then it is difficult to compare the rates of violence in the military and civilian sectors. I also want to clarify two points. The first is a comment from Laura Miller a moment ago, which made me worry that I might have been misinterpreted. Earlier I made a comment about the sheer rarity of the phenomenon of violence that follows coming out of the closet. I hope everyone understands I was not trivializing the actual incidents themselves, which can be extremely serious for the individual targets of any violence. My point was only in terms of the military's ability to carry out its mission. And the second point I want to clarify relates to a common misunderstanding of the cohesion chapter in the RAND research. Those conclusions were not drawn solely from civilian research. The military's own research fails to link social cohesion to performance. In fact, cohesion and performance are correlated more weakly in military studies than in sports studies. . . .

Mady Segal: In terms of the research that should be done, I would like to express a few cautions about the way questions are asked and how they are interpreted. Especially when you are trying to find evidence of incidents of violence and this statistic of the proportion of people who have witnessed certain behavior, there is no way to extrapolate from that information how many incidents actually have occurred. When Charlie Moskos examined the proportion of soldiers in the Persian Gulf who knew of sexual relations in their unit, it was an extraordinarily high percentage of people. But it could have been one highly visible publicized case, so questions have to be very carefully worded. I do not think that the Pentagon study that Aaron mentioned asked respondents if they witnessed a beating, but only if they knew about one. Is that right? At any rate, you cannot establish how many incidents have occurred on the basis of how many people know about it or witnessed it, because you do not know how many people were there or what their interpretations of these questions were. What it means to witness could be quite different. They might have seen some footage on television or read about it in a newspaper, which makes them a witness to it. The questions that you want to address have to be very carefully controlled for. I do not have a grand scheme about what should be asked, but the questions should be subjected to strict scrutiny. . . .

Dixon Osburn: First, Laura Miller identified two views on the privacy issue. Some people argue that the gay ban may protect privacy, others that it may not. I would like to interject a third view, which is that the discussion about privacy itself might be a ruse that is based on this irrational fear that gay men in showers will leer and engage in misconduct. This issue could be a red herring, as opposed to one that has to be addressed in terms of putting up partitions. Second, in her conclusion, Laura Miller mentioned that people perceive there will be problems when gay people come out, once the ban is lifted. I would like to just suggest that this argument puts the onus on gay people as opposed to recognizing that there may be some people out there who will engage in misconduct when somebody does come out to them. It is that misconduct we have to be able to target, not the people who actually are coming out. Third, I definitely appreciate the comment on readiness, which is how we look at this issue. We think that "Don't Ask, Don't Tell" does hurt readiness. And fourth, you invited comments on the timing of the lifting of the ban. We do see it as inevitable that policy will be over-turned, but we think it will be within five to ten years, not within the next administration. Ultimately, it will be up to Congress to overturn this policy. It will not matter who is president or commander in chief. It will be up to Congress, which will have to lead the effort to repeal it, and the Congress that will be starting in January is not there.

Miller: Do you have members of Congress working with you now?

Osburn: Yes, at least in terms of communicating with them about what is happening. No one on either side is ready to move or do anything. There would have to be a completely different mix of folks and a bipar-tisan approach to finally get this policy overturned. There may be a pres-ident at that time who will show support for it or may receive it and not object to it, but I still see it as at least five years if not a decade away.

Eden: I see heads nodding when you say it will be members of Con-gress. Is that how women were included in the military to the extent that they have been? What about the racial integration of the military? Was it through congressional act? . . .

M. Segal: Some of the changes with regard to women have come through Congress, especially when situations have developed that they could respond to. In 1948 Congress passed a ban on women flying com-bat missions and serving permanently on combat ships, but pressure from certain members of Congress and advocates for women in the mil-itary led to a repeal of the prohibition after the Persian Gulf war. Cur-rently, Congress is more conservative than the military services on women's role in the armed forces. For example, the military is not responsible for the push toward segregating basic training. Rather, Con-gress is trying to force the services to move backward from where they are. This shift is unusual.

I started studying women in the military in 1973, and looking back at the history, one idea I do have on research would be to take a look at the conditions under which there is successful integration in a unit of openly gay and lesbian members in the unit. We would want to examine both those units in which the gay members are already a part of the unit and respected and then come out, as well as those gay members who join a unit and are already openly gay. A study could look at the condi-tions under which there is successful integration and when there is not.

My hypothesis would be that leadership role modeling and what leaders actually communicate to the members of the unit would have a tremendous impact on whether it was successful. . . .

Lawrence Korb: I agree that military effectiveness is important to consider. A very reasonable military officer once said the military cannot go through all this social change, because it does not think it would pay off in terms of numbers. If someone knew the numbers, then that might lead somewhere. With women we know they are 50 percent of the population, and African Americans are 15 percent. Somehow we have got to get that data on gays and lesbians. We also need data on the U.S. military. There have been people who have come out and stayed in the unit. These units could be studied, as well as those people who were kept in through the courts. I would look there rather than foreign militaries. . . .

Paul Gade: If we look at attitudes and opinions of military service members, then one of the things that we should consider is how important this issue is in relation to others that military personnel are dealing with. I would guess that it is rather far down on the list. There are many issues about military service that bother them much more than this one. It would be useful for us to know the relative position of these issues, so we can get an index of the importance of those issues for members. . . .

Timothy Haggerty: I wanted to suggest an idea for research. We might try and break out people's attitudes by their age and where they are in their service careers. We should see if this issue is a problem anymore for younger service members, or if it is an issue for older leadership. I think it would be a relatively easy way to get information about what might happen in ten or fifteen years, if you are looking at a long process.

Michael Desch: Some of that data might be available in the Feaver-Kohn TISS [Triangle Institute for Security Studies] Project, which asks one question about attitudes about the gay ban and has all sorts of demographic information including military status.[1] . . .

Jay Williams: It is essential to know more about what is happening inside the military. Such research is not meant to validate people's contrary opinions; we simply have to know what they think and why. One factor to consider is generational change, and Leonard Wong did an interesting study on Xers versus boomers in the officer corps, which I recommend.[2] Second, do not underestimate the resistance of the military to being studied by people they consider outsiders. Only the army and the Coast Guard fully cooperated with this Triangle Institute study and the Center for Strategic and International Studies [CSIS]. It is hard to imagine a friendlier group than CSIS to study the military. A military service chief allegedly said, "If you want to know about my service culture, ask me. Don't survey my people." This attitude means it will require political courage and outside direction to see that these studies do in fact occur and are taken seriously. . . .

Nathaniel Frank[3]: I share an appreciation of the scholarly debate, and I learned a lot from it, but I almost get the sense that the discussion has been largely about implementation. Of course, I will be very pleased when we can really have that discussion in earnest, but I am still left a little fuzzy as to whether the rationale for the gay ban is based on evidence. It may be unfair to ask for a consensus, but do the scholars in the room, especially the ones who are more resistant to overturning the policy, feel that the rationale is based on evidence? Laura Miller mentioned that there is at least some consensus that there is evidence that there would be some conflict if the ban were overturned. It seems to me there is much more evidence that military effectiveness would not be harmed. Is it fair of me to ask for that kind of consensus? Could some of those scholars speak to this question?

Miller: The data suggest that the number of people who would come out would do it so slowly that it would be more of a unit-level problem rather than an issue that would unhinge the military's ability to fight and win wars. It would not be a large-scale problem that would jeopardize our abilities. It would be more likely that unit-level commanders would have to deal with the problem.

Williams: The answer is somewhere in the middle. Lifting the ban will not be as horrendous as the opponents believe, and it will not be as problem-free as the proponents hope. You can do it smart, or you can do it stupid. If you do studies, then you do it smart.

NOTES

1. See Peter Feaver and Richard Kohn, *Soldiers and Civilians: The U.S. Military, American Society, and National Security* (Cambridge, Mass.: BCSIA-MIT Press, 2001).

2. See L. Wong, *Generations Apart: Xers and Boomers in the Officer Corps* (Carlisle Barracks, Pa.: Strategic Studies Institute, U.S. Army War College, 2000).

3. Nathaniel Frank is senior research fellow at the Center for the Study of Sexual Minorities in the Military.

Appendix:
The "Don't Ask, Don't Tell" Law

107 STAT 1671, PUBLIC LAW 103-160–NOV. 30, 1993
SUBTITLE G—OTHER MATTERS

SEC. 571. POLICY CONCERNING HOMOSEXUALITY IN THE ARMED FORCES.

(a) CODIFICATION.—(1) Chapter 37 of title 10, United States Code, is amended by adding at the end the following new section:
"Sec. 654. Policy concerning homosexuality in the armed forces

"(a) FINDINGS.—Congress makes the following findings:

"(1) Section 8 of article I of the Constitution of the United States commits exclusively to the Congress the powers to raise and support armies, provide and maintain a Navy, and make rules for the government and regulation of the land and naval forces.

"(2) There is no constitutional right to serve in the armed forces.

"(3) Pursuant to the powers conferred by section 8 of article I of the Constitution of the United States, it lies within the discretion of the Congress to establish qualifications for and conditions of service in the armed forces.

"(4) The primary purpose of the armed forces is to prepare for and to prevail in combat should the need arise.

"(5) The conduct of military operations requires members of the armed forces to make extraordinary sacrifices, including the ultimate sacrifice, in order to provide for the common defense.

"(6) Success in combat requires military units that are characterized by high morale, good order and discipline, and unit cohesion.

"(7) One of the most critical elements in combat capability is unit cohesion, that is, the bonds of trust among individual service members that make the combat effectiveness of a military unit greater than the sum of the combat effectiveness of the individual unit members.

"(8) Military life is fundamentally different from civilian life in that

"(A) the extraordinary responsibilities of the armed forces, the unique conditions of military service, and the critical role of unit cohesion, require that the military community, while subject to civilian control, exist as a specialized society; and

"(B) the military society is characterized by its own laws, rules, customs, and traditions, including numerous restrictions on personal behavior, that would not be acceptable in civilian society.

"(9) The standards of conduct for members of the armed forces regulate a member's life for 24 hours each day beginning at the moment the member enters military status and not ending until that person is discharged or otherwise separated from the armed forces.

"(10) Those standards of conduct, including the Uniform Code of Military Justice, apply to a member of the armed forces at all times that the member has a military status, whether the member is on base or off base, and whether the member is on duty or off duty.

"(11) The pervasive application of the standards of conduct is necessary because members of the armed forces must be ready at all times for worldwide deployment to a combat environment.

"(12) The worldwide deployment of United States military forces, the international responsibilities of the United States, and the potential for involvement of the armed forces in actual combat routinely make it necessary for members of the armed forces involuntarily to accept living conditions and working conditions that are often spartan, primitive, and characterized by forced intimacy with little or no privacy.

"(13) The prohibition against homosexual conduct is a longstanding element of military law that continues to be necessary in the unique circumstances of military service.

"(14) The armed forces must maintain personnel policies that exclude persons whose presence in the armed forces would create an unacceptable risk to the armed forces' high standards of morale, good order and discipline, and unit cohesion that are the essence of military capability.

"(15) The presence in the armed forces of persons who demonstrate a propensity or intent to engage in homosexual acts would create an unacceptable risk to the high standards of morale, good order and discipline, and unit cohesion that are the essence of military capability.

"(b) POLICY.—A member of the armed forces shall be separated from the armed forces under regulations prescribed by the Secretary of Defense if one or more of the following findings is made and approved in accordance with procedures set forth in such regulations:

"(1) That the member has engaged in, attempted to engage in, or solicited another to engage in a homosexual act or acts unless there are further findings, made and approved in accordance with procedures set forth in such regulations, that the member has demonstrated that—

"(A) such conduct is a departure from the member's usual and customary behavior;

"(B) such conduct, under all the circumstances, is unlikely to recur;

"(C) such conduct was not accomplished by use of force, coercion, or intimidation;

"(D) under the particular circumstances of the case, the member's continued presence in the armed forces is consistent with the interests of the armed forces in proper discipline, good order, and morale; and

"(E) the member does not have a propensity or intent to engage in homosexual acts.

"(2) That the member has stated that he or she is a homosexual or bisexual, or words to that effect, unless there is a further finding, made and approved in accordance with procedures set forth in the regulations, that the member has demonstrated that he or she is not a person who engages in, attempts to engage in, has a propensity to engage in, or intends to engage in homosexual acts.

"(3) That the member has married or attempted to marry a person known to be of the same biological sex.

"(c) ENTRY STANDARDS AND DOCUMENTS.—(1) The Secretary of Defense shall ensure that the standards for enlistment and appointment of members of the armed forces reflect the policies set forth in subsection (b).

"(2) The documents used to effectuate the enlistment or appointment of a person as a member of the armed forces shall set forth the provisions of subsection (b).

"(d) REQUIRED BRIEFINGS.—The briefings that members of the armed forces receive upon entry into the armed forces and periodically thereafter under section 937 of this title (article 137 of the Uniform Code of Military Justice) shall include a detailed explanation of the applicable laws and regulations governing sexual conduct by members of the armed forces, including the policies prescribed under subsection (b).

"(e) RULE OF CONSTRUCTION.—Nothing in subsection (b) shall be construed to require that a member of the armed forces be processed for separation from the armed forces when a determination is made in accordance with regulations prescribed by the Secretary of Defense that—

"(1) the member engaged in conduct or made statements for the purpose of avoiding or terminating military service; and

"(2) separation of the member would not be in the best interest of the armed forces.

"(f) DEFINITIONS.—In this section:

"(1) The term 'homosexual' means a person, regardless of sex, who engages in, attempts to engage in, has a propensity to engage in, or intends to engage in homosexual acts, and includes the terms 'gay' and 'lesbian'.

"(2) The term 'bisexual' means a person who engages in, attempts to engage in, has a propensity to engage in, or intends to engage in homosexual and heterosexual acts.

"(3) The term 'homosexual act' means—

"(A) any bodily contact, actively undertaken or passively permitted, between members of the same sex for the purpose of satisfying sexual desires; and

"(B) any bodily contact which a reasonable person would understand to demonstrate a propensity or intent to engage in an act described in subparagraph (A)."

(2) The table of sections at the beginning of such chapter is amended by adding at the end the following:

"664. Policy concerning homosexuality in the armed forces."

(b) REGULATIONS.—Not later than 90 days after the date of enactment of this Act, the Secretary of Defense shall revise Department of Defense regulations, and issue such new regulations as may be necessary to implement section 654 of title 10, United States Code, as added by subsection (a).

(c) SAVINGS PROVISION.—Nothing in this section or section 654 of title 10, United States Code, as added by subsection (a), may be construed to invalidate any inquiry, investigation, administrative action or proceeding, court-martial, or judicial proceeding conducted before the effective date of regulations issued by the Secretary of Defense to implement such section 654.

(d) SENSE OF CONGRESS.—It is the sense of Congress that—

(1) the suspension of questioning concerning homosexuality as a part of the processing of individuals for accession into the Armed Forces under the interim policy of January 29, 1993, should be continued, but the Secretary of Defense may reinstate that questioning with such questions or such revised questions as he considers appropriate if the Secretary determines that it is necessary to do so in order to effectuate the policy set forth in section 654 of title 10, United States Code, as added by subsection (a); and

(2) the Secretary of Defense should consider issuing guidance governing the circumstances under which members of the Armed Forces questioned about homosexuality for administrative purposes should be afforded warnings similar to the warnings under section 831(b) of title 10, United States Code (article 31[b] of the Uniform Code of Military Justice).

Selected Bibliography

Belkin, A. (2002). "Breaking Rank: Military Homophobia and the Production of Queer Practices and Identities." *Georgetown Journal of Gender and the Law* 3, no. 1: 83–106.

———— (2000). "Gays and Lesbians in the Military." In *Oxford Companion to American Military History*. New York, N.Y.: Oxford University Press.

Belkin, A., and J. McNichol (2001). "Homosexual Personnel Policy of the Canadian Forces: Did Lifting the Gay Ban Undermine Military Performance?" *International Journal* 56, no. 1: 73–88.

———— (2002). "Pink and Blue: Outcomes Associated with the Integration of Open Gay and Lesbian Personnel in the San Diego Police Department." *Police Quarterly* 5, no. 1: 63–95.

Belkin, A., and M. Levitt (2001). "Homosexuality and the Israel Defense Forces: Did Lifting the Gay Ban Undermine Military Performance?" *Armed Forces and Society* 27, no. 4: 541–566.

Benecke, M., and K. Dodge (1990). "Military Women in Nontraditional Job Fields: Casualties of the Armed Forces' War on Homosexuals." *Harvard Women's Law Journal* 13: 215–250.

Bérubé, A. (1990). *Coming out Under Fire: The History of Gay Men and Women in World War Two*. New York, N.Y.: The Free Press.

Bérubé , A., and J. D'Emilio (1984). "The Military and Lesbians During the McCarthy Years." *Signs* 9, no. 4: 759–775.

Britton, D. M., and C. L.Williams (1995). "'Don't Ask, Don't Tell, Don't Pursue': Military Policy and the Construction of Heterosexual Masculinity." *Journal of Homosexuality* 30, no. 1: 1–21.

Bronski, M. (1995). "Identity, Behavior, and the Military." *GLQ* 2, no. 2: 307–317.

Burg, B. R. (1984). *Sodomy and the Pirate Tradition*. New York, N.Y.: New York University Press.

Burrelli, D. F. (1993). *Homosexuals and U.S. Military Policy*. Washington, D.C.: Congressional Research Service.

Butler, J. (1997). *Excitable Speech: A Politics of the Performative*. New York, N.Y.: Routledge.

Cameron, C. (1994). *American Samurai: Myth, Imagination, and the Conduct of Battle in the First Marine Division, 1941–1951*. Cambridge, U.K.: Cambridge University Press.

Cammermeyer, M. (1994). *Serving in Silence*. New York, N.Y.: Viking.

Carey, J. J. (1993). *The Christian Argument for Gays and Lesbians in the Military: Essays by Mainline Church Leaders*. Lewiston, N.Y.: Mellen University Press.

Carpenter, C. T., and E. H. Yeatts (1996). *Stars Without Garters: The Memoirs of Two Gay GIs in WWII*. San Francisco, Calif.: Alamo Square Press.

Chauncey, G., Jr. (1985). "Christian Brotherhood or Sexual Perversion? Homosexual Identity and the Construction of Sexual Boundaries in the World War One Era." *Journal of Social History* 19, no. 2: 189–211.

Davis, J. S. (1991). "Military Policy Toward Homosexuals: Scientific, Historical and Legal Perspectives." *Military Law Review* 131: 55–108.

De Hart, J. S. (1999). "Containment at Home: Gender, Sexuality, and National Identity in Cold War America." In *The Cold War and American Culture*. Eds. J. B. Gilbert and P. J. Kuznick. Washington, D.C.: Smithsonian Institution Press.

D'Emilio, J. (1983). *Sexual Politics, Sexual Communities: The Making of a Homosexual Minority in the United States, 1940–1970*. Chicago, Ill.: University of Chicago Press.

Dyer, K. (ed.) (1990). *Gays in Uniform: The Pentagon's Secret Reports*. Boston, Mass.: Alyson Publications.

Faderman, L. (1991). *Odd Girls and Twilight Lovers: A History of Lesbian Life in Twentieth-Century America*. New York, N.Y.: Columbia University Press.

Flynn, T. (1995). "Of Communism, Treason and Addiction: An Evaluation of Novel Challenges to the Military's Anti-Gay Policy." *Iowa Law Review* 80, no. 5: 979–1047.

Gibson, E. L. (1978). *Get off My Ship: Ensign Berg vs. the U.S. Navy*. New York, N.Y.: Avon Books.

Gilbert, A. N. (1976). "Buggery and the British Navy, 1700–1861." *Journal of Social History* 10, no. 1: 72–98.

Hall, R. (1993). *Patriots in Disguise: Women Warriors of the Civil War*. New York, N.Y.: Marlowe & Company.

Halley, J. (1996). "The Status/Conduct Distinction in the 1993 Revisions to Military Anti-Gay Policy." *GLQ* 3, nos. 2–3: 159–252.

Harris, S. (1989–1990). "Permitting Prejudice to Govern: Equal Protection, Military Deference, and the Exclusion of Lesbians and Gay Men from the Military." *New York University Review of Law and Social Change* 17, no. 1: 171–223.

Herbert, M. S. (1998). *Camouflage Isn't Only for Combat: Gender, Sexuality and Women in the Military*. New York, N.Y.: New York University Press.

Herek, G. M., J. B. Jobe, and R. M. Carney (eds.) (1996). *Out in Force: Sexual Orientation in the U.S. Military*. Chicago, Ill.: University of Chicago Press.

Hippler, M. (1989). *Matlovich: The Good Soldier*. Boston, Mass.: Alyson Publications.

Holobaugh, J. (1993). *Torn Allegiances: The Story of a Gay Cadet*. Boston, Mass.: Alyson Publications.

Hull, I. (1996). *Sexuality, State, and Civil Society in Germany, 1700–1815*. Ithaca, N.Y.: Cornell University Press.

Humphrey, M. A. (1990). *My Country, My Right to Serve: Experiences of Gay Men and Women in the Military, World War II to the Present*. New York, N.Y.: HarperCollins.

Jackson, D. (1993). *Honorable Discharge: Memoirs of an Army Dyke*. San Francisco, Calif.: The Christie & Stefin Company.

Kaplan, D. (1999). *David, Jonathan and Other Soldiers: Identity, Masculinity and Sexuality in Combat Units in the Israeli Army*. Tel Aviv, Israel: HaKibbutz HaMeuchad Press.

Kavanagh, K. (1995). "Don't Ask, Don't Tell: Deception Required, Disclosure Denied." *Psychology, Public Policy, and Law* 1, no. 1: 142–160.

Kier, E. (1998). "Homosexuals in the U.S. Military: Open Integration and Combat Effectiveness." *International Security* 23, no. 2: 5–39.

Lane, A. (1994). "Black Bodies/Gay Bodies: The Politics of Race in the Gay/Military Battle." *Callaloo* 17, no. 4: 1074–1088.

Lowry, T. P. (1994). *The Story the Soldiers Wouldn't Tell: Sex in the Civil War*. Mechanicsburg, Pa.: Stackpole Books.

Mazur, D. (1996). "The Unknown Soldier: A Critique of 'Gays in the Military' Scholarship and Litigation." *University of California, Davis Law Review* 29, no. 2: 223–281.

Meyer, L. D. (1996). *Creating GI Jane: Sexuality and Power in the Women's Army Corps During World War II*. New York, N.Y.: Columbia University Press.

Miller, L., and J. A. Williams (2001). "Do Military Policies on Gender and Sexuality Undermine Combat Effectiveness?" In *Soldiers and Civilians: The Civil Military Gap and American National Security*. Eds. Peter D. Feaver and Richard H. Kohn (Cambridge, Mass.: MIT Press), pp. 386–429.

Moskos, C. C. (1993). "From Citizens' Army to Social Laboratory." *Wilson Quarterly* 17, no. 1: 83–94.

Murphy, L. R. (1988). *Perverts by Official Order: The Campaign Against Homosexuals by the United States Navy*. New York, N.Y.: Harrington Park Press.

National Defense Research Institute (1993). *Sexual Orientation and U.S. Military Personnel Policy: Options and Assessment* (MR-323-OSD). Santa Monica, Calif.: RAND.

Osburn, C. D. (1995). "A Policy in Desperate Search of a Rationale: The Military's Policy on Lesbians, Gays, and Bisexuals." *University of Missouri–Kansas City Law Review* 64, no. 1: 199–236.

Pond, F. (1993). "A Comparative Survey and Analysis of Military Policies with Regard to Service by Gay Persons." In *Policy Concerning Homosexuality in the Armed Forces, Hearing Held by Senate Armed Services Committee*. 103d Congress, 2d session. Washington, D.C.: U.S. Government Printing Office.

Ray, R. D. (1993). *Military Necessity and Homosexuality*. Washington, D.C.: Brassey's.

Rimmerman, C. A. (ed.) (1996). *Gay Rights, Military Wrongs: Political Perspectives on Lesbians and Gays in the Military*. New York, N.Y.: Garland Publishing.

Schneider, J. (1997). "Militarism, Masculinity and Male Sexuality in Germany 1890–1914." Ph.D. dissertation, Department of German Studies, Cornell University, Ithaca, N.Y.

Scott, W. J., and S. C. Stanley (eds.) (1994). *Gays and Lesbians in the Military: Issues, Concerns, and Contrasts.* New York, N.Y.: Aldine de Gruyter.

Shawer, L. (1995). *And the Flag Was Still There: Straight People, Gay People, and Sexuality in the U.S. Military.* New York, N.Y.: Harrington Park Press.

Shilts, R. (1993). *Conduct Unbecoming: Gays and Lesbians in the U.S. Military.* New York, N.Y.: Fawcett Columbine.

Steffan, J. (1992). *Honor Bound: A Gay Naval Midshipman Fights to Serve His Country.* New York, N.Y.: Avon.

Stiehm, J. H. (1992). "Managing the Military's Homosexual Exclusion Policy: Text and Subtext." *University of Miami Law Review* 46, no. 3: 685.

Tatchell, P. (1995). *We Don't Want to March Straight: Masculinity, Queers, and the Military.* London, U.K.: Cassell.

Theweleit, K. (1987). *Male Fantasies: Women, Floods, Bodies, History.* Vol. 1. Minneapolis, Minn.: University of Minnesota Press.

——— (1989). *Male Fantasies, Male Bodies: Psychoanalyzing the White Terror.* Vol. 2. Minneapolis, Minn.: University of Minnesota Press.

Thomas, K. (1993). "Shower/Closet." *Assemblage* 20: 80–81.

Vaid, U. (1995). "The Mainstream Response: Don't Ask, Don't Tell." In *Virtual Equality.* Ed. U. Vaid. New York, N.Y.: Anchor Books.

Valdes, F. (1994). "Sexual Minorities in the Military: Charting the Constitutional Frontiers of Status and Conduct." *Creighton Law Review* 27, no. 2: 384–475.

Webber, W. S. (1993). *Lesbians in the Military Speak Out.* Northboro, Mass.: Madwoman Press.

Weber, R. (1997). "Manufacturing Gender in Commercial and Military Cockpit Design." *Science, Technology, and Human Values* 22, no. 2: 235–253.

Wheelwright, J. (1989). *Amazons and Military Maids: Women Who Dressed as Men in Pursuit of Life, Liberty, and Happiness.* London, U.K.: Pandora Press.

Williams, C. J., and M. S. Weinberg (1971). *Homosexuals and the Military: A Study of Less Than Honorable Discharge.* New York, N.Y.: Harper & Row.

Williams, K. (1994). "Gays in the Military: The Legal Issues." *University of San Francisco Law Review* 28, no. 4: 919–955.

Wolf, M. *Another American: Asking & Telling.* (Unpublished play).

Wolinsky, M., and K. Sherrill (eds.) (1993). *Gays and the Military: Joseph Steffan Versus the United States.* Princeton, N.J.: Princeton University Press.

Zeeland, S. (1993). *Barrack Buddies and Soldier Lovers: Dialogues with Gay Young Men in the U.S. Military.* New York, N.Y.: Harrington Park Press.

——— (1995). *Sailors and Sexual Identity: Crossing the Line Between "Straight" and "Gay" in the U.S. Navy.* New York, N.Y.: Harrington Park Press.

——— (1996). *The Masculine Marine: Homoeroticism in the U.S. Marine Corps.* New York, N.Y.: Harrington Park Press.

Zuniga, J. (1994). *Soldier of the Year: The Story of a Gay American Patriot.* New York, N.Y.: Pocket Books.

The Contributors

Geoffrey Bateman is assistant director of the Center for the Study of Sexual Minorities in the Military. He is currently working on a study of the impact of openly gay and lesbian service personnel on U.S. service members in multinational forces.

Aaron Belkin is director of the Center for the Study of Sexual Minorities in the Military and assistant professor of political science at the University of California, Santa Barbara. He is author and coauthor of studies of gays and lesbians in foreign militaries and coeditor of *Counterfactual Thought Experiments in World Politics* (Princeton University Press, 1996).

Christopher Dandeker is professor of military sociology in the Department of War Studies at King's College, London, and has written widely on the theme of armed forces and society, as well as on social and political theory. His publications include (with T. Johnson and C. Ashworth) *The Structure of Social Theory* (Macmillan, 1984), *Surveillance Power and Modernity* (Polity, 1990), and (as editor) *Nationalism and Violence* (Transaction, 1998). Recently, he has published "The United Kingdom: The Overstretched Military" in *The Postmodern Military* (Oxford, 2000). Currently, his research concerns strategic personnel policy and the evolution of military culture. A fellow of the Inter-University Seminar on Armed Forces and Society (IUS), he is also a member of its council and an associate editor of *Armed Forces and Society*.

Michael C. Desch is associate professor and associate director of the Patterson School of Diplomacy and International Commerce at the University of Kentucky. He is the author of *When the Third World Matters:*

Latin American and U.S. Grand Strategy (Johns Hopkins University Press, 1993), *Civilian Control of the Military: The Changing Security Environment* (Johns Hopkins University Press, 1999), and editor of *From Pirates to Drug Lords: The Post Cold-War Caribbean Security Environment* (Albany State University Press, 1998). He has also published numerous scholarly articles in journals such as *International Security*, *Armed Forces and Society,* and the *Journal of Strategic Studies.*

Lynn Eden is senior research scholar at the Center for International Security and Cooperation at Stanford University and has published two books on life in small-town America. In the field of international relations, she has written on U.S. foreign and military policy, arms control, organizational issues, and the social construction of science and technology. Her publications include "The End of Superpower Nuclear Arms Control" in *Security Without Nuclear Weapons? Different Perspectives on Non-Nuclear Security,* edited by Regina Cowen Karp (Oxford University Press, 1992); and "The End of Cold-War History? A Review Essay" in *International Security* (summer 1993). She is also coeditor of *Nuclear Arguments: Understanding the Strategic Nuclear Arms and Arms Control Debates* (Cornell University Press, 1989) and *The Oxford Companion to American Military History* (Oxford University Press, 2000). Her current project, *Constructing Destruction,* examines the damage caused by nuclear weapons in the past century and how and why the U.S. government has underestimated its impact.

Melissa Sheridan Embser-Herbert is associate professor of sociology at Hamline University. Her publications include *Camouflage Isn't Only for Combat: Gender, Sexuality, and Women in the Military* (New York University Press, 1998); and "Guarding the Nation, Guarding Ourselves: The Management of Hetero/Homo/Sexuality Among Women in the Military" in *Minerva: Quarterly Report on Women and the Military* (1997). She has also given numerous talks on gender and sexuality in the military and currently serves as chair of the Section on Sexualities of the American Sociological Association.

Avner Even-Zohar is retired from the Israel Defense Forces and is currently the director of the Campus Division of the Israel Center in San Francisco.

Paul A. Gade is chief of the Research and Advanced Concepts Office at the U.S. Army Research Institute for the Behavioral and Social Sciences. He is a fellow of the American Psychological Association and the Inter-University Seminar on Armed Forces and Society and past president of the APA Division of Military Psychology.

Bronwen Grey is director of the Defence Equity Organization for the Australian Defence Force.

Timothy J. Haggerty is associate director of the Center for the Arts in Society at Carnegie Mellon University. In 1995 he worked as a research associate on the RAND study *Sexual Orientation and U.S. Military Personnel Policy: Options and Assessment*. His current research examines the changing role of the press in nineteenth-century New York.

Steve Johnston is retired from the British army and currently serves as chair of the Armed Forces Lesbian and Gay Association in London.

Lawrence J. Korb is vice president and Maurice R. Greenberg Chair, director of studies, and director of national security studies at the Council of Foreign Relations in New York City. His areas of interest and expertise include national security organization, policy, and process; U.S. foreign policy, arms control, and defense budget; and NATO. His books include *American National Security: Policy and Process* (Johns Hopkins University Press, 1993), *The Fall and Rise of the Pentagon* (Greenwood Press, 1979), and *The Joint Chiefs of Staff: The First Twenty-Five Years* (Indiana University Press, 1976). He has taught at Georgetown University, the University of Pittsburgh, and the U.S. Naval War College, as well as serving as both director of the Center for Public Policy Education and senior fellow of the Foreign Policy Studies Program at the Brookings Institution.

Robert MacCoun is professor in both the Boalt School of Law and the Goldman School of Public Policy at the University of California, Berkeley. He has published numerous essays on drug use, drug dealing, and drug policy; judgment and decisionmaking; legal disputing, dispute resolution, procedural and distributive justice; and effects of sexual orientation and gender on group performance. His books include (with P. Reuter) *Drug War Heresies: Learning from Other Vices, Times, and Places* (Cambridge, 2001), as well as collective authorship of *Sexual Orientation and U.S. Military Personnel Policy: Policy Options and Assessment* (RAND, 1993).

Steve May was elected to the Arizona House of Representatives in November 1998 and served two terms as state representative. From 1993 to 1995 he served in the U.S. Army's First Infantry Division as a nuclear, biological, and chemical defense officer. In 1995, he was honorably discharged but was recalled to the U.S. Army Reserve in February 1999. In July 1995, the U.S. Army began proceedings against Lieutenant May under "Don't Ask, Don't Tell." He fought the attempted discharge and the secretary of the army intervened to allow him to finish his tour of duty. He was honorably discharged in April 2001.

Diane H. Mazur is professor of law at the University of Florida, College of Law. Her areas of interest include military service and its relationship to equal protection, citizenship, political participation, and ethics. From 1979 to 1983, she served as captain in the U.S. Air Force in aircraft and munitions maintenance. Her recent publications include "Rehnquist's Vietnam: Constitutional Separatism and the Stealth Advance of Martial Law" in *Indiana Law Journal* (July 2002); "Word Games, War Games" in the *Michigan Law Review* (May 2000); and "Sex and Lies: Rules of Ethics, Rules of Evidence, and Our Conflicted Views on the Significance of Honesty" in the *Notre Dame Journal of Law, Ethics, and Public Policy* (2000).

Laura Miller is social scientist at the RAND research corporation. From 1997 to 2002 she was assistant professor of sociology at UCLA. Her publications include "Do Military Policies on Gender and Sexuality Undermine Combat Effectiveness?" with Jay Williams in *Soldiers and Civilians* (BCSIA-MIT Press, 2001); "From Adversaries to Allies: Relief Workers' Attitudes Toward the U.S. Military" in *Qualitative Sociology* (summer 1999); "Not Just Weapons of the Weak: Gender Harassment as a Form of Protest for Army Men" in *Social Psychology* (1997); and "Fighting for a Just Cause: Soldiers' Attitudes on Gays in the Military" in *Gays and Lesbians in the Military* (Aldine de Gruyter, 1994).

Deborah Mulliss is director of personnel equity policy for the New Zealand Defence Force.

Rob Nunn currently serves in the Royal Navy. After his discharge in 1992 for being gay, he returned to service after the United Kingdom lifted the ban on gays and lesbians serving openly.

C. Dixon Osburn is executive director of the Servicemembers Legal Defense Network, a legal and political advocacy organization that he cofounded in 1993 for service members harmed by "Don't Ask, Don't Tell." He has received numerous awards for his dedication to providing legal assistance to thousands of service members and publishing numerous reports on the effects of the policy.

David R. Segal is a distinguished scholar-teacher, professor of sociology, affiliate professor of government and politics and of public affairs, and director of the Center for Research on Military Organization at the University of Maryland. His books include (as coeditor) *The Postmodern Military* (Oxford University Press, 2000); *The Transformation of European Communist Societies* (JAI Press, 1992); and, with Mady Wechsler Segal, *Peacekeepers and Their Wives* (Greenwood Press, 1993). He has authored and coauthored numerous journal articles on military leadership, youth and the American military, multinational forces and operations, and the exclusion of sexual minorities from the military.

Mady Wechsler Segal is professor of sociology at the University of Maryland, faculty affiliate of the Women's Studies Program and the Center for International and Security Studies at Maryland (CISSM), and associate director of the Center for Research on Military Organization. She has served on numerous advisory committees to the military and Congress on issues related to military personnel and family, sexual harassment, military training, and gender. Her recent research has focused on military personnel issues, with particular attention to military women and military families. Her publications include "The Military and the Family as Greedy Institutions" in *Armed Forces and Society* (1986); "Women's Military Roles Cross-Nationally: Past, Present, and Future" in *Gender & Society* (1995); with Bradford Booth, William W. Falk, and David R. Segal, "The Impact of Military Presence in Local Labor Markets on the Employment of Women" in *Gender & Society* (2000); and with David R. Segal, *Peacekeepers and Their Wives* (Greenwood Press, 1993).

John Allen (Jay) Williams is professor of political science at Loyola University, Chicago, and is executive director and a fellow of the Inter-University Seminar on Armed Forces and Society and chair of the Academic Advisory Council of the National Strategy Forum. His writing includes work on civil-military relations, military professionalism and leadership, military forces missions, defense organization, and strategic nuclear policy. He is coauthor (with Sam C. Sarkesian and Stephen J. Cimbala) of *U.S. National Security: Policymakers, Processes, and Politics*, 3d ed. (Lynne Rienner Publishers, 2002). He coedited (with Charles C. Moskos and David R. Segal) and contributed to *The Postmodern Military: Armed Forces After the Cold War* (Oxford University Press, 2000). His other projects include coauthoring (with Sam C. Sarkesian and Fred B. Bryant) *Soldiers, Society, and National Security* and coediting (with Sam C. Sarkesian) *The U.S. Army in a New Security Era*.

Index

About the Book

Conservatives and liberals agree that President Bill Clinton's effort to lift the military's gay ban was perhaps one of the greatest blunders of his tenure in office. Conservatives argue that Clinton should have left well enough alone; liberals believe that he should have ordered the military to accept homosexuals rather than agreeing to the compromise "Don't Ask, Don't Tell" policy. In this groundbreaking book, experts of both persuasions come together to debate the critical aspects of the gays-in-the-military issue.

The participants consider whether homosexuals undermine military performance, whether they threaten heterosexual privacy, and whether the experiences of militaries in other countries have relevance for the United States. They also explore the human, organizational, and dollar costs of the present policy. Belkin and Bateman provide a thorough context for the transcripts of the deliberations, as well as a discussion of the implications of the participants' conclusions for current U.S. policy.

The project participants: Aaron Belkin, Christopher Dandeker (UK), Michael C. Desch, Lynn Eden, Avner Even-Zohar (Israel), Paul Gade, Bronwen Grey (Australia), Timothy J. Haggerty, Melissa Sheridan Embser-Herbert, Steve Johnston (UK), Lawrence J. Korb, Rob Mac-Coun, Steve May, Diane H. Mazur, Laura Miller, Deborah Mulliss (New Zealand), Rob Nunn (UK), C. Dixon Osburn, David Segal, Mady Segal, John Allen Williams.

Aaron Belkin is assistant professor of political science and director of the Center for the Study of Sexual Minorities in the Military, at the University of California, Santa Barbara (CSSMM). He is coeditor of *Counterfactual Thought Experiments in World Politics*. **Geoffrey Bateman** is assistant director of CSSMM.